*f*P

MADDY DYCHTWALD

Cycles

HOW WE WILL
LIVE, WORK,
AND BUY

THE FREE PRESS
NEW YORK
LONDON
TORONTO
SYDNEY
SINGAPORE

*f*P

THE FREE PRESS
A Division of Simon & Schuster, Inc.
1230 Avenue of the Americas
New York, NY 10020

For information about special discounts for bulk purchases, please contact Simon & Schuster Special
Sales: 1-800-456-6798 or business@simonandschuster.com
Designed by Karolina Harris
Manufactured in the United States of America
10   9   8   7   6   5   4   3   2   1
Library of Congress Cataloging-in-Publication Data
Dychtwald, Maddy.
   Cycles: how we will live, work, and buy/Maddy Dychtwald.
     p. cm.
   Includes index.
   1. Consumer behavior—United States. 2. Lifestyles—United States. 3. Cycles. 4. Civilization—
Forecasting. 5. Life cycle, Human—Social aspects. 6. Life cycle, Human—Psychological aspects.
I. Title.
HF5415.33.U6 D94 2003
303.4—dc21
2002040892
ISBN 13: 978-0-7432-2615-8   ISBN 10: 0-7432-2615-1

To Ken, Casey, and Zak—
You bring love and magic into my life.

CONTENTS

ACKNOWLEDGMENTS

Many heartfelt thanks to all the wonderful people who have helped transform *Cycles* from an idea into a book.

Ken Dychtwald for showering me with love, support, mentorship, a critical eye, and unending patience. He is the perfect soul mate and partner.

Casey Dychtwald for being the most perfect daughter and challenging me every step of the way.

Zak Dychtwald for being the most perfect son and a "wise old soul."

Sally and Ray Fusco for not only bringing much love and joy into my life but also providing great fodder for my book.

Richard, Linda, David, and Joel Kent for being an essential ingredient in my life and family with their constant love and lifetime friendship and support.

Pearl, Seymour, and Alan Dychtwald whose love helps define the word *family* for me.

Gerry Sindell for providing me with focus, insight, and warm friendship.

Doris Michaels for her enthusiasm and advice, and for finding me the best home for this book.

Dominick Anfuso for believing in my ideas and giving me free rein to develop this book.

Julie Penfold for being my rock and editing with brilliance and compassion.

Greta Mart and Beth Harrington for their diligent, thorough research assistance.

Dawne Bernhardt, Jayme Canton, Meryl Comer, Sandie Dorman, Dennis Jaffee, Don Mankin, and Leda Sanford for providing astute editorial input.

Luke Van Meter for terrific graphic images.

Mary Plescia for her willingness to help and support me in making my life work.

My dear friends Gayle and Jayme Canton, Sandie and Kenny Dorman, Nancy and Danny Katz, and Jane and Neal Katsura who are always there with encouragement, love, and smiles.

Age Wave, Inc., and everyone who has been part of our company over the years, for being the source of much joy, frustration, learning, and many of my original ideas.

CYCLES

Reinvention. Liberation. Opportunity. That's what this book is all about. Validation, too, since many of us are already experimenting with *cycles* in our own lives. We just might not have known it until now. But, as this book shows, we are all part of this human revolution, shaping it and being shaped by it at the same time. In these pages, I'll show you how that's happening, and explain what it means to you, the marketplace, and the workplace.

The concept for *Cycles: How We Will Live, Work, and Buy* was born from my work as an entrepreneur, consultant, public speaker, and cofounder of Age Wave, a think tank and consulting firm created to guide companies in product development and marketing to boomers and mature adults. Like most endeavors of real value, I learn as much—or more—from my clients and audiences as they learn from me. Over time, I noticed that when I would talk about the concept of living a "cyclic" versus a "linear" life—whether it was in client meetings, keynote presentations, or focus groups—people perked up. Whether they were 25 or 55, this idea resonated with them and left them exhilarated about the possibilities. In fact, many felt they could identify with this emerging trend and were already embarking on such an approach to their own lives.

These busy men and women realized that they were no longer adhering to the strict, linear outline of life events that has been the model for civilization to this point: birth-education-work-marriage-family-retirement-death. Instead, they were naturally gravitating toward a more *cyclic* approach to life where these stages and activities are revisited throughout a lifetime. Many were going back to school at 35, crafting new careers at 52, starting a family at 45, or getting remarried at 76. The *circle of life*, it seemed to them and to me, had begun to replace the straight-and-narrow path.

Was this a passing trend or a sea change? Over the years, as my work widened and deepened, I kept returning to this notion of a new Life-Cycle paradigm. The questions and examples kept coming and I began to piece together enough anecdotal evidence to confirm that the old linear way of life was, indeed, giving way to a new model for many people. And I began to wonder what the implications for all of us would be if a huge part of the population transformed the notion of how adult life should be lived. I formed some hypotheses, dug into the research, and eventually, answered my own question: Life as we've known it is indeed in the beginning stages of a profound and systemic paradigm change. In *Cycles*, I'll show you the who, what, when, and where . . . and also the why.

REVOLUTION

The personal, social, political, and economic ramifications of this shift are huge. We are at the dawn of a new era, nothing less than a LifeCycle revolution that will change the very essence of who we are . . . as humans and as consumers. It promises to shake up everything we do, and to change how and when we do it.

At its essence, this LifeCycle revolution is a release from the age-old assembly line of life passages that each ended with a door sealed shut to prevent us from ever turning back. For instance, this prescribed linear path insisted that:

- Youth (and exploration and free-spirited play) is just for the young.
- Education comes just once before real life begins, and old dogs can't learn new tricks.
- Marriage always lasts a lifetime.

- Having and raising children is the primary purpose of adult life.
- Retirement (and obsolescence) comes at age 65.
- Following the straight and narrow is the only appropriate life path.

At one time, these rules and their related passages made perfect sense. Life was considerably shorter and less complex then than it is now, so using age to define the activities we were involved in seemed appropriate and even helpful. Age-based determinism provided a roadmap of exactly what we should be doing with our lives at any given point along the continuum. And the business world sensed the obvious: Aiming products and services at consumers based on their age would quickly and precisely score a hit. And since people established most of their values and preferences when they were young, targeting youth made total sense.

But times have changed. We're living in a new century with new challenges and opportunities. We're facing new enemies, fears, hopes, and dreams in an ever-shrinking and increasingly volatile world. Economic and technologic complexities enable us to perform almost any task from almost anywhere. Life expectancy has skyrocketed to 77, and promises to edge even higher. New generations of highly educated, self-reliant men and women are seeking challenges, adventures, relationships, and meaning throughout their lives, at every age. As a result, we're starting to question the wisdom of living life through a series of age-driven life passages with no turning back. And, we're no longer buying products and services based on this long-held, overgeneralized *age-defines-the-person* and *youth-is-the-target* model.

DEMOGRAPHIC DESTINY

By now, the fact that we are in the midst of a great societal shift seemed certain to me. Which led me to my next question: Why? Why this particular change, at this particular moment in time? My answer, this time, came easily: demographics. It's really the underpinnings of this Life-Cycle revolution. Because a number of powerful demographic forces begun decades ago are intersecting right now, we're seeing profound lifestyle changes take place that are, increasingly, inevitable.

Before your eyes begin to glaze over, let me confess: I never would have guessed that one of my passions in life would be demography. In my mind, it always seemed like a technical science for data lovers and "propeller heads." But, as I learned, the number-crunching aspects of demographics are just the tip of the iceberg. It's really the powerful changes looming just beneath the surface that truly fascinate me.

I've come to appreciate that demographics is the engine that drives most social and lifestyle trends. It makes sense, then, that understanding demographics opens a window on the future, giving us a preemptive view of coming big-picture truths. Because demographics is based on hard, established data, it is predictable. It can draw a reliable picture, based on a foundation of fact, of who we are becoming. In these unpredictable times when the speed of change keeps increasing and global dynamics can create so much uncertainty, it's reassuring to know that we can count on demographic change to unfold just as we expect. It can help make the future easier to understand and make decisions about. Sure, there will be surprises like economic downturns, terrorist attacks, and technological innovations, but who we are becoming and what we'll require along the way is an eventuality that's already set in motion. If we open our eyes to what our changing realities are, we can get a view of the future: *our* future, our family's future, society's future, and, of course, the future direction of the consumer marketplace.

THE CYCLES OF LIFE REPLACE THE STRAIGHT-AND-NARROW PATH

When I decided to write *Cycles*, I wanted to examine the essence of this lifecycle revolution from its known beginnings to its projectable future. I felt that many of us were already embarking on more cyclic life paths, but we're so busy with the *doing* of it, we may not be cognizant of the effects this sea change is creating for our overall society. I also realized that it might be reassuring to know we're not alone and certainly not in error in this new way of living our lives; others are taking divergent paths, too, leading the way with great success. These role models help crystallize some of the opportunities this new circle of life is creating for personal pursuits and commercial enterprises of all kinds.

Cycles takes you through this journey using a clear and practical approach, featuring a chapter-by-chapter analysis of the pivotal aspects of the LifeCycle revolution and their impact on you, society, and business-at-large. First, I'll describe how we're breaking free of the outdated assembly line of closed-door life passages. Second, I'll draw a picture of the new lifecycle model that is emerging—a more flexible, open-door approach to life's options. Third, I'll connect the dots to business, describing many of the ways that these changes should impact the marketplace and workforce in the decades to come.

Because demographics is essentially the jumping off point for both my work and this book, **Chapter One** explains the unique demographic shifts we're experiencing right now and how they will alter our reality. Not too long ago, we could discern much of what there was to know about a person based primarily on his or her age. For instance, a 24-year-old woman usually was married or seeking that union with visions of children in her near future. Although she might be employed, it was usually in just a job, not a career. She was struggling to set up her own household with her husband and had clearly finished all of her education and was never going back. Her focus was domestic. Today, that same 24-year-old woman could likely be involved in a Chinese menu of activities and relationships. Maybe she's married, maybe not. Maybe she never wants to get married. Maybe she's serious about a career or hasn't yet found her vocational preference. Children? Maybe in 10 or 20 years; maybe with a mate or, if she really wants to, she can go through artificial insemination and have a child on her own. Maybe she'll go back to school soon or take a year off to travel. The point is that, in defining *her*, age is almost irrelevant. In a nutshell, this chapter asserts that age no longer defines our limits, who we are, or the choices we can make.

Chapter Two describes one of the most essential ingredients in a cyclic life: lifelong learning. In our new LifeCycles, learning and education are no longer the exclusive province of the young. I'll describe how *knowledge power* is freeing us up to question the status quo of our lives and, ultimately, to experiment with new life and career paths as well as new products and services throughout our lives. In this chapter, the connection to business will become obvious on two fronts. First, I'll show how the business of education will take many divergent forms, expanding innovatively and exponentially in the years ahead. Second,

I'll put to rest the tired assumptions about consumers and brand loyalty of old as we begin to understand a new, highly educated, and ever-changing consumer.

Chapter Three explores careers and how the world of work is transforming to suit our more cyclic selves. Men and women now have the freedom to pursue cyclic careers rather than just one career path that lasts a lifetime. This new freedom, of course, has its pros and cons. On the one hand, with evolving technologies and skill requirements and an increasingly fluid labor pool, the psychological and financial security inherent in having one job for life is slipping away. As a result, we must face the challenge of planning for our long-term financial future and short-term health care without depending on a lifelong corporate relationship. On the other hand, work will no longer be limited to those between the ages of 18 and 65. We'll see people cycling in and out of the workforce—sometimes by choice, sometimes not—and we will need to plan for these (often unexpected) sabbaticals. We will also see ageism in the workplace melt away—just as racism and sexism are slowly disintegrating—to make way for the emerging multiracial, multiethnic, multigenerational workforce.

Chapter Four explores how love and romance will be impacted by our more cyclic lives. In the old linear life model, love and romance were traditionally the brief pregame show for marriage and family. We married young and pragmatically; that marriage lasted a lifetime and its primary purpose was to build a nest for raising children. No one ever imagined that "'til death do us part" could mean 50 years of togetherness—or more. Nor did the authors of that fateful phrase imagine that *both* partners in a marriage might continuously reinvent themselves.

The lifecycle revolution is morphing the institution of marriage to better fit the new length, styles, and rhythms of our lives. Chapter Four explores how we are cycling in and out of love, reinventing the institution of marriage. Cyclic monogamy is one of the outcomes. Margaret Mead said it best, referring to her own love life, "I've been married three times. All successful." This chapter will also explore some of the ways that many of us are maintaining, reinventing, or freshening up a single, magical, meaningful relationship that does last a lifetime. Either path toward love and romance takes work, commitment, and a lot of consciousness, which opens the door to some tremendous commercial ramifications, as you'll see in this chapter.

As a natural follow-up to love and romance, **Chapter Five** looks at the virtual family. As the nuclear family continues to shrink in popularity, extended longevity is creating a world where many generations are alive at once, living much longer, and all in need of different forms of family support. The sandwich generation that was a new phenomenon just a decade or so ago has become a worldwide double-decker with far-reaching personal, social, and commercial ramifications. Concurrently, the depth and breadth of the concept of *family* has expanded to include midlife parenting, blended families, friends as surrogate family, and every other derivation we can conceive of. In the new cyclic lifestyle, we can relax and know that we're not weird or missing out if we don't have a traditional, nuclear family unit. There is no more *average* family; in the new era of virtual families, nearly anything goes. And to think that business still defines family, its number one bull's-eye, primarily as young family formations! Talk about missing the mark!

Chapter Six examines play and recreation and how they are becoming a more integral aspect of our identity throughout our lives. "People are defining themselves now more by how they play than by how they work," according to journalist Howard Means, co-author of *The Banana Sculptor, the Purple Lady, and the All-night Swimmer: Hobbies, Collecting and Other Passionate Pursuits.*[1] Now that play is no longer considered something exclusively for the young or the retired, new forms of leisure are emerging, influenced strongly by the boomers' values and attitudes. The opportunity to reinvent ourselves through hobbies, play, relaxation, and recreation is a major component of our cyclic life paths. This chapter describes a variety of forms such reinvention can take and the opportunities it creates for each of us individually, as well as for the business community at-large, particularly those in the travel/leisure and hobby/craft industries.

In the linear-life model, aging, disease, and death were tightly linked. This interrelationship partly explains why we dreaded getting older; we knew . . . and feared . . . what was just around the corner. Today, modern medical research has shown us that aging and disease are two distinct experiences. Yes, our bodies can wear out, just like cars do, if they're not properly maintained, but aging and disease do not have to go hand-in-hand. Furthermore, disease—even life-threatening conditions such as cancer, heart disease, and AIDS—no longer leads inevitably to death. Today, advances against most illnesses can lead to recovery, offering us the opportunity to cycle back into an active life, with a new perspective and greater appreciation of all it has to offer.

The first part of **Chapter Seven** focuses on the newly emerging model of healthy aging and how adults are maintaining and regaining their vitality to cycle back into an active life, a process young people also embrace with enthusiasm. The second part of this chapter explores the antiaging revolution that is swiftly gaining momentum. Both parts of the chapter link directly to the vast commercial opportunities being created for health care, wellness, fitness, beauty, personal care, rejuvenation, and beyond.

Chapter Eight reminds us that, in the linear-life model, the last stage of life was retirement, a removal from work to rest, reflect, and prepare for death. Traditional retirement was meant to be short and to provide the opportunity for the old and no longer *useful* members of society to recede from the mainstream while the young took over the reins. Even today, according to *Webster's Unabridged Dictionary*, retirement is defined as "to disappear or recede; to withdraw."

This definition made sense when life was short, work was physical, and the number of young people vastly outweighed the older members of society. Today the average retiree spends almost 20 years in retirement, is a member of the wealthiest segment of society (thanks in part to the many programs put in place by the government) and is supported by a diminishing number of younger workers. This system will definitely undergo some needed change and the commercial worlds of financial planning, employee benefits, and retirement living will respond in kind. We'll look at these and other new and far-reaching ramifications of retirement re-envisioned in this chapter.

The final chapters, Chapter Nine and Chapter Ten, put all of these pieces together to form a cohesive picture of what the lifecycle revolution means to your future as an individual and to our collective future as a society. **Chapter Nine,** *The Cyclic Self,* takes a broad look at what cyclic lifestyles will mean to us all in our everyday lives. While it offers us tremendous opportunities, the cyclic life will also challenge us at every turn. This chapter discusses how these seven core truths affect each of us:

- We are longevity pioneers on a new life path: the cyclic life path.
- We need to adapt to a *dynamic* versus a *static* lifestyle.
- We must be willing to be beginners at any age.
- The rhythm and cadence of life will change.
- Setbacks and detours are inevitable.
- Late bloomers may bloom best.
- The pressure's off.

Chapter Ten, *The Cyclic Society,* is intended to help those of us who are in the business of understanding the public and determining what it wants. How can we respond profitably to the cyclic consumer? And how will the cyclic life impact the workplace? This is brand-new territory and we are all pioneers. So how does a business reach a cyclic consumer today? Here are seven guideposts to keep in mind:

- Embrace the new ageless consumer.
- Target lifestyle and LifeCycle, not age.
- Reinvention is a constant.
- Empower consumers.
- Needed: LifeCycle navigation.
- Target freedom and security.
- Optimize a cyclic workforce.

The traditional linear view was great for business because product developers and marketers knew exactly what activities people were likely to be involved in just by knowing how old they were. If we were in the insurance business, we'd target young families—18- to 34-year-olds—exclusively. If we were in the education business, it was young people—under 25—exclusively. If we were in the retirement planning and investing business, we targeted people primarily in their 50s. Not anymore. For those who enjoyed those easy days of marketing to populations that were marching lockstep through the predictable stages of life—that's all over. We are fast becoming cyclic consumers in a cyclic society.

Whether you're reading this book to get a sense of where your own life might be headed or as a professional looking for business ideas, my hope is that you will find something that *you hadn't really thought of quite like that before* within these pages. Get ready for the cyclic life path, because here it comes!

THE PATH TO LIFECYCLE LIBERATION

We are at the dawn of a LifeCycle revolution. Spurred by the convergence of a number of powerful cultural, technological, and demographic forces, the way we live, work, and buy is beginning to change radically. At its essence, this revolution is a release from the invisible age-related constraints in values, attitudes, and expectations about the reality of life that have enslaved us throughout time. Prescribed by society for centuries, these boundaries have defined our lives and what we've done at each stage of life. Among other things, they dictated that youth was just for the young, that education comes just once before real life starts, that marriage should last a lifetime, and that retirement comes at age 65. They've also telegraphed to business what products and services we might need at what stages of life.

At one time, these rules may have made perfect sense. Dan Levinson's groundbreaking research and Gail Sheehy's illuminating book *Passages* outlined these predictable life passages based on chronologic age and told us what to expect and how to prepare for each one. Levinson was the first after Erik Erikson to theorize that development did not end at adulthood but continued throughout life. Sheehy's idea was that if we could understand adult LifeCycles and the fact that most people experienced the same things at roughly the same age, we could understand and gain comfort from what we were feeling about where we were in life.

This age-based model of life could also provide a window for business leaders to better understand and target their consumers. Within this paradigm, marketing and sales were, likewise, simplified into a predictable pattern of age-based marketing. If we knew how old someone was, we had a pretty clear idea of what they were doing in their life and which products and services they might purchase. "Aim products and services at consumers based on their age" became the battle cry of Madison Avenue. It was a successful model of age-oriented marketing, made even more intense by the belief that *everyone* formed their brand preferences in youth and remained loyal to them for life.

Well, things have changed. We no longer live life in a series of predictable life passages. We're breaking free of age-related lifestyle expectations that defined us. We're no longer buying products and services based on this neat age-oriented marketing model. And we're no longer as set in our ways. Welcome to the dawn of LifeCycle liberation!

A REVOLUTION IN THE MAKING

In the quarter-century since *Passages* first appeared, there have been tectonic changes in the landscape of human experience. First, average life expectancy has been on the rise and, with the help of emerging biotechnology and new medical breakthroughs, it will increase substantially in the years ahead. Second, we used to be primarily a young population. Not anymore. Adults fifty and over are now the fastest growing segment of our population, growing twice as fast as the overall population. At the same time, we see the number of young adults—18- to 34-year-olds—actually shrinking in size. Last, the largest single population group ever to share a set of common values—boomers—now dominates our culture, not as rebellious teenagers, but as midlife adults. As they continue to mature, their influence on the attitudes and values of younger generations seems to be growing. And we can be sure that the boomers have no intention of aging like their parents or grandparents did.

All of these enormous changes are transforming the way we think about some long-held social conventions such as education, marriage, parenting, and retirement, and their locations and timing in our lives. Since Sheehy wrote her important but increasingly obsolete book, there has been a groundswell of support for the idea that there is life after youth. No longer do we assume that we open ourselves to education just once when we're young: now we know we might return to it continuously as demanded by work, family, or personal interests. Like it or not, many of us don't necessarily say "'til death do us part" just once either. After all, when marriage was originally conceived, no one expected it to last for 50, 60, or even 70 years. Cyclic monogamy has become the norm, with most people enjoying two or even three primary relationships over the span of their lengthening lives. The roles of men and women have loosened up, too, offering us more options. Even the inevitable physical decline that has always gone hand-in-hand with getting older is not quite as inevitable anymore, as examples of healthy aging are popping up everywhere.

What is happening is that we are moving from a rigid *linear* approach to life to a more flexible, *cyclic* life; a new path that isn't as straight *or* narrow as it used to be. There are more curves in the road and a multitude of divergent side paths that some of us might choose to try. Perhaps most important is the fact that the roles and activities we choose are much less likely to be determined by how old we are. It's not unusual to see a 35-year-old or a 65-year-old starting a new career; a 30-year-old or a 70-year-old getting married; a 45-year-old or a 25-year-old graduating from school. Age is no longer the ultimate definer of who we are, what we're doing, how we feel on the inside, what group we're a member of, or the products and services we demand from the marketplace. We are being liberated from a life of one-way passages to a cyclic life with a nearly unlimited set of choices, options, and possibilities available at any age—to anyone with the vision and courage to seize the day.

A life of cycles offers both the challenge and the opportunity for each of us to define—and often redefine—our own future rather than to have our future imposed on us by society's age markers. By liberating our patterns of purchasing from age-dependent factors, we can emerge as *ageless* consumers. There is no more easy-to-find Pepsi Generation and, contrary to popular opinion, you *can* teach an old dog new tricks. The age-segregated mass market is dying, and in its place, a vibrant new LifeCycle- and lifestyle-based marketplace is emerging.

It's a bit like discovering the world is round when all along we were sure it was flat. The social institutions we've put into place and the assumptions about work and career, marriage, parenting, retirement, and even illness are all shifting, coming unhinged from their moorings. If we recognize this fact and understand the new options before us, we can comfortably make choices to help us navigate life's new cycles. How do we figure out who our market is? What kinds of products and services will be in demand? Who are the new arbiters of cultural hipness? These are the questions we're just starting to ask as we move into the new world of LifeCycle liberation.

WHY THIS REVOLUTION? WHY NOW?

Powerful demographic forces drive this revolution and we need to understand them. The word *demography* sounds complicated and boring. And, if you go by the technical definition, "the science of vital statistics," your eyes might quickly glaze over. But look closer, back to its original meaning, and it comes alive. Demography derives from the Greek *demos*, which means "people" and *graphic* which means "to write." So, originally, demography meant "writing about people." I think of demographics as "the science of understanding people and populations through vital statistics."

Many business, economic, and political leaders believe if you can grasp demographic trends, you can anticipate future trends in terms of consumers, economics, and public policy. I take it one step further. I think demographics can open a window into tomorrow—our tomorrow, our customer's tomorrow, even our employee's tomorrow—so that the future becomes easier to understand, more predictable, and easier to make decisions about. The wonderful benefit of making sense of the unknown in this way is that the fear of the future is reduced, and we can more readily take charge of our own plans for tomorrow. It may even give us a feeling of hope that it's never too late. After all, if we have a clearer picture of what the road ahead looks like, it's that much easier to travel with ease and comfort. We might also get the feeling that our time to shine may be in front of us rather than behind us, no matter how old we might be.

So what new demographic forces are reshaping our lives and the marketplace? There are three unprecedented trends at work. First is the ever compounding *longevity revolution*, the result of dramatic advances in medicine and biotechnology; second is the steady *decline of the youth society* based on both the declining birth and mortality rates; and last is the impact of the *pioneering values, attitudes, and traits of the boomers* as they continue to revolutionize maturity. (This generation has transformed every stage of life through which they've passed.) The convergence of these three forces is transforming who we are and who we can become; moreover, it will liberate us from yesterday's oppressive *act your age* rules and limits.

The Longevity Revolution

We are the first humans to experience long life en masse. Until now, young people have almost exclusively dominated the planet. Aided by technologic breakthroughs in the life sciences, medicine, and health care, people are living longer and better than ever before.

Throughout most of history, death came early to many. Life was short and brutish for all but the privileged classes; older people were a rarity. If we go back to the year 1000, the average life expectancy was only 25 years. (See Figure 1.1.) At the time of the signing of the Declaration of Independence in 1776, the average life expectancy was only 37 years. Just 100 years ago, the average American could expect to live to age 47 and the median age was 17. In fact, throughout 99 percent of human history, the average life expectancy was under age 18. Think about that in perspective: during the 4,500 years from the Bronze Age to the year 1900, life expectancy increased less than it did in the twentieth century.

Today we are living longer and better than ever before. In the twentieth century alone, average life expectancy went up 29 years. Right now the average American will live to age 77 and the median age is almost 36. And the United States isn't even at the head of the list of nations when it comes to longevity, but ranks thirty-fifth of nations worldwide. (See Figure 1.2, which shows a sampling of, but not all, countries.)

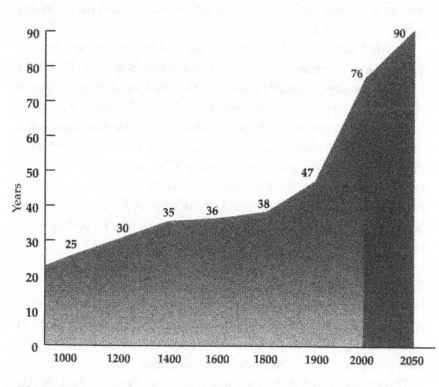

Figure 1.1
Life Expectancy at Birth
1000–2050
Source: United States Bureau of the Census, 2000.

WAGING THE WAR FOR LONGER LIFE

How have we waged the war for longer lives? We employed continual technologic innovation and improvements in every aspect of medicine and public health. First, we attacked death in the early years of life. As a result of sanitation improvements, advances in public health, better nutrition, and a varied diet made available by the invention of refrigeration, infant mortality rates and childhood death rates decreased dramatically worldwide in the late nineteenth and early twentieth centuries. Then medical and pharmacologic breakthroughs such as antibiotics and immunization helped us overcome infectious diseases such as pneumonia, diphtheria, smallpox, polio, and tuberculosis.

The next battle in the war for increased life expectancy was begun in

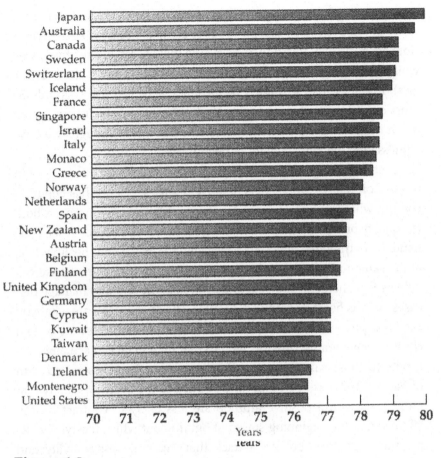

Figure 1.2
Life Expectancy Worldwide
Source: United States Bureau of the Census, International Data Base, 1998.

the late twentieth century. Once we had control of acute, infectious diseases, we began to focus attention on diseases that are slow moving, debilitating, and tend to occur in life's second half—chronic, degenerative diseases such as arthritis, diabetes, heart disease, and cancer. While still a far cry from successful, progress has been developing on this front—so death rates among older age groups are 50 percent lower than they were a century ago.

Combating these chronic, degenerative diseases has required a highly refined medical system relying primarily on high-tech weapons of war. Our detection systems have evolved so that we can now discover many conditions before they cause major damage. Over time, we've developed highly specific drugs to combat diseases like hypertension, heart disease, and kidney disease so that we can live relatively well while controlling a particular disease. When I was just a child (in the '60s), my uncle had a sudden heart attack and died. He was only 35 years old. Today, that same heart attack probably wouldn't have meant death because of the tremendous technologic breakthroughs we have witnessed in the management of heart disease.

Lifestyle management is emerging today as another potent tool in the war on many chronic, degenerative diseases. Science has begun to confirm what many of us suspected: how we live our lives impacts both the quality of our health and how long we live. We've begun to see first-hand the detrimental effect smoking cigarettes has on our health while, at the same time, learning that a simple thing like regular exercise can help us feel energetic and vital and even help prevent and manage diseases such as heart disease and diabetes. The saying, "You are what you eat," has proven to be true; a low-fat diet can help prevent certain chronic, degenerative diseases while a diet high in fat can actually contribute to those same diseases. Even stress has been associated with disease. In fact, recent studies have pointed to the likely possibility that individuals with a positive attitude are less likely to contract cancer. We're still at the beginning stages of figuring out which lifestyle habits are the right ones, but it's a track that's gaining respectability and acceptance.

The life sciences are becoming even more effective in developing new and improved tools to prevent and manage disease. Biotechnology is still in its early stages of development, but holds the promise of extending life expectancy. Stem cells hold the hope of growing new organs when the old ones wear out or stop working effectively. New biotech tools are being developed that offer the promise of combating diseases that are closely associated with aging such as Alzheimer's, arthritis, and osteoporosis.

Even aging itself could someday become a thing of the past. Modern cellular research, boosted by exploding genomic understanding, has begun to hint that the so-called biologic clock could possibly be reset. As a result, we may, in our lifetimes, be able to slow down or even halt our own aging process through impending biotechnology break-throughs to increase life expectancy even more.

This kind of future science may sound like science fiction, but it may very well help shape how long many of us will live. One thing is clear: The increasing velocity of medical and biotech breakthroughs will in all likelihood continue to help us add both years to our lives and life to those years.

THE FUTURE OF LONGEVITY

In many ways, increased longevity is like a dream come true. Throughout history, men have fantasized and schemed for long life with eternal youth. Even the ancient Egyptians, obsessed with planning for the afterlife, were responsible for the first documented antiwrinkle recipe—discovered in the Ebers papyrus and believed to have been written in 1530 B.C. In the Middle Ages, Lucas Cranach the Elder painted a famous picture of a spectacular spring where wrinkled old women plunged in at one end and young beauties came out at the other. Ponce de Leon bumped into Florida while searching for the fountain of youth. Almost every culture has a myth or legend related to the fountain of youth, but we're the first to experience long life en masse.

Have we gone as far as we will go? Will life expectancy plateau at its present levels? Although there is much controversy concerning the potential life span of humans, there are some indicators of how long we might live. Renowned cell biologist Leonard Hayflick of the University of California has believed for a half century that human cells have a finite number of times they can divide before dying off. His ground-breaking discoveries, now well accepted, explain that each living cell has a biologic clock that controls the aging process and how long we live. Based on a growing body of scientific research, Hayflick believes humans have the potential to live to somewhere between 100 and 120 years.

According to John Rowe and Robert Kahn in their book *Successful Aging,* "in almost every species, the oldest age observed is approxi-mately six times the length of time from birth to maturity. In the human case, this argues for a life span of 108 or 120 years, assuming that the age of complete biological maturity is 18 to 20. On the other hand, many scientists now feel that it is unlikely that there is any fixed life span limit."[1]

According to even the most conservative estimates, average life expectancy will continue to rise over the next several decades. The National Institute on Aging predicts that by the year 2050, average life expectancy will be somewhere between 90 and 95. Demographer James Vaupel describes the future of longevity as "a new paradigm of aging in which average life expectancy could reach one hundred or more."[2] In the United States there are already more than 50,000 people over the age of 100 while worldwide there are 250,000. Doctors Rowe and Kahn project that there will be over 600,000 centenarians in the United States alone by the middle of the twenty-first century. And it is projected that the number of centenarians worldwide will increase sixteenfold by 2050.[3]

We see the pioneers of this super-longevity trend already beginning to appear. San Francisco Bay Area resident Chris Mortensen died at the age of 115 in 1998. Mortensen was the "world's oldest man with a verifiable birth date of 1882." When he was 96, Mortensen moved into a retirement community where he was often seen riding his bicycle. He lived independently until 110. In order to better understand longevity, John Wilmoth, a demographer at University of California/Berkeley became friendly with Mortensen during the last few years of his life. At age 37, Wilmoth said, "I had spent more than ten years studying changes in longevity in kind of an abstract scientific way. Chris, in a sense, was a data point. Meeting him changed my perspective. Suddenly my 88-year-old grandma wasn't that old anymore."[4]

The one thing that seems clear is that many of us might live a lot longer than we've planned. We may see 100 or 110. Sixty will seem young in a life that spans more than a century. You may just hit your stride at 80. The term *late bloomer* will take on a whole new meaning. We'll have more time to live, freeing us up to do all that we want to do instead of just all that we have to do.

The era of long life is upon us. We are entering unexplored terrain, creating a world of long-lived humans. As we've put to rest the fear of dying young, a mounting concern is the polar opposite—living too long—outliving our health, money, and purpose in life. The problem is that few of us have ever contemplated living a century or more, and we have no real model for how to do it. However difficult, we will need to create one.

This longevity revolution will require new ways to think about many of the things that we each take for granted in our daily life. Some of the cornerstones of our thinking—how old is old? When do we retire? How many careers can we have in one lifetime? How long is a life?—will be challenged and, ultimately, give way to new beliefs about what extended life can hold for us. New products and services will be required and business will develop new methods to help customers access products and services easily, conveniently, and in ways responsive to their needs. Many generations will be alive at once, all vying for the attention of both business and government. As pioneers at the forefront of this unprecedented longevity revolution, we will each help define the future and many of the multibillion products and companies of tomorrow. We will release ourselves from a life of predictable passages and break free of age-related lifestyle expectations to pioneer a life of cycles and lifestage liberation. It won't always be easy but it promises to be interesting, challenging, and, at moments, exhilarating.

Shifting Demographic Plates

Another demographic force reshaping our lives is that the overall composition of the general population is changing, altering the landscape and mindscape of our world as emphatically as an earthquake. Who we were was *young*.

Just 100 years ago, the median age was 17. We were a youth-focused world for all the right reasons. Everything from the clothes we wore to the way we designed our communities was geared to meeting the needs of young people. Even the way life was organized. Few worried about what to do after the kids grew up because most didn't live long enough to have that problem. Social Security and Medicare? The concept had little relevancy because of the small number of adults over 65. Entitlements were for the young, not the old. Free education was the *big* entitlement. The world was youth focused, as it should have been, then.

That youth focus followed us into the twentieth century as well. Health care for young families with children was a top priority. Marrying young, learning a trade while still in one's teens, creating job opportunities for young people and education for their even younger children . . . these were some of the key needs of our youth-focused culture.

Not surprisingly, the big sellers were products that glorified the spirit of youth. Clothing that enhanced young bodies, transportation designed for young spirits, homes designed for young families, and an educational system designed for young minds. These were just some of the products that were a logical outcome of living in a youth-focused world.

But the world is morphing. Although who we *were* was young, who we *are becoming* is mature. According to the United Nations, both birthrates and mortality rates are now declining, radically changing the age structure in most countries worldwide.[5] In other words, while more of us are living longer, we're also not reproducing ourselves at the rate we once were. Demographer Carl Haub states it clearly, "Population decline due to low fertility is a new phenomenon."[6] As recently as post–World War II in the United States, the birthrate was 3.8; today it is only 2.06, the minimum replacement level. Italy has the distinction of having the lowest fertility rate of any country with a birthrate of 1.2. In fact, it's the first country ever to have more people over age 65 than under age 25, followed by Germany, Greece, and Spain.[7] China has a strict policy on family size and is proud that its birthrate has dropped from 6.7 in 1950 to 1.8 today. Japan's is 1.39. Even developing nations have lowered their fertility rates by as much as 50 percent over the last few decades. This worldwide paradigm shift is moving the pendulum of people from youth toward the middle and later years of life.

The net result is that the youth segment of our population—which has traditionally been where most population growth took place—is shrinking in size while the mature age segments are growing. This dramatic swing is shifting the focus of every aspect of our lives from popular fashion to the average age of college students, from the kinds of foods we eat to our society's political priorities. Our new composition of fewer youths and more older adults is just the opposite of what we've traditionally seen in the demographic makeup of our world, and this trend is projected to continue, recalibrating the balance of power away from youth, toward the later years.

So what is the specific demographic makeup that is changing what we look like? In the year 2000, the youngest age group—those from birth to 17—consisted of 70 million people, the largest population of young people to appear since the post–World War II baby boom generation.[8] However, it represents not just U.S. births but the constant in-migration of children and young families moving into the United States. If this were not the case, this age group would be a shrinking population group.

The young adult population group—age 18 to 34—is the smallest of any age group, with only 55 million people in the United States.[9] That has never before been the case. Historically, this stage of life has always been the bull's-eye of American business; the group most coveted by marketers; the group influencing society and culture the most. However, for the first time ever—due to declining birthrates in the '70s and '80s—this has become a shrinking demographic segment. As a result, the young adult age group is steadily diminishing in size, spending power, and, ultimately, importance.

While the young adult population is declining, the midlife age group is growing in size, gaining strength in numbers and financial power. It is where the growth and, consequently, the power in the United States is migrating. The 35- to 54-year-old population segment is comprised mostly of those born during the post–World War II baby boom and known as baby boomers. Seventy-eight million strong, it represents one-third of the entire U.S. population. Based on sheer size alone, it's an influential group. As we will soon see, this population impacts the overall culture more than any other and will continue to do so for decades to come.

The 55-plus age group has become the fastest growing segment with almost 60 million people.[10] As life expectancy continues to rise, this age group will remain the fastest growing, with rising financial and political strength.

As birthrates remain on the decline and people continue to live longer, our world is shifting from one dominated by youth to one steadily filling up with midlife and older adults. Although our world is no longer youth dominated, that reality hasn't fully sunk into our collective attitudes and mind-set. For example, youth is still defined as the *in* place to be in our culture. We still cling to the basic assumption that the first 40 or 50 years is where the action is and then life becomes a slow descent; life after 50 is the *over the hill* years. Our center of gravity has moved from youth to midlife, but our perceptions of life have remained somewhat stagnant and stuck in the past reality.

Businesses continue, out of habit, to think that the youth market is still where the action is. They continue to think that adults are over the hill, that they have but one shot at consumers, when they're young: "Catch them in youth, and you'll have them forever."

But, as we're about to see, that is no longer the case. The world will steadily transform to better match the size and the shape of who we are becoming. And the boomers will help ignite this transformation toward a more cyclic way of life.

Boomers: Pioneering the Cyclic Life

As the cultural epicenter moves from youth to midlife and beyond, the character and values of consumers will change, influenced strongly by the boomer generation. In researching and studying the different generations, it has become clear that although boomers are a huge and highly diverse group, there is a set of values, attitudes, and expectations that are generally shared within the overall group. In fact, boomers were the first generation to exemplify certain traits that have been adopted by younger generations and even sometimes by their elders. Let me add that boomers are not always admired or even liked by other generations. In fact, they're often resented, for the very reason that they are followed. That is, there are so many of them, their sheer size and confluence of core values and attitudes influence the attitudes and values of the overall society. Boomers will be the pioneers creating the path into the second half of life that future generations will follow.

Boomers entered life after a series of tumultuous, dark moments in history. During the 1930s and early 1940s, couples had few children. Worldwide economic depression, followed by a devastating World War, led to low birthrates. But that all changed after the Allies, led by the United States, won World War II. Suddenly, the economy was expanding as it never had before; prosperity became a reality. Hope and optimism replaced despair and hopelessness. Believing the future held great promise, young men and women rushed to get married and help build a new, better world. Ninety-two percent of those people of marriageable age went to the altar, and more than 84 percent of those had children, averaging nearly four births per couple. As shown in Figure 1.3, between 1946 and 1964 we had 76 million live births in the United States alone. That translates to one-third of the entire U.S. population, born in an 18-year period. Similar population explosions took place throughout Australia, Canada, Great Britain, France, and New Zealand.

What soon became evident was that the boomers were a magnetic force field that held the attention of our entire culture. Wherever the boomers moved along the life span, their needs, interests, and desires created trends that reverberated throughout society.

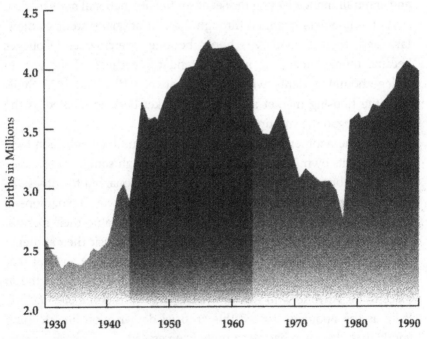

Figure 1.3
The U.S. Baby Boom, 1946–1964
Source: United States Bureau of the Census, 2000.

Smart businesses saw that these boomers were a potent marketplace phenomenon, affecting product purchases more than any other age group. When they were babies, Dr. Spock became the first millionaire author by advising parents how to raise them. The strong single-family home market and the development of the suburbs were driven by the desire to give boomers a better life. They contributed to the growth of pediatric medicine, the baby food and diaper delivery business, the positioning of Kodak cameras as a way to capture young families, the ever-burgeoning life insurance market. Wherever they were in the life span, boomers created havoc and market opportunity by their sheer numbers.

Early television executives were quick to realize that boomers were a target audience and shaped much of their schedule to entertain young kids. Popular television series of the early '50s and '60s included *Leave It to Beaver, Father Knows Best*, and *Ozzie and Harriet*. In the '50s and '60s, for the first time ever, all Americans were tuned into the same information and entertainment, planting the seeds for the first national mass market.

As the boomers migrated through the educational system, elementary and then secondary schools became overcrowded. Colleges became more demanding in their standards because of the glut in college-bound students, which tripled between 1965 and 1975. Similarly, the housing market and the job market became inflated as the boomers began the "nesting" cycle of life.

When the boomers hit their teenage years, suddenly rebellion took on a life of its own. Every generation goes through some sort of rebellious behavior as part of asserting their own persona, but to witness 76 million people rebelling at once created a worldwide revolution—a youth revolution. "Don't trust anyone over 30" became their mantra, jeans and long hair their uniform, and rock 'n' roll music their anthem.

During this period, our obsession with youth became so total that the overall culture embraced this message, and youth became the *in* place to be. Anyone who was not young, was considered *over the hill*. Even as the boomers crossed this artificial demarcation line defining youth, that obsession has never quite been erased.

As free-spending teenagers, boomers continued to fuel the economy. The *Pepsi Generation* was born because American adolescents gulped 25 percent of all soft drinks. They invented rock 'n' roll and were responsible for 43 percent of total record sales. They bought 53 percent of all movie tickets and soon became the target market for new business ideas such as fast food. According to boomer historian Landon Jones, "Advertisers intensified this generation's self-awareness. Being isolated as the first target market has made the boomers avid consumers."[11] At the same time, being earmarked as an incredibly attractive consumer group has given them tremendous power as a generational force.

In many ways, that is the greatest strength of this generation: their collective power. The boomers are a lot like the phenomenal Pando Aspen Grove in Utah. Fly over Pando and the naked eye views a large, beautiful grove of aspen trees, but looks can be deceiving. This aspen grove is really just one organism, sharing the same root system. The boomers, too, are large in numbers and seemingly diverse, but they share a common set of values and attitudes from which much of their power emanates. As individuals, boomers have never held any more or less clout than previous generations. But, as a generation, they have pruned themselves to be an all-powerful organism.

In 1969, *Time* magazine singled out this generation as their Man of the Year, an honor usually bestowed on significant world leaders. It was the first time ever that a generation had been singled out for its leadership power. And the boomers demonstrated that power.

Today, not one person of that first generation to chant, "Don't trust anyone over 30," is under the age of 30. In 1996, the first boomers started to turn 50. From that moment forward, every eight and a half seconds, another boomer celebrates a 50th birthday. Ten thousand people each day cross the threshold to the second half of life.

Not surprisingly, as this happens, the concept of *over the hill* will be redefined. So will a lot of other things such as: how old is old, what is attractive, how long will we work, what kinds of products and services will we want, which is the target market to be coveted, what is retirement, and how we will organize our lives. Maturing boomers will see to that.

The boomers, as a collective, will use their power to reinvent the second half of life. It's time. And, as we've repeatedly seen, the boomers have the magnetic power to create new trends and accelerate social change. Reinventing maturity is next in line and that's exactly what they will do.

BOOMER TRAITS

For such a large population, boomers share a surprising number of the same experiences, attitudes, and values. Because they are the magnetic core of our society, these values and attitudes are transferred by osmosis to the overall population. They have already laid the groundwork to defy every cultural stereotype there is on aging and how to live the second half of life. That's their nature as rule breakers, one of their key traits that falls directly out of the fact that boomers are much more highly educated than previous generations.

Based on their educational background and their intellectual curiosity, boomers have done what well-educated people do—question authority and the status quo. In older generations, such as the mature generations born before World War II, individuals tended to respect authority and follow the rules set down by society. Boomers broke this rule and set the precedent for future generations to question authority as a matter of course. They're rebellious by nature and like to do things differently than those who came before.

The parents of boomers who, themselves, were rule-followers and comfortable with conformity, raised their children to believe in themselves and think of themselves as unique or special. One result of that message is that many boomers feel it their right and obligation to "do life"in their own way. This individualistic nature of boomers makes them fundamentally different from their parents, no matter how old they are.

Although it was their parents who fed them the message, "you're special" as they grew up, boomers' parents didn't always like the way this message manifested in their children's personalities. They considered their individualistic nature to be self-centered and narcissistic. They started to label the boomers the Me Generation and resented their attitude. But what some call narcissistic or selfish might also be described as self-reliant and entrepreneurial—two key survival skills for the fast-paced and quickly changing twenty-first century.

Boomers are social entrepreneurs, experimenters, and innovators by nature and nurture. Usually experimentation and innovation is something associated primarily with the young, but boomers have broken this rule, too. With every step they have taken, they have created innovation in the social, lifestyle, business, and economic life of our entire society.

It's no surprise that boomers ended up protesting as teenagers and exploring a spectrum of alternative lifestyles as adults such as delayed marriage, divorce if the marriage didn't work out, delayed childbearing, and alternative ways to practice religion. They have changed the role of women, expanded the definition of *family*, and transformed the workplace. Boomer entrepreneurs such as Steve Jobs and Steve Wozniak launched a technology revolution from their garages, which became a force of change for our entire economy.

If boomers are nothing else, they are control freaks. They enjoy regulating the social and lifestyle barometer or the direction our society is moving. They take pride in the fact that wherever they are in the cycle of life, their needs and interests become central themes for the entire culture. We can almost bet that they aren't about to give up that role willingly as past generations have done when they reach their more mature years. The boomers won't accept the downward descent stereotypical of the second half of life as a fait accompli.

According to my husband, Ken Dychtwald, in *Age Power*, "The assumption that boomers would migrate through life's stages in exactly the same way as the more traditional generations before them proved to be way off base. Much more indulged, boomers are more inclined to question the status quo and more willing to speak out and challenge authority than any previous generation."[12] Throughout their lives, boomers haven't really behaved like their parents and grandparents and are not about to start now just because they are crossing the traditional threshold of youth. They will strive to age differently. Remember, they created the youth culture and feel it their privilege to bring the concept of *youth* with them into the second half of life. They will not accept the long-held belief that older people are past their prime; they disavow the commandment to "act your age"; they will live, work, and buy in a more cyclic approach to life.

What does that mean? Business will need to adjust its attitude toward maturity if it is to effectively woo the newly empowered mature consumer which, by the way, will soon represent the majority of consumers.

Boomers will be the pioneers that clear the paths for the cyclic life, merging the spirit and excitement of youth with the experience and perspective of maturity to create an entirely new hybrid—a kind of youthful wisdom or even *ageless aging*. In so doing, they will lay the foundation for a new approach to living with the space for continual reinvention—a more cyclic approach.

EVOLUTION OF THE CYCLIC LIFE

When the three demographic forces—*(1) the longevity factor, (2) a youth society giving way to a more middle-aged world, and (3) the magnetic force of boomer values and attitudes*—intersect, one of the most basic implications that results is that boomers opt to "do life" on their own terms rather than by the old linear-life formula. This is creating a new model of how we'll live; a model that gives us the freedom to design our lives to fit our personal needs and desires.

Sociologists have long told us that society organizes life into a linear-life pattern where three clear stages of life are defined. Education, the first stage, prepares us for our main roles in life. The second stage is the major part of life: work and family. The final stage of life was originally designed as a short period of rest and reflection before death, but that has now evolved into a longer period of leisure activity. Life was seen as orderly, linear, and predictable; this created a straightforward roadmap of life. You might veer off the prescribed path, but at least a roadmap existed to beckon you back. This linear pattern was sensible in a society where people lived short lives and showed a deep respect for following the rules and outside authority.

The linear view was great for business because marketers knew exactly what activities consumers were likely to be involved in just by knowing how old they were. If, for instance, you were in the education business, you could target your products to young people and only young people. They were the market. If you were in the insurance business, you targeted young families—18- to 34-year-olds—exclusively. Within this predictable life pattern, age alone was the primary factor in understanding and targeting the market. That was all we needed to know.

Now a more cyclic approach to life is already beginning to evolve where the stages of life—education, work and family, and leisure—are reshuffling and reappear multiple times throughout each lifetime. A new life of cycles is replacing the straight and narrow linear path of yesterday.

For business, those easy days of marketing to populations that were marching lockstep through the predictable stages of life is over! We are seeing women opting to raise a family after they reach 40; men and women of all ages reinventing their careers; an avid interest in learning at 20, 40, and even 70; and we're even seeing budding romance and love among those at the far end of the age spectrum, 80-year-olds and beyond.

This new model tells us "just because you're down, it doesn't mean you're out," "comebacks are not only possible, but probable," "life is what you make it," and other hopeful messages to imply we can all bloom innumerable times in life, adorned in different colors and patterns each time.

As a result, education is no longer something just for the young. Retirement is not just for the old. Marriage, career, parenting, and leisure pursuits are all being transformed, creating opportunities for some and challenges for others. If you can see it coming, the new cyclic model is like a breath of fresh air liberating us at every turn. This far-reaching LifeCycle revolution introduces new values, attitudes, and expectations that break loose the shackles that have restrained us throughout time.

According to a Yankelovich Monitor survey, 42 percent of consumers agree with the statement, "If I had a chance to start over in life, I would do things much differently."[13] And many of us are. Harbingers of reinvention are popping up all around us. We've all watched Regis Philbin come back from a bout with heart disease to rev up his career as the host of the recently canceled *Who Wants to Be a Millionaire?* For a while, he was treated almost like a rock star, with men of all ages copying his style of dress. Maybe he'll come back once again. Most of us shared Katie Couric's pain as she courageously helped her husband (and, later, her sister) unsuccessfully battle colon cancer. We supported her as she grieved and finally overcame this tragedy, beginning to build a life as a single working mother, dating for the first time in years. She updated her hairstyle, became a blond, renewed her contract with the *Today* show for millions, and found a cute boyfriend. She has since fallen in and out of love again, and we're cheering her on as she continues to discover and rediscover herself. And Carlos Santana reinvented his rock 'n' roll career, winning eight Grammies including album of the year for *Supernatural* at the 2000 Grammy Awards. By partnering with a variety of hip young musicians such as Rob Thomas of Matchbox 20, Lauryn Hill, and Dave Matthews, he created an album that was loved by young and old selling more than 21 million copies worldwide. What helps make this comeback even more impressive is that it was produced and orchestrated by then 67-year-old Clive Davis.

This revolutionary cyclic model of living will unhinge many of the basic expectations that businesses take for granted. For example, we could take three 50-year-old men, all in the same socioeconomic category, even in the same career, and find they have very different needs based on the LifeCycle events they are moving into. One, for instance, might be very traditional, with kids already out of school. He hopes to take an early retirement and live a traditional retiree lifestyle. He's a perfect target customer for golf clubs, a retirement home in a warm climate, and long-term care insurance. But don't try selling those products to the second man. He hates his job and wants to quit to become an entrepreneur. He's looking for a contractor to renovate and add an office onto his home, home office equipment, and a good small business health insurance plan. Not the third 50-year-old. He just got married to a younger woman who wants to start a family. He's shopping for fertility treatments, a bigger home, a minivan, and term life insurance.

Age no longer defines who we are, what we are doing with our lives, and what we might be demanding from the marketplace. As we will soon see, the boomers will be the first generation to extend the number of working and spending years to remain part of mainstream society far longer than any preceding generation. We need to look at LifeCycle events and where people are in the cycle of their own lives rather than at their chronologic age as a method of understanding the new adult consumer.

In the chapters that follow, we will look at every aspect of our lives—from learning to recreation, from romance to the family—to envision how the LifeCycle revolution will change the way we live, work, and buy. We will explore some of the ways this revolution will impact each of us, and the products and services we demand from the marketplace. And, of course, we will explore its impact on business.

LIFELONG LEARNERS

In the old linear model of life, education was a gift granted only once and only to the young. It was considered a necessary first step toward adulthood that ended abruptly before work-life began. In the LifeCycle revolution, education becomes an essential component to living a long life well, a tool for continual reinvention and better living, no matter how old someone is. It's a deep well many of us are likely to revisit several times throughout our life. Andrew M. Rosenfeld of Unext.com, a leader in Web-based education, says it best: "Static education is a thing of the past. You can't fill up your tank at age 25 and then coast without needing a refill."

The cyclic life offers us the opportunity to distribute and integrate education into our whole lives, not just into our youth. We may choose to accelerate, eliminate, or defer certain segments of the existing education system as we see fit. For example, college or higher education used to be viewed as something young adults pursued immediately after high school to help set their course for real life. It was designed to provide them with the tools needed to live a better, richer life. Although the U.S. Department of Education reports that two-thirds of last year's high-school graduates are pursuing higher education this year, that's not necessarily how it will work anymore. "In 2001, *The Journal of Higher Education* reported that taking a year off between high school and college is a small, but growing, trend."[1]

We may go back to college or another higher education program that enhances our work or lives several times over the course of our lives. We may choose to work or travel before we pursue college or graduate school. It will be our choice to decide at what points along the way we will want and need to enhance our education, but it will be an essential ingredient in the cyclic life offering us the opportunity for continual reinvention. Cyclic learning is here to stay.

THE ROOTS OF LIFELONG LEARNING

Three converging forces are coming together simultaneously to create a society that puts a high premium on lifelong learning:

1. Increased longevity
2. A knowledge-powered economy
3. A love of learning

Increased Longevity

When we step back to think about it, it makes perfect sense that lifelong learning is becoming the new status quo. As people live longer lives, the need for updated knowledge and changing skill sets will grow dramatically, especially given the rapidly increasing speed of change in today's world. For example, in the last 20 years, we've seen the workplace alter the way it does business through the development of fax machines, voice mail, e-mail, overnight delivery service, and the whole world of computer technology. Imagine what a woman who has devoted the last 20 years to raising her children would have to contend with if she were to consider reentering the workforce. Even with a college degree or a business degree, the work environment and the tools used for efficiency would have become almost unrecognizable. Or imagine, as we live longer, that we might be working until age 70, 75, or even older. And then factor in the chance we might decide to change careers.

These new realities require continuous updating and learning new information as well as developing skills to help us cope in a quickly changing world. Continued learning throughout life will become an essential tool rather than an occasional endeavor.

A Knowledge-Powered Economy

At the same time that life expectancy is rising and the rate of change is accelerating, a new economic model has taken root: a knowledge-powered economy. In such an economy, more information, ideas, and concepts are being produced than manufactured goods. Obviously, manufactured goods such as cars, clothes, and soap are still valued commodities, but, relying on new and constantly improving knowledge-based innovations, these products are manufactured and distributed using fewer human resources and more automated tools.

Management expert and Claremont University professor Peter Drucker describes this shift, "In the 1950s, people who worked to make or move things were still a majority in all developed countries. By 1990, they had shrunk to one-fifth of the workforce. By 2010, they will form no more than one-tenth."[2] On the other side of the coin, the U.S. Labor Department reports that professional and managerial jobs make up 60 percent of the new jobs; such jobs employ 70 percent of the college graduates in the workforce. One result of these shifts is that many jobs and career paths will disappear while others will morph in new directions. The U.S. Department of Education declared in the year 2000 that "60 percent of all new jobs in the twenty-first century will require skills that are possessed by only 20 percent of the current workforce." For example, the need for bank tellers dropped dramatically with the innovation of ATM machines. Many tellers were forced to learn and develop new skills for fresh career paths. The same is true for telephone operators. It's not often that a live operator helps us anymore. At the same time, new career paths appear on the horizon based on the development of new technologies and other knowledge-based innovations. Database administrators and systems analysts barely existed 20 years ago; today they're two of the fastest growing jobs in America, according to the U.S. Department of Labor that reports 20 million net jobs were created in the six-year period ending in November 1999.

Not only is our knowledge-based economy ever evolving, its strength is determined to a great extent by the intelligence and creativity of those who are actively involved in it. We are, after all, the source of new discoveries, innovations, and applications of knowledge. To stay current, all of us will need to invest in the continual acquisition of information and skills throughout our lives.

Federal Reserve Chairman Alan Greenspan, speaking at a Labor Department–sponsored summit on the future of the workforce, emphasized this fact in June of 2001. In his keynote speech, rather than focus on interest-rate policy, he stressed how crucial it was for the United States to continue to invest in research and scientific breakthroughs, especially at leading American university research centers where new innovations often are the outcome of that research. Greenspan said, "If we are to remain preeminent in transforming knowledge into economic value, the U.S. system of higher education must remain the world leader in generating scientific and technological breakthroughs, and in preparing workers to meet the evolving demands for skilled labor." He added, "The days when a high school or college education would serve a person throughout his working life are gone. Learning will increasingly need to be a lifelong activity."[3]

With cyclic careers becoming more common, lifelong learning becomes a necessity rather than a luxury. Cyclic careers are a primary driver of the trend toward lifelong learning. Unless we continuously upgrade our capabilities and go back to the well of knowledge regularly, we each will become as obsolete as many of the no-longer-used manufacturing techniques or products of a century ago. Knowledge power will rule the coming decades.

A Love of Learning

"Being the perfect teacher requires the perfect student." In order to have a society where lifelong learning becomes the status quo, we need to value and enjoy learning.

Boomers were the first-ever well-educated generation. In 1950, 75 percent of Americans 55 or older were high school dropouts. Education was considered a luxury reserved for the rich or super smart. In contrast, 87 percent of boomers are high school graduates and 26 percent have college degrees while over half have some college experience. Higher education for boomers was a rite of passage, and for the first time, college and high-powered learning became something for the masses rather than just the elite. (See Figures 2.1 and 2.2.)

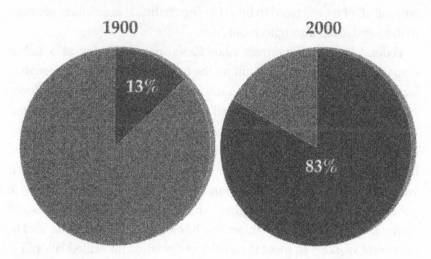

Figure 2.1
High School Graduates
Source: United States Bureau of the Census, 2000.

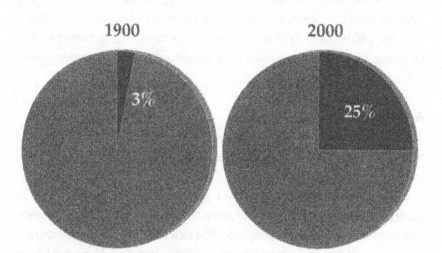

Figure 2.2
College Graduates
Source: United States Bureau of the Census, 2000.

Their thirst for knowledge didn't just go away when they reached adulthood. Boomers continue to hold education as an important value for themselves and their children. More than any previous generation, they see a strong link between learning, self-improvement, life satisfaction, and career success. Sixty percent of boomers firmly believe a formal education is key to reaching the American Dream.[4]

One of the myths supporting the idea that education is primarily for the young was the assumption that the dominant period for maximum capacity learning was life's early years. As many of us suspected all along, this simply isn't the case. Now that there are so many older adults alive at once, science has been able to study this issue to determine if adults can, in fact, continue to learn and grow intellectually as they age. Researchers such as Dr. Helen Neville, a leading expert on brain plasticity working at the Center for the Neural Basis of Cognition in Pittsburgh, Pennsylvania, and Dr. Jay McClelland, co-director at that same institution, have conducted seminal experiments that demonstrate that the adult brain, like the adolescent brain, is capable of significant change, even late in life. This suggests that age is not really an obstacle to learning.

There may be a difference in how we learn as adults, but it's a learning *style* rather than the *ability* to learn. Researchers have found that, on the down side, as we get older our ability to access information we already know might take a little longer. On the up side, our ability to think critically actually improves. And adult learners are often more highly motivated to learn. They're usually seeking education to better their life while young people are sometimes on a preprogrammed education plan as dictated by society and/or their parents. Most important, they have work and life experience that can make abstract principles real and concrete. That can even make them more interesting students from the point of view of their instructors.

Further, scientific data is beginning to point to the fact that education can be a key tool to maintaining health as we age. *The MacArthur Study of Successful Aging* report that the education level of an individual is a strong predictor of sustained mental functioning. Simply put, a person with more education has a higher likelihood of functioning well mentally in the second half of life than does a person with less education. In

addition, this groundbreaking study found that the more we continue
to take part in activities that require mental activity, the higher the likelihood for sustaining mental functioning.

Not only does lifelong learning help maintain better brain function;
it can actually keep us *feeling* younger longer. Researchers Eileen M.
Crimmins and Mark D. Haward of the University of Southern California
have shown a direct correlation between education levels and maintaining physical health, vitality, and a general sense of youthfulness.
Their work demonstrates that highly educated 60-year-olds have the
same rates of disease and disability as less-educated 50-year-olds. In
short, the well-educated will, most likely, age more slowly.

At the same time, many of us have come to believe that doing crossword puzzles or playing cards might help keep our memory and brainpower intact longer. Now, a new study suggests there just might be
some truth to this "use it or lose it" theory. The study, by scientists at
Rush Alzheimer's Disease Center at Rush-Presbyterian-St. Luke's
Medical Center in Chicago found that participating in activities that are
cognitively stimulating is associated with a reduced risk of Alzheimer's
disease. They looked at everyday activities like reading, doing crossword
puzzles, and going to museums among participants in the Religious
Order Study, an ongoing study of aging among older Catholic nuns,
priests, and brothers from several groups across the United States. Scientists discovered that, on a scale measuring cognitive activity—with
higher scores indicating more frequent activity—a one-point increase
in cognitive activity corresponded with a 33 percent reduction in the
risk of Alzheimer's disease. Use it or lose it is an important preventative
health tool.[5]

As we begin to understand that old dogs must learn new tricks to
stay healthy, vital, and relevant, lifelong learning will be a key tool to
enable us to be whom we choose to be, no matter how old we are. We'll
begin to feel less like the second half of life is a downward slide and
more open to the attitude that anything is possible, no matter how old
we are.

As interested as boomers are in their own education, it's not surprising that they have worked hard to provide their children with an even
better education; something all income and socioeconomic levels agree

is a necessity in our fast-paced, knowledge-based economy. In the year 2000, the percentage of 25- to 29-year-olds who completed at least high school rose from 78 percent to 83 percent. Over the same period, the percentage of high-school graduates in this age group who also completed some college increased from 44 to 66 percent, and the percentage who obtained a bachelor's degree or higher rose from 22 to 33 percent. The National Center for Education Statistics has labeled this younger generation *hypereducated*.

Boomer parents have demanded that childhood education become a priority on both local and national political agendas, campaigning for more funds at the local and state level, taking part in classroom activities, and aggressively raising private funds to improve classroom education. For instance, in my community, which is home to about 30,000 people, activist parents help keep class size small, supplement teachers' salaries, provide elective courses such as music and art, and enhance classroom materials by donating almost $1 million annually to the local schools.

Throughout the United States, some parents have taken the quest to improve their children's education even further by banding together to create charter schools or even home schooling their own children. In the last decade alone, the number of children home schooled has gone from 500,000 to 1.7 million.

One thing is clear: the boomers' love of education has successfully been transferred to their children. And, as we move into a more cyclic life pattern, education will span the decades and become a more independent venture to meet our own specific needs and desires. Whether we're 8, 18, or 80, this will be the case. Many of us will take more control over our own education process to customize and enhance the outcome to better meet our needs and expectations.

THE MULTIGENERATIONAL PARADIGM

Today many midlife and older adults have begun to mix school into their real life to advance their personal and business skills and goals. For example, Nancy Donald is 45 years old, married, a graphic designer, and mother of two school-age girls. Nancy's career has always been a big part of her life, but she started to feel frustrated as she saw more and more young designers who worked under her bring multimedia skills to the table that didn't even exist when she was being trained. Without these skills and knowledge base, she knew she would have a hard time advancing in her career. Not only that, she longed to be able to add those skills to her own arsenal. Between family and work commitments, she knew she just didn't have time to sandwich one more thing into her life. However, she decided education had to be a priority or both her work and family life would suffer. So when her daughters enter middle school and high school next year, Nancy will be taking a leave-of-absence from work to start school, too, at Stanford University for her master's degree in multimedia design.

Nancy's two daughters have been talking about how they feel scared and excited to start new schools in the fall. Nancy feels the same way and maybe even more so. She worries that, among other things, she'll be the oldest person in the class, she'll be isolated from her classmates because most of them will be living close to campus while she'll be commuting 45 minutes daily, she won't be easily available for study groups because of her family commitments, and that she just doesn't have the focus to study anymore. She also worries about the impact it will have on her family. At the same time she's excited to have the chance to be immersed in the cutting-edge advancements of her profession, meeting others who will be there, too, and having the luxury to devote time to developing new skills for the next chapter of her career.

Nancy's story is not that unusual. In 1991, an estimated 58 million adults in the United States participated in adult education. By the year 2000, that number almost doubled to an estimated 90 million. Today, more than 40 percent of those enrolled in higher education are part-time students over 25.[6] The average age in community colleges has shot all the way up to 32, and is rising. Some education experts project that the number of college students over age 35 will soon be larger than the number of students who are 18 and 19.

One of the questions that this dynamic forces us to ask is, How are we going to pay for this education? In the old linear-life model, parents usually scrimped and saved to pay for the education of their children to offer them a better life. If the kids were really smart or great athletes, they might even get scholarships to school. And there was always the option of student loans, a variety of student aid programs, or inexpensive community colleges. However, today a new financing device has appeared on the horizon. Just like venture capitalists invest in companies, investors are beginning to research individuals in need of financing their education in exchange for a piece of their future income. Already, a company has appeared in midtown Manhattan, MyRichUncle, that calls itself a "for-profit charity investing in human capital." Cofounders Vishal Garg and Raza Khan loan students between $5,000 and $10,000 per semester with the understanding that they'll get paid back anywhere from .5 to 4 percent of their future earnings for 10 to 15 years. Marie Gjoni was a client who needed tuition for NYU; "Something might have worked out, but I really preferred this," she said, "I see them as a benefactor."[7]

Today graduate school and specialized professional training such as medical school and law school are on the to-do lists of people of all ages rather than only the young who are just graduating from undergraduate school. Many students arrive at medical school with Ph.D.'s or experience in the workplace. The median age among first-year medical students has gone up to age-25; up from age-22 just a decade ago. And women now make up 43 percent of all students, up from just over 30 percent in 1984.

With college admissions becoming even more competitive with the number of applicants per opening growing from 10 to 12 or 13 and all the pressures on young people to take the same road at the same time, some young people might choose to opt out temporarily to get some thinking time and figure out what they really want to do in their lives. They might choose to work or travel prior to their college education while those that are a little older with more life experience might view their goals with more clarity and be more highly motivated to attend graduate schools that are highly competitive and filled with pressure.

The traditional model of education told us that this wasn't right; education must come first or it won't happen at all. The new model of lifelong learning tells us that delaying education doesn't mean putting it off forever, but integrating it into our entire lives in a more comfortable manner. As a growing number of young people feel less pressure to continue their formal education immediately after high school, a real slice-and-dice approach to higher education will emerge.

Kristen, for instance, is a college senior whose major is premedicine. Ever since she was a child, she has wanted to be a pediatrician. But she's been so focused on her studies for so many years that she decided to take a year's break to clear her head and relax a little before entering the even more intense period of study required by medical school. Her college advisor suggested that she might want to defer medical school even longer so she can explore life a little more and be certain that pediatrics would be the best place for her. He suggested working in a preschool for a year, as a nanny, or even volunteering in an inner-city school tutoring program. He said, "You're going to be a doctor for a long time. A few years exploring the world prior to medical school might make that experience even richer. It would certainly make you more sure that medicine and, in particular, pediatrics is the right career direction for you."

Kristen isn't alone. Twenty percent of Harvard undergraduates take off some time from school, often even before they head to Harvard. Dean of Admissions William R. Fitzsimmons encourages the practice.[8]

As our process of education begins to span the decades, some educators are questioning the duration of our traditional four-year high school model. Maybe, they propose, we need to shorten or redesign the "education only" segment of life to better meet the needs of who we are becoming: lifelong learners.

What becomes clear is that a love of learning and an understanding of *how* to learn might be the most important skills that primary education can give us. For some, that may take longer than for others. For still others it might require a less traditional path. For instance, AmeriCorps offers the chance for students to take time out from school to give their time and energy to a menu of volunteer opportunities. This can include anything from tutoring local kids to building new homes for families; from restoring coastlines to helping families traumatized by domestic violence. They provide a modest living allowance, health insurance, student loan deferment, and training. Plus, after service is completed, students receive a $4,725 education award to help pay for college, grad school, vocational training, or to pay off student loans. Other programs, such as those offered by Outward Bound, National Civilian Community Corps, the Global Service Corps, and Dynamy, offer young people the chance to integrate volunteering, work, or creative learning experiences into their traditional education years. These programs are beginning to sprout up all over the United States, Canada, Australia, New Zealand, the United Kingdom, and other westernized countries.

Another shift that takes place in a lifelong pursuit of education is that the pressure involved with the choice of career specialization begins to melt away. I remember when I was getting ready to go to college, my parents told me I had to choose a major that would lead to a clear career path. I couldn't have two or three majors; I had to choose just one. That was a fear-inducing and paralyzing thought to me. I had at least five or six career paths that I could see myself taking, but none of them were related and each would require a different educational emphasis. In addition, I had no idea what was really involved with any of the career paths I had in mind. They were really fantasy career paths based on nothing but a hunch that I might like them. I eventually chose something I never pursued, changed my major numerous times, and felt like I squandered much of my time in college. The inertia that it created contributed to the more than four years it took me to complete college.

In a lifelong learning model, these pressures dissipate substantially. For one thing, we no longer have to feel our learning has to lead to just one career choice. We may specialize in one thing and then move on to a far different career. So-called frivolous choices such as being a poet or a model seem less threatening to check-writing parents when we accept that a frivolous choice might be an essential first step in the lifelong process of self-discovery rather than the entire focus of life. The fear component of making a lifelong mistake is tempered when we know that we need not be bound by the educational choices we make at 18.

Lifelong learning offers all ages and incomes a chance to continually open their minds. It's not just young and midlife adults who pursue learning; it's older adults as well. And their pursuit is not usually based on preparation for careers or enhancing job skills, but on the love of learning itself. Much of this learning is taking place through a broad spectrum of programs in community colleges and university extension programs as well as top-tier centers of education. More than 1,000 colleges in the United States encourage mature adults to take classes and almost 200 schools have developed programs specifically for older learners. Harvard University, for example, has developed the Institute for Learning in Retirement where mature adults pay a pittance to take a class at Harvard. They've had students as old as 95 attend classes.[9]

Mature adults, however, aren't limited to learning in the traditional school environment. Elderhostel, for example, is a Boston-based, nonprofit program that offers mature adults the chance to combine learning with travel. They offer an entire catalog filled with course selections available at a diverse cross-section of college campuses around the world. The over age-60 students live in dorms, eat together in the dining halls, attend classes, and generally have a wonderful time.

One Elderhostel couple who attended a variety of programs over several years describe their experience this way:

"We've carved linoleum; found a beaver dam; climbed around mountains, temples in India, a Roman bath in Wales, and over the remains of an amphitheatre in England; sailed on Loch Lomond in Scotland; ridden in an ancient outrigger canoe in the bay out of a palm-shaded lagoon near Kona, Hawaii; and found giant pinecones at 7,000 feet in Idlewild, Colorado. Ed played jazz piano with fellow students at two Elderhostels at Chapel Hill, North Carolina, and in shows on Friday nights at many other Elderhostels."[10]

In 1975, Elderhostel had 220 students at five sites. By 1988, that number grew to 170,000 students in 1,000 sites in 37 countries. In the year 2000, over a quarter million students attended learning programs in more than 10,000 sites in 100 countries. Elderhostel isn't the only program that combines leisure and learning for mature adults. National Geographic, Earthwatch, and other organizations focused on nature and the environment have begun sponsoring field trips that combine travel and learning to sites all over the world. Often they bring distinguished anthropologists, ornithologists, historians, and naturalists along to remote locales to lead discussions and field tours. Although these programs are not specifically aimed at mature adults, more than any other age group those are the people who have the time and money to attend. A key attraction of travel programs like these is that there are no spectators; each traveler joins in to participate, actively learning and contributing at the same time.

The process and timing of education have already begun to shift and change form, showing us the early signs of the future of lifelong learning. The LifeCycle revolution will transform education from a onetime early lifestage into a cyclic experience that returns throughout our lives, no matter how old or young we might be.

TOWARD A RETOOLED MODEL OF EDUCATION

Now that the door to education can be unlocked more easily throughout our lives, the pressure to get it all in when we're young will begin to recede. Most of us will be cycling in and out of education at *every* stage of life. This will beg for a retooling of the very system in which we learn. The 2,500-year-old Socratic method of teaching face-to-face to an exclusively young population is in definite need of more than just a superficial facelift. In this era where lifelong learning is essential to our future, a new model of education must take shape.

This new model will enhance the best of the Socratic model to take advantage of the new power tools that advancing technologies offer us. At the same time, education will become more democratic and less ageist, offering options for learning that accommodate a variety of different ages, incomes, and social and lifestyle needs. In all likelihood, education will become an increasingly for-profit industry, catering to various adult populations whenever and wherever their interests are piqued.

For years, we've heard rumblings about *distance learning,* but it's never amounted to much . . . until now. The Internet and other technologic innovations have led to the formation of *virtual universities* that provide lifelong learning on demand, interactively, freed from the physical confines of the traditional classroom.

The number of students taking advantage of virtual universities is growing by 33 percent every year. Enrollment is expected to hit 2.2 million by 2004, according to International Data Corporation.[11] Offering an incredible variety of courses through the Internet, virtual university learning provides students with the opportunity to take accredited

courses and interact regularly with teachers, without time-intensive
travel, rigid schedules, and difficulty getting into popular classes. We
can still listen to lectures, talk with teachers and other students during
chat times, take tests, write papers, and get grades and credits. Through
broadband access and video streaming, we even get the chance to take
a class with a popular teacher who might otherwise be available only in
a rigidly scheduled, direct face-to-face interaction.

The virtual university can hold appeal to people of all ages, but its
advantages are most immediately understood by those who have other
commitments in their lives that prohibit them from pursuing a traditional education. Alan Spindell is a typical virtual university student
who might not have had the chance to learn and ultimately to change
careers without the aid of the Internet and distance learning. A 40-
something New Yorker, married with a teenage daughter and a toddler,
Alan was a stockbroker who realized he no longer enjoyed his work. He
longed to be a teacher, helping high-school kids realize their potential.
To do so, he had to go back to school himself to get an education
degree. That was a near impossibility: Alan's wife also worked long
hours which meant that Alan had a lot of family responsibilities, such as
helping his older daughter with her homework after school and picking
up his youngest from day care. So he enrolled in www.suny.edu, which
is part of the state college system in New York. Late at night, Alan is on
the Internet working his way through the comprehensive curriculum he
needs to earn his master's degree.

Bill Reid, a 29-year-old military retiree, is another example of a non-
traditional student who chose still a different direction. He wanted a
degree through a classroom experience rather than a virtual one, but he
didn't want any of the traditional trappings he associated with school.
"At my age, I didn't feel like sitting in line at the bursar's office, filling
out paper work, or finding that a class I want wasn't available," said
Reid. Instead, Reid opted for the University of Phoenix, a for-profit university competing head-to-head with traditional universities and colleges, but with strategic differences.[12]

Rather than positioning itself primarily with the young, the University of Phoenix takes the opposite tack, requiring its students to be at
least 23 years old and already employed to be considered one of its

68,000 students in 15 states. Although some courses are taught online, the classes are typically given face-to-face from convenient locations like malls or office buildings near where the students live in suburban communities. The curriculum is developed at the corporate headquarters rather than by individual teachers, and delivered by a freelance group of part-time professors hired to teach each six-week class rather than by tenured professors with long-term relationships with one school. The cost of those courses is slightly higher than similar courses at public universities, but the courses are designed to be delivered in the most efficient way possible so students can complete their education sooner than at a traditional university. "Our model was designed from the ground up for a working adult student," says Todd Nelson, president of the Apollo Group, the parent company of Phoenix.

While startups such as Phoenix Online, Unext, eCollege, and Jones University repackage and deliver courses taught at established universities, many top-tier schools such as Stanford and Columbia see the opportunity to increase their revenue by linking with for-profit companies or designing curriculum themselves to deliver courses online. In 1998–99, only 48 percent of colleges and universities offered distance-learning programs. But by 2000–2001, 70 percent reported having such programs. There are no dorms, no sporting events, and little social interaction, but by the year 2000, more than 1.3 million students were enrolled in college-level distance-learning classes for credit. MIT even offers all its courses online at no cost. There was so much disagreement on how much to charge for the courses, they decided to offer all courses online for free but with no college credits or degrees.

A hybrid model combining the best of all elements could be more common in the coming years. Fordham University's Transnational MBA program offers a glimpse of this model, geared to time-pressured adults. It blends the best of the face-to-face traditional learning model with the best of the Internet. During a four-month semester, students meet face-to-face one weekend a month. Between those meetings, they use the Internet for course reading and lectures, submitting papers and taking part in class discussion and group work online. Most of the employees/students work for large multinationals such as IBM or Chevron. "We try to emulate what it's like for people in transnational organizations," says Ernest J. Scalberg of Fordham's Graduate School of Business Administration. With that in mind, students are highly motivated to learn to work together virtually since they'll need to do that in their everyday work life.

Although university and college degrees will be the goal for some learners, others will seek short bursts of pure knowledge gathering. There's been a steady growth of clinics, camps, and certified programs in the last five years that aim to meet this need. Universities across the United States interested in additional revenue now offer special programs for adults during the summer and at various breaks in the school year. Some also offer professional development certificate programs during the school year. Several years ago, my husband, Ken, enrolled in Harvard University's Business School for a weeklong class on how to be an effective board chairman. He lived in the dorm with fellow students and ate bad food in the school cafeteria. He attended challenging classes throughout the day and stayed up late studying. In the evenings he was also part of a study circle that worked on a weeklong team project. At the end of the week, he felt he had gained more real knowledge than he had in an entire semester of college previously because he knew what he wanted to learn in advance. He also felt that his peers were so smart and had such a vast bank of experiences that he learned as much from them as he did from the professors.

CAREER UPDATING AND CORPORATE TRAINING

With the quickly changing demands of the workplace and the need to reeducate the workforce every three to five years, corporate training and career updating needs will grow even more rapidly than they have over the last decade. That's saying a lot. The corporate training market has grown by over 25 percent per year for the past seven years with over $66 billion spent annually on training and education in the United States alone. Fully 65 percent of the college-educated workforce has participated in employment-related training in the past 12 months.[13] According to *The Economist*, "The $50 billion spent annually on education and training by companies accounts for about half of America's total spending on higher education."[14]

One outcome of this increasing demand for high-quality training and job skill updates is that we will eat up self-paced interactive learning tools, especially those that combine entertainment with education in an easy-to-use format. We've all gotten so used to television, as well as computer and video games, that combining an element of entertainment with learning messages is an obvious method to draw in learners and hold their ever-shortening attention spans. For instance, Gameware, an interactive learning subsidiary of Bankers Trust, has developed training programs on everything from derivatives trading to managing the reduction of sexual harassment in the workplace using formats such as card games, 3-D mazes, races, and even video games modeled after *Doom* and *Quake*. Marc Prensky, one of the innovators, describes his goal "to bring the excitement of Nintendo and computer gaming to the dry and boring world of executive training."[15]

A training program developed for Cadlab, a corporate client who needed to teach industrial engineers how to use a new piece of 3-D design software, uses a video game format that sounds a lot like a PlayStation game. It's called *The Monkey Wrench Conspiracy*, a tribute to author Edward Abbey. The trainee takes on the role of an intergalactic secret agent sent on a rescue mission to deep space and the Copernicus space station. The mission requires the secret agent or trainee to save the station from alien hijackers. The agent or trainee has to design all the tools necessary for a successful rescue. If the trainee's designs don't work, he dies, a rather direct indication that the employee's training isn't yet complete.

Career training not only keeps employees better equipped and more confident in their responsibilities but also improves job retention. According to a 1998 survey by the Gallup Organization, workers say they are more likely to stick with companies that invest in training programs. Eighty percent of workers agree that the availability of company-sponsored training programs is a strong factor in deciding whether to accept a new job.

PacifiCare Health Systems found this out and did something about it. This large HMO medical system based in California, Oregon, and Texas, began to notice a serious retention problem several years ago, when their annual turnover rate hit an all-time high of 29 percent.

Probing under the surface of this problem, they discovered that what staffers really wanted—and didn't feel like PacifiCare was offering them—was career development in the form of continuing education and training. Once PacifiCare recognized the problem for what it was, they took steps to correct it immediately and, as a result, saw employee turnover rates plummet.

As employees become more interested in their own training, corporate universities have become an essential part of many innovative companies throughout the country, including McDonald's Corporation, General Electric Company, and Federal Express Corporation. In 1988, there were fewer than 400 company-sponsored universities in the United States; today there are more than four times that number, according to Corporate University Xchange, Inc., a New York–based research firm.[16] Classes can last anywhere from one hour to three weeks. They can be highly interactive or self-paced. What they all have in common is that they give employees the chance to learn skills and information they need to move ahead on their career tracks.

Many adult learners will want customized learning experiences designed to meet their specific needs and fit in with their hectic schedules. In the past few years, there has been noticeable growth in the business of personal coaching and education. Equal parts educator, mentor, shrink (without the medical credentials), and friendly confidante, personal coaches can help individuals gain skills or knowledge in an accelerated fashion, set professional goals, and even learn how to work through transitions in personal and business life. As 76 million boomers migrate through midlife, many will seek out this kind of customized personal counsel. At the same time, as tens of thousands of echo boomers take the plunge into the world of young adulthood, there's a good chance they will take their cue from their parents and seek customized tutoring and coaching to help them navigate their complex options.

BEING THE BEST WE CAN BE

An entire industry of lifelong education focused specifically on self-improvement—mental, emotional, spiritual, and practical—has been steadily growing for decades and is about to surge. From evening courses at the Learning Annex to weekend self-discovery workshops at Esalen Institute, many of us diligently pursue knowledge to realize more of our human potential. Remember, back in the '70s, the boomers made Werner Erhardt and his program, *est*, a household name; in the '80s they helped Tony Robbins start a global empire based on discovering *Personal Power*; and in the '90s they helped turn the *Chicken Soup* books into a self-help industry of its own, complete with books, television shows, calendars, and journals. As we all try to navigate an extended life with few role models on how to do so effectively, we will seek regular infusions of knowledge to help us improve our capacity for productivity, personal effectiveness, or just plain having fun.

In response, how-to books, packaged courses, television shows, face-to-face and Internet-based learning experiences will continue to gain popularity and cover every imaginable subject. For example, as men have become more active participants in parenting their children, learning programs have cropped up to help them do so more effectively. "The Boot Camp for New Dads" program in Southern California is an example of a learning program that might never have worked with previous generations. Yet it's been a success with boomers and younger parents alike. Started by Greg Bishop, a Los Angeles–based trauma center consultant, Boot Camp is aimed at rookie dads, old and young. The program offers both practical pointers such as how to change a diaper and warm a bottle and psychological insights into coping successfully with in-laws.

As boomers' kids navigate the teenage years, the demand for workshops and clinics on subjects like coping with teens, coping with parents, talking to your children about drugs, negotiating effectively with parents, inspiring your children to greatness, and managing parents effectively will bring about a whole new generation of information and advice on coping with the rebellious years, for kids and adults alike. Already Workman Publishing is continuing its successful parenting series of infant/toddler handbooks with *What to Expect When You're a Teenager* while Stephen Covey, author of the bestseller *The 7 Habits of Highly Effective People*, inspired his own son, Scott, to write a book, *The 7 Habits of Highly Effective Teens*.

EDU-SALES

A variety of industry sectors—from financial services to health care, from travel and leisure to retail stores—are beginning to capitalize on our avid desire to learn continually. Innovative companies are beginning to build client and customer relationships as well as to increase sales by providing us with fabulous learning experiences. It's becoming an effective method of both retaining customers and acquiring new ones. It is, in fact, a viable way to create brand loyalty in a marketplace that is fickle and quick to change. Following are a few examples of how this works.

The Retail Sector

Home Chef was one of the first to offer a full curriculum of readily available, reasonably priced cooking classes where students can sign up for anything from a single session to a 12-week, full-immersion cooking school. One of the great benefits Home Chef has realized is that cooking school students tend to buy a lot of cooking supplies and equipment to help them duplicate recipes they learn, and they tend to buy these items at the store where they take the class. Home Chef has even expanded their product line to include teacher/chefs available on a freelance basis to either turn a dinner party into an event where everyone helps with the cooking or to just plain cater a dinner party.

Home Chef didn't invent this model. Weight Watchers and Jenny Craig had already perfected a similar setup. Both of these diet programs have long included packaged food for sale to their clients. In fact, packaged food sales have been the critical aspect of their business model which offers clients the education and support program first, and the tools with which to execute it second.

Home Depot applied a similar model to their customer base, realizing that informed do-it-yourselfers buy more than those intimidated by the task. They now offer in-store classes on a variety of common do-it-yourself projects such as how to build a wood deck or how to caulk windows properly.

BarnesandNoble.com launched Barnes & Noble University in July 2000, offering more than 35 free courses online. Their goal was to get students to buy the course books from BarnesandNoble.com. The results exceeded expectations. In just one week, 20,000 students registered to take courses. According to Powered, the provider of the educational courses for BarnesandNoble.com, almost one-quarter of all students enrolled in the courses purchased books from the site.

Expect to see this model for increased sales and expansion of the customer base applied to other retail sectors. For instance, we'll see more wine stores offering wine appreciation courses and wine tastings while nurseries offer classes in caring for roses or designing edible gardens. We'll see more local sporting good stores offering hiking tours and skateboarding classes. Those companies that want to increase demand for their products will work hard to get consumers interested in them through learning.

Financial Services

Savvy brokers, agents, and financial services companies have begun to wake up to the fact that one of the key benefits they can offer clients and prospects is sound financial education and advice. In the past, employees received guaranteed benefits, often including pension funds, which were funded and managed by their employers. It was all handled for them. That simply isn't the case today. If we're lucky, we might have a 401(k) fund available through our workplace where we can contribute a portion of our salary voluntarily. If we contribute regularly, our employer will match funds, but we're primarily responsible for funding our pensions and managing the funds in investments. Fifty percent of the working population report that the complexity of financial information, investment choice, and financial decision making make them unsure of what to do and so they often don't invest at all. This suggests a strong marketplace need for a range of financial literacy and education programs.

In addition, the rising number of single and professional women has generated a whole new investor class seeking to take charge of their finances. A Yankelovich Partners study done for Oppenheimer Funds found women were in even more dire need of financial education than men. Forty-seven percent of women age 21 to 34 were identified as not very knowledgeable at all concerning investing, versus 38 percent of men. The same study reported that almost half of all women in this age group reported living from paycheck to paycheck.[17]

Ann Kaplan, a Smith College trustee and alumni who is now a partner at Goldman Sachs, saw this situation as a call to action. She says, "Women will never be seen as a force in our global economy unless they have financial management skills for both their professional and personal lives." She decided this process ought to be started at the earliest stages of life. As one of the first female partners at Goldman Sachs, Ann not only put up her own money but convinced Goldman Sachs to do the same to launch a financial literacy program at Smith College. Based on further research Kaplan did on her own, she discovered that a few grammar, middle, and high schools have started to offer basic financial education to their students. These can serve as a model for other schools to adopt. However, she also noticed that financial education at the college level and beyond barely existed. In response, she decided to create Smith College's first *Women's Financial Education Program*. The program consists of four courses: (1) financial decision making, (2) current events and how they impact financial markets and individual investors, (3) entrepreneurship, and (4) principles of analyzing financial data and asset allocation.[18] This program might serve as a model for progressive financial service companies and independent financial planners.

Although many financial professionals already offer courses that relate directly to their product lines or to general investing, unfortunately they usually talk about investing in terms of the traditional linear life track where all events are age-based. One financial services company that's attempting to do it differently is AIG/SunAmerica. Recognizing that we are living more cyclic lives where saving and investing are more complex issues, they hired Age Wave to design a seminar that some of their representatives could use to build relationships with clients and prospects. The result was "LifeCourse Navigation: Charting Your Course to Retirement Freedom," a seminar that describes, among other things, the longevity revolution and the cyclic life that many of us are beginning to live (www.lifecoursenagivation.com). The goal is to help clients envision the opportunities, challenges, and financial preparation needed to live their lives with financial independence in our quickly changing, more cyclic world.

Lifelong financial planning that helps a person navigate though *cycles* is what we will all need and want. Those who provide such education will be critical sources of empowerment for people in dire need of financial literacy. As people gain the knowledge and confidence they need to take charge of their financial futures, they will more readily purchase financial service products. Overwhelmingly, they will make that purchase with those they trust: the financial companies and planners who invested in their clients with education and advice.

Health Care

Increasingly health care professionals will be asked to take on the role of health educators. As consumers become more proactive in their health information gathering, they have already made health information sites the most popular websites today. Advice lines linked to a doctor's practice have already become efficient tools in pediatric medical practices to help parents cope with the routine illness of a child without a costly visit to the doctor. Parents of patients can call nurse practitioners 24-hours a day to ask questions related to health, then essentially self-diagnose simple health issues such as a cold or ear infection.

This style of patient education and advice will increasingly flow over to the adult side of the market, with particular emphasis on intergenerational and geriatric medical advice. As midlife adults cope with the illnesses of their parents, they will often be asked to intervene on their behalf, even when their parents live far away. The first enabler in that effort will be easy access to information on a parent's illness and the parents' medical practitioners. A 24-hour advice line can be the most efficient way to access that information. More and more, we will see these services being offered on either a fee-for-service basis, for an annual fee, or as a supplement to a health insurance or HMO plan. Many of these services are already beginning to offer more than advice and act as a nationwide referral service to qualified physicians and health care specialists of all kinds.

One of the outcomes of advice lines is that individuals are more willing to take charge of some aspects of their own health, especially diagnosing medical conditions. As a result, we'll see an expansion in the market for home testing kits. We already have access to over-the-counter tests for pregnancy, AIDS, insulin levels, and more. This is just the beginning. Diagnostic tools will continue to gain popularity and become more available for everything from cholesterol levels to testing for colon cancer.

Travel and Leisure

The leisure travel industry is also orienting around education as a business-building tool. For instance, Club Med, the Paris-based resort company, has successfully reinvented itself more than once. In the '70s, it saw the demographic writing on the wall and morphed from a singles hot spot to a family vacation destination. Now in the 2000s, they are once again seeing the direction the market is heading and responding creatively. At some of their resorts, Club Med has recently added cultural and literary enrichment along with computer and Internet learning workshops. For example, in the spring of 2000, they began experimenting with a new program in their Cancun, Mexico, resort. They invited 20 novelists and essayists to lead week-long literary forums with guests on the beach. As a result of these new amenities, attendance has been rising at Club Med, which is attracting both a new kind of clientele and repeat customers interested in an expanded leisure experience.[19] This trend will accelerate in the decades to come as resort hotels and cruise lines look beyond the usual amenities for offerings that can help guests combine learning with leisure.

The cruise lines offer a great example of education as a tool for social interaction. My family took a cruise to Alaska last summer. Together with our two children, my husband and I boarded a large cruise ship in Vancouver, Canada, to go up the coast of Alaska to view wildlife, watch the glaciers calve, and experience the beauty of this natural environment. We expected the pools, game rooms, movie theatres, and other entertainment extravaganzas, but what we didn't expect turned out to be one of the best aspects of the vacation. A naturalist on board not only showed her slides in organized seminars but also spent a good part of the day pointing out wildlife and sea animals we might never have noticed while we were cruising. One day she pointed out four kinds of whales, explaining the differences between them, their habitat, and eating habits. We learned about the types of bears and saw, firsthand, the impact of global warming on the glaciers. On board, people from age 5 to 95 were all sharing a learning experience far beyond any science lecture that we might have attended. Then we all talked about it together over dinner. It was the first time that I saw my 13-year-old daughter intently involved in conversation with an 85-year-old man. They had something in common to talk about that bridged any kind of generation gap.

Mind Spas

Moving a little further outside the box, we might begin to see spas or fitness centers devoted to maintaining and expanding our mental acuity. Just as the physical fitness movement and fitness centers cropped up over the last 20 years, the "mind fitness" movement will take root and grow in the next 20 years. Some may appear as adjuncts to fitness centers, spas, or health care centers while others will be dedicated mind spas, and still others will be available on the Internet. (Already brain.com offers a series of programs to expand the mind.) These mind gyms will offer everything from creativity workshops to memory-enhancing classes to intelligence training sessions that teach us how to exercise our brains for enhanced functioning to more experimental therapies such as biofeedback. Some of the fringe therapies of the '60s and '70s may be updated and reappear, such as Samahdi tanks for increased focus, clarity of mind, and enhanced meditation. Similar to physical fitness gyms, mind gyms might have snack bars selling smart drinks, smart bars, and other brain food to improve mental acuity and memory. They might even sell substances such as Vitamin E, ginkgo biloba, ginseng, garlic, deprenyl, and even human growth hormone that have been linked in one way or another with improving mental clarity and acuity.

In the LifeCycle revolution, lifelong learning will explode as a tool to build sales and market products and services to customers. Companies in a wide variety of industries will take note and provide that knowledge, building one of the few types of meaningful brand loyalty that will exist.

THE EMPOWERED CONSUMER
AND THE DEATH OF BRAND LOYALTY

The LifeCycle revolution is a key contributor to the observation that traditional lifetime *brand loyalty is dead.* Lifelong learning is a major reason why. As we continually grow, learn, and open up to new ideas, experiences, solutions, and possibilities, we no longer arbitrarily remain loyal to brands that we once chose. Instead, brand loyalty needs to be reestablished in innovative ways, continually.

Many of us will routinely make product-purchasing decisions based on objective intelligence-gathering. "Training in an academic discipline instills a belief in the effectiveness of information in making more enlightened decisions," explains Greg Schmid, director of strategic planning for the Institute of the Future in Menlo Park, California.[20] We will research product choices via the Internet before we buy a camera, a house, a pair of skis, a mutual fund, or any other product where choice is involved. And, with the advent of globalization, a click of a mouse will empower us to purchase products from companies around the world. Instead of accepting a company's claims as truth or a past decision as a lifelong habit, we will do the necessary research to validate brand quality, compare prices, check references, and read independent product reviews.

Some companies build relationships with customers by providing that competitive analysis, even if their brand doesn't come out on top. Progressive Insurance is an example. When prospective clients come to them for quotes, they not only offer their rates instantly but also provide the rates of their competitors, pointing out the differences along the way. Although their prices aren't always the best option for every prospect, they create trust and loyalty with their clients and potential clients.

As we gain confidence in our ever-expanding personal knowledge base, we feel comfortable asking for exactly what we want. Some innovative companies have identified this desire and are working hard to develop customized products designed to meet each customer's individual needs. We see examples in the marketplace such as cosmetics custom-designed to match our skin type, glasses molded specifically to fit our particular faces, shoes designed for our feet alone, and computers designed to our exact specifications. Customized products are still in their infancy, but it's a segment of the market that will grow exponentially if they can deliver on their promise of creating high-quality personalized products. The companies that successfully deliver will create customer loyalty.

One company that does deliver is Polaris Health. Founded by Dr. Andrew Weil, Polaris Health has developed customized vitamin supplements, available directly online from Weil's website, www.drweil.com. The author of bestselling books on integrating nutrition into health and healing, Weil is known for combining his traditional medical training from Harvard with eastern and preventative medicine. He is well respected for his integrity and devotion to the subject and has immediate credibility with many empowered consumers concerned about health and nutrition. Customers start online by filling out a basic health and lifestyle questionnaire that goes well beyond just gender and age and determines which vitamins will be included in their individual packets. To make it convenient for their customers, vitamins are then packaged in a box holding a 30-day supply of individually wrapped doses to be taken three times a day, every day. These custom-designed vitamins based on each customer's health profile are delivered directly to the customer's front door for maximum convenience. At the end of a month, the company automatically delivers a new supply unless customers opt to take a free monthly update that could change their vitamin mix. Their customer care representatives are knowledgeable and friendly, answering any questions or concerns that might pop up, either online or by phone without long waits or delays. It's a sophisticated program that combines individually designed products with ease of purchase, a recipe developed to build ongoing customer loyalty.

Amazon.com is developing tactics to build long-term relationships with customers through mass customization. Amazon.com sells books over the Internet and uses push technology to take each relationship deeper. After someone has ordered a few books, the data that person provides contribute to a picture of his or her reading tastes and buying habits. The company is then able to suggest books that suit that individual's tastes. You can also fill out a questionnaire designating your preferences and receive regular e-mails with recommendations of books you might enjoy. In this way, Amazon.com creates a personal relationship with each customer that manifests in added sales.

Amazon.com's CEO, Jeff Bezos, believes that maintaining brand loyalty into the future requires a whole new level of customer service and a
redeployment of financial resources. In the old business model, 70 percent of resources went to marketing while 30 percent went to creating
good customer service. To succeed in the new business model, Bezos
believes that those numbers need to be reversed. Personalized service
will be a key that unlocks customer loyalty.[21]

CONCLUSION

In the old linear model, education came once in life, when we were
young. Not anymore. In the lifecycle revolution, education is an integral
component of living a long life, a tool for continual reinvention and better living. Throughout our lives, we'll all have the chance to learn everything from how to short stocks to how to skydive, and businesses that
provide these services will prosper. Education will be delivered in new
and innovative ways, offering us all a variety of options on *how* to learn
and creating hybrid models of learning. Corporate training and career
updating will be essential as we require constant intelligence and skill
updates to keep current. A population of lifelong learners will bring
forth a whole new attitude about who we are and what we can be and
do throughout our lifespan.

As a result we are beginning to see the emergence of a more empowered consumer. We, the consumers, will be more in charge of the marketplace than ever before. Knowledge will continue to tilt the balance of
power away from manufacturers toward consumers. As a result, edu-
sales—where education and commerce meet—will become an effective
tool in building customer retention and acquisition.

The traditional brand loyalty so common in the linear life is no longer
alive. It has been replaced by the consumers' constant search for products and services that meet their ever-changing needs. Consumers will
have more knowledge about products, and business will, in turn, need
to have more knowledge about what individual consumers will demand
from the marketplace if they want to build an ongoing relationship with
their customers.

In the past, a single focused career path was considered normal, sensible, and the key to a successful career and a stable life. Those who didn't follow this straight and narrow path were often considered dilettantes, lost souls, or just plain failures. This made sense when life was shorter, more predictable, and the pace of change was slow. Not anymore.

On the linear life path, careers were expected to go in one direction: up. Then, after we reached our highest level of achievement, we had nowhere to go but out. The door to the world of work locked tightly behind us as we entered the next predetermined phase of life—retirement. We were expected to graciously exit at a specific age (around age 65) with little consideration of reentry.

The cyclic life path offers us all the opportunity to have lateral careers similar to Leonardo da Vinci. Although Leonardo da Vinci is synonymous with "famous Italian Renaissance painter" in our minds, he completed only a handful of paintings, including the *Mona Lisa*. He was too busy with his other careers to focus exclusively on painting. We're all familiar with his second career related to painting: he was a sculptor. He also built toys and machines at several points along his cyclic career path. In one of his first job applications (a letter to Duke Sforza) he barely mentioned his talents as a painter or sculptor, but focused on his talents as a "military engineer," describing his ability to build strong, light bridges, create new weapons, and build armored

chariots and warships which could protect the Duke's soldiers from
his enemies.[1] Da Vinci also was an inventor and even studied optics,
attempting to build a device with giant rounded mirrors similar to
those in modern telescopes.

Like da Vinci, our talents and interests might evolve over time and
manifest in different career choices. Cyclic careers may not just go up,
but go out in new and varied directions. This offers up a completely different panorama of choices, including unplanned career interruption,
new career beginnings, workplace reentry, sabbaticals, and opportunities for reinvention at various points along the way. Today the average
worker will have 12 to 15 jobs over the course of a career and stay at
each job an average of 3.6 years, according to research by Walker Information Global Network, a workplace consulting firm, and the Hudson
Institute, a renowned think tank.[2] Transitions and turning points, the
exception in a linear-life arrangement, are becoming the status quo.

ADAPTABLE, PORTABLE SKILLS

Most of us will need to learn to adapt faster and feel more comfortable
making the shift from one set of skills, one job, or one career path to
another . . . and another . . . and possibly another. It will become essential to continuously upgrade and expand our skill sets and make
switches in career direction, giving us the challenge and opportunity to
reinvent ourselves continually.

Certain universal skill sets will be easily transferable from job to job,
no matter how diverse those jobs might be. For instance, negotiating
skills, time management skills, networking skills, communication skills
(both verbal and written), financial planning skills, and relationship
building skills will be needed by all careerists whether their careers be
in high technology or fashion, finance or travel. Other, more focused
skill sets might be applicable only to one particular industry or job. Both
sets of skills will need to be accumulated for a life filled with job change.

In this new mode of cyclic careers, some of us will stay on one broad
career path and continuously ascend to greater heights, sometimes in
one company, but more often, hopping from opportunity to opportunity. For instance, Howard Schultz, founder and CEO of Starbucks, was

manager of U.S. operations for Hammarplast Swedish drip coffeemakers when his passion for the coffee business became evident. He had held a variety of jobs before that, but didn't discover his own interest until then. As part of his job, he flew to Seattle to visit a client, a coffee bean store that sold lots of Hammarplast coffeemakers. That store was Starbucks, and he was immediately taken with the way Starbucks educated their customers on the joy of coffee and the variety and complexity of coffee beans. He left Seattle saying, "God, what a great company. I'd love to be a part of that." He eventually convinced the owners of Starbucks to hire him as the marketing and operations director and moved to Seattle to work there. When Schultz traveled to Italy, he was fascinated with the coffee bars that served as social centers for people to congregate, laughing, drinking, and eating. He decided to transform Starbucks from a coffee bean store to a coffee bar and store. The owner of Starbucks hated the idea, however. So Schultz again changed jobs. This time he became an entrepreneur, starting a local coffee bar, Il Giornale, in Seattle. He did well and soon went back to the owners of Starbucks to buy their business. Again, Schultz changed career paths. He went from owning a coffee bar to founding an international company of rapidly expanding coffee bean stores/coffee bars throughout the world. His goal was still the same, "to serve a great cup of coffee," but his career path kept transforming.[3]

While some of us will follow one broad career path, others will use a job or career path as a jumping off point to plunge into new and different career directions in related fields. For instance, my brother, Richard, was a lawyer. When he was still in college and without much direction, our parents insisted he pursue studies that led directly to a professional career. Being the good son that he was, he did just that and ended up working as a lawyer in Los Angeles. He hated it. Almost everything about it annoyed him—the paperwork, the details, the research. The only things he enjoyed were the negotiations and putting together deals. As a result of his interest in the business deals, he did well. He went from working at a midsize firm to starting his own. After 15 years of 15-hour days, he sold his practice to try his hand at a different career. He began to develop a small investment firm with negotiating and looking for great deals as the primary focus. Now he really loves what he does, and he's the first to say that he could never have built this new career without the knowledge and expertise he gained as a lawyer.

Another career direction for some of us will be complete career reinvention, tapping a variety of latent talents at different moments in our adult lives. Diane Reichenberger took a sudden career U-turn when she realized that her job left her feeling hollow and empty. She had always dreamed of running a big company and planned a career path that would lead her there. Four days after graduation, she started work at Hewlett-Packard Company in the accounting department to gain some basic skills. After she mastered that, Diane began a process of upward mobility, going from job to job, ascending the corporate hierarchy by moving from company to company to further develop her skill sets, knowledge base, experience, and financial rewards. Eventually she got what she wanted and became president of LA Gear, a footwear company.

Although the position represented her personal dream come true, the job itself did not. For the first time in her life, she felt unsure of her goal or direction.

A friend convinced her to go along on a diving trip to Fiji. There were no fax machines, phones, or laptop computers—nothing but her, the other divers, the local people, and the beauty of the islands and the ocean. She was fascinated by the simplicity of life in Fiji and became acutely aware of the peace and ease it could offer. Diane realized she wanted to live a simpler existence, which meant a radically different career path.

She began researching books on career change, and remembered her fascination with women's health when she was in college. She came across a book, *Spiritual Midwifery*, that had impacted her deeply when she was 18 years old. The philosophy of midwifery—offering guidance and support in the birthing process—was one that she wanted to nurture in herself. She said, "I feel like taking a course in birthing might help me to rebirth myself over again."

And that's exactly what she did. At age 40, she enrolled in the National Institute for Midwifery. "Now anything seems possible. I feel like I'm 17 years old again, but I have the confidence and wisdom of being a 40-year-old woman. It's a nice place to be."

Not all cyclic careers are formed from choice. Many of us are forced into it through layoffs. At this writing, many people are losing their jobs and may not get back jobs so fast, certainly not the same ones. The economy, going through a downturn even before September 11, 2001, is now reacting to short-term uncertainty, fear, and distrust that goes much further than anything else we've recently experienced. That's happened before. The last big downturn that took place about 20 years ago created fear first, but then an onslaught of highly entrepreneurial endeavors.

Cyclic careers become even more relevant as we are often forced to assess our own skill sets and apply them to career directions we might never have considered before. "Many are taking the opportunity to reassess their direction, think about changing careers, or go back to school," according to John Van Cleve, a work life consultant at Hewitt Associates.[4] One thing is clear, the job market will be a sea of constant change that each of us will need to learn to adapt to and navigate. We are the pioneers at the forefront of a new era of cyclic careers.

I remember reading *The Secret Life of Walter Mitty* by James Thurber when I was a child. In this wonderful book, Walter Mitty lives a rather ordinary life in reality, but in his fantasies he experiences a wide variety of successful, unrelated careers—from a Naval hydroplane commander to a surgeon to the rich and famous. The story was a fantasy, meant to seem far-fetched and somewhat ridiculous in the linear-life organization of the time. In the cyclic life arrangement, however, we will all get the opportunity to be like Walter Mitty.

We can expect a life filled with ever evolving jobs and career paths, sometimes morphing out of old ones, sometimes coming out of left field. It's new territory, facing things that were never part of the predictable linear life arrangement. The new norm will be *change*, and, if we can get comfortable with that, this new norm will lead to opportunities for ongoing personal growth and satisfaction.

DOWN WITH THE OLD, UP WITH THE NEW

The notion of one job for life is definitely yesterday's job style, not today's. John Hefferman, a Cambridge, Massachusetts, biotech worker, for instance, has had six different jobs since graduating from college in 1979. He says, "My father worked at the same company for 41 years. Back then you stayed at a company for life." He adds that today "You can expect to be laid off at least once."[5]

For most of us, ascending the ladder to success along a one-way, upwardly mobile career path with one paternal employer and no career interruption is as much a fantasy as Walter Mitty's many careers seemed in Thurber's day. So much so that Chris Olson, a Fresno, California–based headhunter reports that when she tried to interest an employer in a prospect who had been at his current job more than 15 years, the employer asked, "What's wrong with him?"[6]

The workplace changes we're experiencing clearly have a lot to do with the changing nature of our overall economy, sudden worldwide political upheaval, quickly evolving technologic advances, and the overall heightened pace of change itself. Together, these factors were largely responsible for the restructuring of the workplace during the 1980s and early 1990s. *Downsizing* and *early retirement* became euphemisms for being fired without fanfare. Today we're experiencing the early signs of recession coupled with a heightened fear of terrorist activities. The net result is that more than ever, our careers belong to us not any corporate entity, and they are ours to develop, nurture, and advance. This is a primary driver of the growing need for lifelong, cyclic learning.

On closer examination, however, we also see that beneath the economic and technologic changes described above are the same demographic forces described in Chapter 1. Helping to transform the nature of the workplace and careers are the longevity revolution; the decline of the youth-focused society; and the pioneering values, attitudes, and traits of boomers.

The Longevity Revolution

As life expectancy continues to rise, most of us will either want to or need to work longer, maybe even a little of both. We will be retiring the notion of retirement as we know it today. This multifaceted issue has so many ramifications that I devote Chapter 9 to it. For now, think about retirement from a purely pragmatic standpoint. When Otto von Bismarck designed the first retirement program for Europe back in the 1880s, the average life expectancy was 45 years. He chose age 65 as the appropriate age for retirement. Today, if we were to calculate the appropriate retirement age using von Bismarck's formula, we would select age 115. Now I'm not suggesting we should all work until age 115; I'm suggesting that the workforce will no longer be limited to people between the ages of 18 and 65.

No longer will society tell us we've outlived our usefulness based on age alone. And, no matter how old or young we are, we will have repeated opportunities to start down new career paths. Imagine being a beginner again at 60! We will cycle in and out of work at our own discretion throughout our extended lives based on our wants and needs. Age diversity in the workplace, beyond anything we have ever experienced, will become common.

The Rise of Age Power and the Decline of the Youth Society

As the median age of the population continues to rise, so does the median age of the workforce. Over the last 30 years, our workforce has been relatively young. (See Figure 3.1.) In 1979, the median age of the workforce was only 34.7. In 1985, the median age of workers was 35. It's projected that by the year 2008, the median age of the workforce will go up to 41. When the first of the boomers begin to hit the traditional retirement age of 65 in 2011, half of all workers will be over age 45. Based on population figures, there will be fewer younger adults than older, creating a shortage of available young workers and a potentially large number of older workers.

As these demographic forces collide, workplace ageism and the so-called *silver ceiling* will begin to dissolve. Labor force participation by people over 55 will need to increase by 25 percent for the United States and other westernized countries to maintain their current levels of productivity. This shift represents a reversal of the trend we've seen between 1970 and 1990, where the workforce participation of people over 55 has actually gone down by nearly 20 percent, costing our economy approximately 2.6 percent per year of the gross national product.[7] It is, however, the direction we will need to move to keep our economy active and remain competitive. Both business and government will need to give older adults incentives to continue to be active in the workforce, and they'll need to modify recruitment, compensation, and benefit plans to recruit and retain them.

Pioneering Values, Attitudes, and Traits of the Boomers

The boomers have already been responsible for many workplace innovations and changes. For instance, they've helped loosen up the dress code, created flextime and the virtual workplace, and flattened out the chain of command. And, of course, women of this generation have radically altered the gender politics of work. Today, women hold almost half of all management and professional jobs. According to the Bureau of Labor Statistics, 62 percent of married women are in the workforce. (See Figure 3.2.)

Boomers won't stop there. They will further change the nature of work by continuing to work far longer than their parents or grandparents did, partially because they want to but also because they'll need to. According to a survey by the Rutgers University Center for Workforce Development, today an astonishing 90 percent of working adults intend to work at least part-time during retirement; nearly 70 percent said they would work even if they had enough money to live comfortably for the rest of their lives.[8] Boomers will also change jobs—even careers—more than any other generation in history.

The impact of this paradigm shift will be felt in every aspect of our work lives. The most potent changes will pertain to the following:

- The emergence of an intergenerational workforce
- Career reinvention
- A shift to a free-agency system and a 100 percent temporary workforce
- The need for new rewards and benefits to attract and retain desirable serial workers

THE INTERGENERATIONAL WORKPLACE

In the industrial age, physical labor was often central to the work we did. We needed strong bodies and that required youth. Today's work

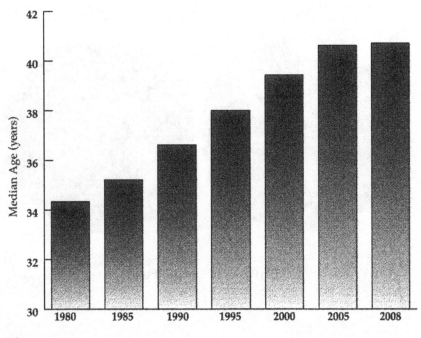

Figure 3.1
Rising Age of U.S. Labor Force
1980–2008
Source: United States Bureau of Labor Statistics, 2002.

involves less physical labor but more intelligence-gathering, strategic planning, thinking, and social skills. Experience clearly counts; so does sound judgment and a high level of commitment to quality. These are traits that, according to a recent study by AARP, define the older worker and grow with time and experience.[9]

Our bias against older workers has been based on the old model of work where strenuous physical labor was key. Because most older adults were past their prime and ready to go out to pasture by age 65, they were unceremoniously pushed along the assembly line of life into the next predetermined life phase: retirement. There was no revolving door back into the workplace for most. As we move into a more cyclic approach to life, this age bias will become a relic.

My stepfather, Ray Fusco, is an example of how cyclic careers can work, and how an intergenerational workforce holds the potential to

1900   2000

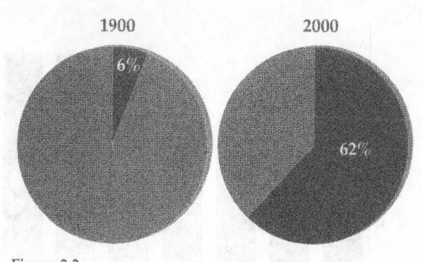

Figure 3.2
Married Women in the U.S. Labor Force
Source: United States Bureau of the Census, 2000.

function more effectively than a homogenous one. Ray had a successful first career as a cameraman and then producer for ABC Sports, where he worked for most of his career. Like many men of his generation, he retired at age 65. When he reached retirement age, he realized he just hadn't saved enough money to live the lifestyle he enjoyed while working. So he started a second career as an entrepreneur. He noticed that the movie studios desperately needed a reliable, cost-effective means of organizing publicity interviews in one locale rather than sending the stars of movies on a whirlwind tour that required valuable time and money. Ray did some research, figured out how to coordinate all the moving parts, and, with a business partner, started a company to answer this need as a way of supplementing his income and having a little fun during retirement.

One of his biggest challenges was the fact that the entertainment industry identified itself as a very *young* business, and he knew he ran counter to this stereotype. Creativity and being in touch with the pulse of young America were prized traits strongly associated with youth. The public relations departments of the major studios were run primarily by people under 35; they would be the pool of prospective clients Ray would have to convince to hire him in his new approach to publicizing movies, and those would be the clients he would have to work with over time.

At 67, he found that his age and experience could work to his benefit. Many of his prospective clients were, at first, surprised to hear such an innovative approach to their business from a man with gray hair. At the same time, they were impressed with his depth of knowledge and his practicality. He could save them money and valuable star time, maybe even improve the level of publicity per movie. His wisdom, experience, and savvy helped him gain their respect and trust. They also liked his easygoing yet self-assured style and the fact that he listened to them and took their input seriously, even though he was twice as old as most of them. His age ultimately helped them feel secure enough to take a risk on a new approach to publicizing movies. One of his favorite aspects of his new career is interacting with a wide variety of talented people ranging anywhere from 18 to 80. In fact, he's found that working with young people helped him feel energized while his clients felt reassured to have someone older and experienced that they could turn to for advice, especially in such a high-stress business.

The company has grown to be the largest producer of promotional junkets for the major studios in the United States. Although his work isn't full time in the traditional sense of the word, this postretirement career has ended up being far more lucrative and even more engaging than his first career.

Even a career in professional sports, acknowledged as a short career cycle exclusively for the young because of the wear and tear on the body, is being revolutionized by this attitude that it's never too late to return to or even start a new career. Michael Jordan is the one we hear the most about but how about Jim Morris, a Texas high-school teacher, who started his baseball career at age 35? Morris did double duty as one of his high school's favorite science teachers and the varsity baseball coach. In 1999, the former minor league pitcher was trying to pump up his bedraggled team so he dared them to aim much higher than any of them thought possible. He promised that if they stretched themselves to win the district championship (which they stood little chance of doing), *he* would try out for a major league baseball team. No one ever expected to see it happen, but when the team won, off the 35-year-old Morris went to the Tampa Bay Devil Rays' cattle call. Once there, he fared much better than anyone expected and began his new career as the oldest baseball rookie in 40 years. Although elbow surgery and tendonitis cut his baseball career short, it opened the door to still other career directions, including a book, *The Oldest Rookie,* that continued its life as a Disney movie starring Dennis Quaid. Morris says, "The kids I was supposed to be teaching wound up teaching me a lesson: Never shut the door on your dreams."[10]

Not only are we cycling in and out of the workforce well into our later years, many kids are venturing into the workforce while they're still in school. In fact, teenage entrepreneurs are becoming increasingly common; especially as technology savvy and innovation are not necessarily age-driven skills. Nancy F. Koehn, associate professor of business administration at Harvard Business School, says, "There's not a period in history where we've seen such a plethora of young entrepreneurs." According to Computer Economics, Inc., a Carlsbad, California, research firm, about 8 percent of all teens—about 1.6 million in the United States—are making some money on the Internet.[11] Most of it comes in the form of small commissions to help companies link to larger sites, but some of it is serious money. In the year 2000, *YoungBiz* magazine began ranking the top 100 entrepreneurs between the ages of 8 and 18 and found that the top four had incomes averaging more than $400,000.

For example, Michael Furdyk, a Toronto-based teen, got a lot of media attention a few years ago when he sold his website, MyDesktop.com, for more than $1 million while still in high school. Afterwards, he started a comparison shopping service, BuyBuddy.com, where he's hired his father, Paul, as CEO. Paul had been a managing partner for product marketing in Canada for NCR and brought seasoned business experience to his son's imaginative company.

Although Internet and technology ventures seem to dominate teen business success, at the tender age of 11, Rich Stachowski of Moraya,

California, came up with the idea for a toy that eventually became a whole line of innovative water toys: underwater walkie-talkies called water talkies. His parents thought it was a creative idea and saw the possibilities, so his father and some family friends invested time and money to bring Rich's idea to the toy market, and they all did well by believing in and investing in an 11-year-old's creative invention.

The result of some of us starting work earlier and many of us working well past age 65 is that the workforce is becoming far more age diverse. We may have bosses and mentors who are chronologically younger than we are but from whom we can learn a lot. At times, we might see a very young worker on a team with someone old enough to be his or her father or even grandmother. Most importantly, compensation will be based on merit—how well a job is performed—rather than on age and seniority. Performance not age will be the measure of worth and compensation. Just as we developed skills to accommodate women in the workplace and racial diversity in the workplace, we will increasingly need to develop skills, tolerance, and understanding to thrive in an age-diverse workplace.

CAREER REINVENTION

Reinvention will be a ticket to personal fulfillment. When we're young and trying to figure out who we are and what would be an appropriate fit for our talents and abilities, we're expected to make big career decisions that will last a lifetime. Happenstance often dictates the career path we select. Parents, too, influence our decisions, sometimes more than we'd like. It's often hit or miss. When the linear approach to life prevailed, society encouraged us to stay on whatever career path we started in our youth, no matter what. If it was secure, predictable, and would put food on the table, it made little difference whether we liked what we did or not. It was the linear way of life.

Diligence, sobriety, and hard work were considered virtues and working with one employer for life was the status quo. In the new cyclic life, we're beginning to demand a redefinition of the purpose as well as the arrangement of work in our lives. Chances are most of us will need to figure out what we want to do several times in our ever-evolving

cyclic lives. We'll have to get comfortable with the idea of new begin-
nings and starting over. For instance, after being laid off, Bonnie Ulmer
took a summer intern position at Triad Communication in Washington,
D.C., to learn new skills. She was 56 years old. And she has company. In
Chicago, a midlife lawyer interns at a television station while in New
York a former business executive interns as a pastry chef.[12]

Frequent job change, a sign of instability in the past, can mean finding the right path and getting ahead. Career change was rarely even
heard of in the past; now it's becoming an opportunity to reinvent our
lives. In fact, some of the fastest growing jobs today didn't even exist 15
years ago. Work exits and reentry were often a signal of trouble. Today
they're a sign that we are innovative, hard-charging, and fulfilled.

Sometimes midlife or mature adulthood provide the opportunity to
rethink what we might really want to do with our lives, including defining our career paths. Barbara Sher in her book, *It's Only Too Late If You
Don't Start Now*, believes "midlife is a time to create the life you want,
not the one that society has ordered for you. What you do today, this
hour, will be your ticket to happiness. It's a major beginning."[13]

Sometimes renewal means moving back rather than forward. Neal
Stern began realizing this at age 40. Neal had started his career as a
video producer. Relying on his natural entrepreneurial skills, he built his
own small company, developing industrial films. However, his day-to-
day responsibilities had become more administrative than hands-on.
He began to feel resentful that his employees got to have all the fun
producing films while he handled all the management details and hassles. It became clear to him that he no longer enjoyed what he did. It
had become a grind. "I've invested more than 15 years building my
company and my reputation in this industry, but I see myself working
for at least another 30 years. There's no way I want to continue down
this unfun path for 30 more years."

So Neal decided to take a leap backwards. He sold his business and
started pounding the pavement, looking for more personal satisfaction.
It was a big risk for him to leave the security of his own company; he
had a family to support. But he decided it was a bigger risk to continue
to do something that "burned him out rather than fired him up." He
knew he loved the work of producing video and film, but he also knew

he hated the management part of the job. After several months searching for a job and several false starts in new jobs, he got a job working for
a major television production company where other executives handled
the management details and Neal got to do what he loved most, producing video and film hands-on. He started out making less money, but
was exhilarated by his work for the first time in many years. It was a
chance to start life on a fresh new path. "The money will come," he said,
"but even if it doesn't, I feel passionate again about going to work
everyday. I feel very lucky." Like Neal, many of us will be cycling in and
out of work over a 50-year span. That's a long time to be committed to
one career path, especially if we don't enjoy it.

Don't think it's just older or midlife adults who rethink goals and
direction. Michelle Conlin had enjoyed her work for the 10 years she
had been a hairdresser. The 30-year-old hairdresser developed a loyal
clientele who followed her from salon to salon. However, she began to
seriously rethink her career after the World Trade Center collapsed. She
said, "I felt so helpless. What I really wanted to do was help out somehow, but I didn't have the skills that were needed. I knew from that
moment forward that I had to find a new career, something more
important than cutting and coloring." Michelle decided to go to nursing
school. She cut back her work hours so she could continue to have
enough money to live on while she went to school. After she gets her
degree in nursing, she plans to travel to distressed regions that really
need her new skills.

THE FREE AGENCY SYSTEM: TOWARD
THE 100 PERCENT TEMPORARY WORKFORCE

The paradigm shift toward temporary work is producing a new *free
agency system* of employment. Sometimes it will be within one company, but more often than not, it will mean moving from one project to
another with more than one employer. Sometimes a job will last for
five years; other times, for five months. We may never meet our co-
workers face-to-face (they could be from the other side of the world)
or we may be working side-by-side, depending on the needs of each
project. And we will be evaluated based on our contribution and abil-

ity to collaborate successfully with others rather than on office politics
or how close to the power source we might be. Even within an organization, more of us will be working on a series of projects rather than
just one lifetime job.

Interestingly, the entertainment industry frequently uses this type of
fluid work model in which people involved with one project then move
on to the next. It's common in this sector for workers to take time off
between projects and, often, switch work terms as demands and needs
shift. Not too long ago, the entertainment industry was dominated by
the big studio system, controlling nearly all employees working in that
industry, with few exceptions. For someone who screwed up or stepped
on the wrong toes, the euphemism, "You'll never work in this industry
again," definitely applied. The entertainment industry slowly broke free
of that confining model however, and has evolved into a more entrepreneurial free agency system.

Here's a simple description of how it works in the entertainment
industry. If, for instance, Spike Lee is going to produce a movie, he
brings together a group of people that he knows with talents that complement his and with whom he likes to work, such as actor John Turturro and cameraman Mekhi Phifel. Each professional Lee hires
collaborates for months with him on a specific project. Lee, in turn, provides a compensation package for work on this project and this project
only. When the project is completed, they all go their separate ways.
Although Spike Lee tends to use many of the same people on most of
his films, Turturro and Phifel are responsible for not only finding their
next jobs but also creating their own benefits package and advancing
their careers.

Over the last several years, this model has been gaining momentum
throughout other sectors of the business world. According to a 2000 poll
done by EPIC/MRA, a market research firm in Lansing, Michigan, 26
percent of the workforce was composed of free agents. They project that
by the year 2010, more than 40 percent of the workforce will identify
themselves this way.[14] A Harris Interactive and Opus 360 poll reports that
more than half of those who think of themselves as free agents say they
have improved both their earnings and their quality of life by working in
this manner. More than 80 percent say the best part of this setup is their

ability to make their personal lives and families a higher priority.

As in any free-market system, the strong will thrive in this environment. "People are much more likely to get what they are worth—they will participate directly in the downside and the upside results of their work," according to Christopher Myer, director of the Center for Business Innovation at Cap Gemini Ernst & Young.[15] We could very well see a formally structured system emerge, rating and trading human talent on an open market not dissimilar to the markets we see for corporations, Nasdaq and NYSE. Some of us will trade ourselves on the big boards such as NYSE while others will opt for smaller, niche markets. Services of the best and the brightest will go to the highest bidder. In April 2000, at the height of the dot-com era, we saw an attempt at an auctionable labor pool when a group of 16 Internet employees tried to auction themselves off as a group on eBay to the highest bidder. Although it didn't succeed and dot-coms have since crashed, it's an idea that could very well take hold in one form or another.

We will probably see many of the bells and whistles associated with the entertainment industry's free-agency system meander over to the world of business. We already do. For example, casting directors and agents aren't so different from headhunters and personnel recruiters. The recruitment business will be on the rise with many niche companies appearing as the need for companies to quickly expand and contract their workforces continues and we reinvent our careers every so often. Employment counselors and psychologists will also be in greater demand as free agents continually add skills to their resumes and search for the hottest jobs that meet their growing talents. Many entrepreneurs or executives have already hired public relations experts as part of their staffs. That, too, will become more common with workers trying to distinguish themselves from the masses. Personal managers, packaging ideas with personnel, and syndication deals won't be too far behind.

Neal Lenarsky, in fact, is a personal manager for free agents in business. Based in the Los Angeles area, Lenarsky has a background working as a human resource executive. Disenchanted with his job, in 1996 he reinvented his own career and started Strategic Transitions to help executives figure out new career paths and take the steps necessary to move successfully down that path. He spends hours with his clients helping them determine what they really want to do. Lenarsky coaches them to improve their resume and interview skills, add much needed skill sets, and even alter their expectations of what they might receive as a compensation package from a new job. Then he sells those clients through his vast network of contacts. Like agents and managers in the entertainment industry, Lenarsky gets a small percentage of each of his client's ongoing salary for as long as the relationship lasts. And, no, he definitely doesn't go away after a client is hired. He and his clients understand that each job is just one step along the cyclic career path. He says, "If you let outside forces manage your career, you will lose control. I look at people as products, and great products need great branding, marketing, and distribution."

Another tool used routinely in the entertainment industry is the employment contract. We've all heard about the perks of stardom that are outlined in these contracts such as a fitness trainer and gourmet chef, but this tool has been used at all levels of employment in that particular industry to protect employees. Until now, however, it's something that has been reserved for mostly high-level executives in most other businesses. As we evolve toward a free-agency system, that's quickly changing. Employees are seeking more than mere stock options that might never be worth much; they're looking for guarantees if they are terminated without cause. This might mean that employees who are pink-slipped in an economic downturn, corporate change of direction, or for some other reason that has nothing to do with their job performance might get a perk such as being able to remain on the corporate health plan after leaving, vesting stock options and money in retirement plans, or even being forgiven a loan provided when they were hired.[16]

In a free-agency system, associations and networks will gain importance as we feel more loyalty toward colleagues than any one employer. Our network of contacts and colleagues will become a lifeline into the job market. For instance, if a producer is putting together a crew for a movie, chances are one of his first hires would be a line producer who might have a whole list of trusted colleagues that he would recommend to fill a variety of other crew positions from cameraman to grip. In similar fashion, networking groups will proliferate and develop along niche fields of interest. Having access to the latest and greatest developments in a specific industry and field will be highly desired. Learning how to negotiate effectively with employers will be a much-needed tool. So will working in teams and learning how to effectively deal with constantly evolving new technology. Associations will also be a valuable source of employment opportunities and inside information on the culture of a specific employer. They will offer employers the opportunity to one-stop-shop for employees to fill jobs that are available immediately.

As the free-agency system evolves and refines, new products and services will arise to meet the complex demand of free agents who will be responsible for continuously building their skill base, planning their career paths, and designing their own benefits packages and long-term saving and investing programs. Job transition insurance may become an innovative new product in response to the changing nature of careers. Disability insurance has been available for decades, but as more of us embark on serial careers, we may be willing to pay for a policy that would help us through unexpected or sudden job transitions.

As free agents, we will each be in charge of navigating the more complex work environment. More than ever, we will need to rely on a team of trusted advisors to guide us through the complex choices that will be ever-changing in a cyclic life. For instance, business managers and financial planners, once serving the rich and famous exclusively, will be in demand by many more of us. As health benefits and pension programs migrate toward our own control and portability rather than our employer's, we'll need experts to help us navigate the maze of financial and health-benefits decisions we'll need to make continuously throughout our quickly changing lives.

New Benefits for Cyclic Workers

"People are now the primary source of competitive advantage," says Edward Michaels, a director of McKinsey & Company.[17] As a result, employers will have to work hard to retain the services of talented, cyclic workers, offering them more of what they really want, including flexible, customizable, and portable benefit programs that can travel with them from job to job and can change as their needs change.

For example, some companies have already begun to experiment with cafeteria-style benefits programs where employees are given a set amount or a voucher along with a menu of choices for both health and pension benefits. At Carlson Companies, a travel, marketing, hospitality, and food-service company in the Minneapolis area, employees are given allowances that they can spend on a menu of different health plans with a wide variety of doctors and hospital groups. Although employees are responsible for selecting their plan, they get the advantage of choosing from a coalition of contracts Carlson selected as the best programs and plans at preferred rates.[18] In addition, they can choose from a menu of benefits and self-select those that are relevant to their particular lives and specific needs.

A variety of companies, including AT&T, Owens Corning, and Empire Blue Cross/Blue Shield, have eliminated traditional pension programs entirely and replaced them with cash-balance plans. Typically, an employee will get a 4 to 8 percent of salary credit toward a pension program of their choice, a desirable alternative in a more cyclic life. All the interest that accrues is theirs, as is the cash balance. The advantage is that as employees leave jobs, their pension can travel with them. "These new plans pay people for what they bring to the firm today, not for what they brought to the firm yesterday. Basically, they're designed to take away the incentive to stay a long time," explains Ethan Kra, chief actuary at William M. Mercer.[19]

In *Age Power*, my husband, Ken Dychtwald, describes a portrait of a Portable Pension Program (PPP) that could be established in the United States to replace the Social Security System and a variety of other pension programs available through employers. Ken believes, "Under such a plan, you would start accumulating benefits, and have rights to them, the day you start working. If you stop working, the value of your pension would be deposited into your federal PPP account, which could be managed by the government or perhaps by private companies set up for this purpose, much as IRAs are now handled. For periods when you were out of the workforce, or if your employer did not provide a pension program, you could contribute a certain tax-deductible amount of your savings or salary to the account."[20] As we switch jobs, our new employers would contribute so that our pensions could be cumulative and in our control throughout our lives, encouraging each of us to build our own pension, no matter who our employers are or what our work situations might be.

As more of us embark on cyclic career paths, portable, cafeteria-style health benefits and cash-balance pensions could become the norm. Coalitions and clubs of like-minded individuals may form to take advantage of group rates and discounts. Industry specific associations or networks will offer these benefits and maybe even use them as a profit center. Using the entertainment industry model as an example again, the Writers Guild and the Screen Actors Guild both offer these kinds of benefits to their members. Benefits could also be offered through clubs organized for the very purpose of providing free agency workers with one-stop counseling and shopping for health and pension benefits and planning.

CREATING LOYALTY ON THE CYCLIC WORK PATH

One thing has become clear: money alone doesn't buy employee loyalty. Even during difficult economic times, today's employees want more flexibility, stimulation, and opportunities for continued personal growth. In August 2000, a study released by a New Jersey consulting firm, People3, pointed out that the companies experiencing the highest rates of turnover of information technology professionals were, in fact, providing higher than average salaries. But those big paychecks weren't creating a sense of loyalty at all. Another study released in May 2000 by the Radcliffe Public Policy Center found that earning a high salary came in sixth on the list of priorities for all workers. The number one priority for those in their 20s and 30s was a family-friendly work schedule while those in their 40s chose challenging and rewarding work and those over 50 chose satisfying relationships with co-workers. Although the priorities differ slightly by age, they all point toward a desire to be treated with respect, to be challenged and stimulated by the work, and to grow professionally while still maintaining a "life."[21]

Cyclic workers also want the option to design their work life to better fit into their overall life while still maintaining a sense of job security. Work hours and days no longer need to be exclusively etched in stone and dictated by the greater society: 9 to 5, five days a week. That remnant of the industrial age and manufacturing process is dissolving as it becomes less relevant to success. In 1985 only 12 percent of American companies offered any form of flextime. Today that figure has nearly quadrupled to 58 percent of firms, up from 51 percent in 2000.

Dawson Personnel Systems, a temporary staffing company in Columbus, Ohio, finds that giving away time instead of money as a bonus to employees not only improves morale and creates loyalty, but can boost the bottom line. They have seen double-digit sales increases over a two-year period due largely to their policy of acknowledging sales goals through extra time off rather than extra money. The vice president of Dawson, David DeCapua, saw his sales reach new highs immediately after offering his sales staff the opportunity to leave work at 2:00 p.m. for the rest of the month after they reach their sales targets for a particular month.

Even in those companies restricted by a manufacturing process, placing employees' time at a high premium pays off. Sarasota, Florida–based Aladdin Equipment, a pool and spa replacement parts manufacturer, shortened their production schedule to four and a half days per week so employees could have a half-day off to take care of personal business or just kick back. The move resulted in a 10 percent increase in productivity and a 50 percent decrease in absenteeism.[22]

For some, the ultimate flex perk is telecommuting. Although not for everyone, those who can effectively mesh work with home life are often even more productive than those working full-time from the office. They feel so appreciative of the opportunity to spend more time with their family that they work even harder at home than they might in the office. Plus, in this era of terrorism, telecommuting even offers the benefit of feeling safer. According to the International Telework Association & Council (ITAC), the number of people who telework—or do work from some place other than a traditional office—is expected to reach 30 million by 2004.[23]

Sabbaticals, too, have been gaining popularity in the flexible workplace. Long an academic tradition, sabbatical programs were first established at Harvard University in 1880. Today the majority of universities offer paid sabbaticals to faculty members so that they can have the time to take a break to pursue research, writing, or their own brand of learning. That concept has begun to migrate over to the world of business. According to a 2001 survey by The Principal Financial Group, "more than half the employees of small and midsize companies say they long for a sabbatical."[24] Sarah Ryerson, for example, took three months off from work at The

GEM Group, a marketing-services company based in Atlanta, to tour Tibetan monasteries and U.S. National Parks. "I feel loyalty to the company . . . I know I will return more motivated for the job and already look forward to sharing my experiences with my colleagues," says Ryerson, who checked in regularly with her boss via e-mail along the way.[25]

Another approach to retaining talented employees is limiting employee reductions during difficult times. Instead of just firing employees during an economic downturn, a few companies are experimenting with alternate solutions. For instance, Cisco Systems didn't just fire Sandra Hodgin even though she lost her finance job there. Cisco gave her a two-month vacation followed by a one-year finance position working for a group of northern California women's shelters. Although she only gets one-third of her previous salary, she still receives her benefits, a laptop computer, and full access to the company gym. Hodgin says, "I'm still employed. It's great."[26] Both she and Cisco hope the economy will turn around by the end of her 14-month experiment so she can come back to work full-time for them again.

As the job market becomes more fluid, employers will have to work harder to attract the best employees, keep morale up, raise productivity, and lower absenteeism, all without being bogged down by a large workforce. Employees will be looking far beyond cash to incentives that keep them motivated, productive, and committed to an employer.

CONCLUSION

The cyclic life will offer us the chance to be many different people in our work lives. A job is no longer a life sentence. It's an opportunity to figure out what we can do best and then move on. Midlife may provide a new beginning for some while maturity may offer a chance to blossom in a new career for others. Sometimes we'll choose it; sometimes it will be forced upon us. Cyclic careers will mean repeated career reinventions; work exits and reentry; being a beginner in midlife; sabbaticals; and flexible work options, compensation, and benefits. The possibilities will be unlimited when a linear progression upward is no longer the only desired career path.

4

LOVE CYCLES

In the linear life arrangement, romance and the mating game were designed for the young with one goal in mind: marriage. The institution of marriage has always been the building block of the family and hence, of society. In the old lifestyle model, marriage came early and lasted a lifetime. If we didn't marry by a certain age, say our early 30s, we were denigrated by society, labeled a bachelor, or even worse, an old maid.

For most of its history, the primary purpose of marriage was to create a nest to raise the next generation before sending them off to do the same thing. Marriage also provided a system of legal rules to handle the granting of property rights. If love and romance happened to be present, so much the better, but they were considered bonuses rather than essentials.

In the 1500s, marriage was seen as a way "to prevent men and women from sins, for companionship, and procreation."[1] Years later, the Puritans described marriage as "the highest and most blessed of relationships." Happily married herself for decades, Queen Victoria noted, "Marriage is no amusement but a solemn act." And in the twentieth century, a sunny and optimistic marriage boom preceded our record-breaking baby boom, where 9 out of every 10 people who could marry did marry. No matter how we've described it, sometimes it worked out well; sometimes it didn't. In either case, life was short and we stuck out our marriages no matter what. Not anymore.

The LifeCycle revolution is causing the institution of marriage and the concepts of love and romance to morph to fit the new styles and rhythms of our more cyclic lives. For some, one love will renew itself many times throughout a long life, growing deeper and more evolved. For others, love might blossom several times during different Life-Cycles—and with different partners. Some might not find love until the second half of life while others may experience it only in fleeting relationships along the way. Still others may consciously decide to remain happily single throughout their life spans, without the stigma of failure attached. In any case, the choice will be ours, with the variety of options vastly increasing.

LIFELONG SOUL MATES

Back when the Puritans were extolling the virtues of lifelong marriage, the average marriage lasted only about 12 years because adult life spans were so short.[2] Today's lifespans bring new meaning to the idea of lifetime commitment.

My husband and I recently attended a 60th anniversary celebration for his parents. A few years before that, we attended a party celebrating his aunt and uncle's 70th anniversary. Obviously, the longevity revolution is adding years to our love lives along with our life spans. When the traditional marriage vows were written to include the phrase "till death do us part," no one ever dreamed that could mean upwards of 50 years. But, according to the U.S. Census Bureau Office of Marriage and Family, of those married in 1930, 26 percent were still together after 50 years.

What I've noticed from observing the durability of my in-laws' relationship is that as they've gotten older, they seem to have grown closer to each other rather than farther apart. When I asked my mother-in-law about this, she explained that her generation's family values made it unacceptable to divorce, so when things got difficult in her marriage, she tried to solve the issues rather than leaving the relationship. Sometimes that was very frustrating, but ultimately, it added such depth to the relationship that she "couldn't imagine life without him." One of her comments that struck me as enlightened was, "You need to learn to manage expectations and realize that anything good takes work."

Whether we remain in a relationship for 50 years or 50 months, in a legal marriage, or in a live-in relationship, long-term relationships take work, a realization that nothing is perfect, and an acceptance that we all change continually. Natalie Low, Ph.D., a clinical psychologist and instructor at Harvard, has been married for more than 50 years and agrees with my mother-in-law's perspective. She says, "The facts of life are very grinding, so the reality of marriage is grinding. There is no obvious course to follow, so couples just have to keep working."[3] *And* managing their expectations.

According to research, a successful long-term relationship includes sharing, accommodation, and companionship, whether we're young or old, rich or poor, straight or gay. Also mentioned frequently as relationship cornerstones are qualities such as trust, open communication, psychological intimacy, laughter, touch, sexual compatibility, psychological and social support, and, of course, heartfelt love.

The latest research studies probe a little deeper and suggest that those who expect the most from their marriages are often the ones who work the hardest at them and, therefore, end up with the strongest relationships. When married couples take on traditional gender roles or form effective partnerships, that, too, can lead to relationship success. Qualities that often lead to divorce include contempt, criticism, defensiveness, and stonewalling. Even subtle facial expressions like eye-rolling during an argument can be a strong indicator that a relationship isn't working.[4]

Remaining in one primary relationship and maintaining positive ideals throughout a lifetime were simpler when life was short and there were few alternatives. Until very recently, people stayed together to raise their children, and then either one or both partners died. During the vast majority of the relationship's entire duration, both partners were in the same lifestage—parenting—and that was their shared and primary goal. Today, marriages often don't even include children, many of those by choice.

At the same time, the median age for venturing into first marriages has been rising steadily since the mid-1950s. "Today people know they are going to be married until they are 80. So 40 is the new 30" in terms of marriageable age, says Marcus Matthews of Kaagan Research, a market research firm. According to the U.S. Census Bureau, the proportion of 20-to-24-year-old American women who have not yet married doubled from 36 to 73 percent while the proportion of unmarried female 30-to-34-year-olds more than tripled from 6 to 22 percent over the past three decades.[5] That means many well-educated young women are opting for careers prior to marriage so they can establish that LifeCycle before developing a meaningful—and time-consuming—love relationship. Significantly, it may also mean that a greater number of women and men are choosing to remain single indefinitely, an option I'll discuss in more detail in the "Solo Flyers" section that follows.

Although we're marrying later, we're also divorcing more regularly. Half of all marriages end in divorce. According to the U.S. Department of Commerce's *Current Population Reports*, the divorced population is the country's fastest growing marital status category with the number of divorced people quadrupling from 1970 to 1996. Eighty percent of those who divorce remarry, and second marriages statistically fair just as poorly. Apparently, cycling in and out of monogamous relationships doesn't necessarily make us better at them.

Long-term relationships, whether bound by legal marriage or not, will themselves become cyclic, with their own ebbs and flows, and those that endure the test of time will be more secure knowing that such changes are inevitable. For instance, some couples with enduring relationships might live one love cycle as a couple in a long-distance relationship.

In my own marriage, my husband and I spend a lot of time apart due to work obligations that involve travel. I've had friends ask me, "How can you stand being apart so much?" The truth is that it has its difficulties, but overall, I enjoy having both a life with my husband and a life without him. It helps me appreciate him and not take the relationship for granted. And I like the fact that it gives me some time to be just me rather than half of "Maddy-and-Ken." I also notice that he appreciates me more after we've had some time apart. He gets time to miss me. And that's been good for our relationship.

Other couples might experiment with shifting roles and responsibilities. Donna and Bob Jamison were both highly educated with meaningful careers when they met in Boston in their late 20s. She had taken a business path while he dedicated himself to a nonprofit career. About the time they decided to marry, Donna got a lucrative job offer in California. Together, they decided she would take it while Bob would stay home with the kids, if they were lucky enough to have them. Six years later, they have a wonderful daughter, Diana, and are both happy with this reversal of the traditional roles. I recently saw Bob at a kickboxing class where he was busy swapping information with a woman on the best after-school dance programs for their young daughters. He did mention, however, that he and Donna were, again, thinking of changing roles so that she could get some more time with Diana, and he could start rebuilding his career.

Some couples committed to long-term romance find unique ways to continually refresh their bond throughout the years of change and growth. For instance, at this writing, my husband and I have been married for 19 years and had 20 weddings. We had such a great time at our first wedding that Ken suggested we create a romantic tradition of our own: remarry every year in a different location through a different religious ritual. I was touched and delighted that he felt so tenderly about our marriage, so no matter what else is going on in our lives, every year just the two of us take off for a romantic destination and renew our vows on our anniversary.

We find that sometimes we're in a good place together when that time of year rolls around, and sometimes we're not. But the very process of assessing where our relationship stands and where we'd like it to be going has become a pivotal component in our tradition, a kind of housekeeping and goal-setting exercise in one. A few years ago, we put the ritual off for a month, and we found it had a very negative impact on our relationship. Things that had been building up all year didn't have a chance to come out in the open because we were both so busy and disconnected from each other. We never again missed our anniversary renewal of vows.

We've had every kind of service you can imagine, from two singing rabbis in Berkeley to a female Mexican judge accompanied by a mariachi band in Cabo San Lucas, from a t'ai chi ceremony in Big Sur to a skiing judge in Vail. This annual pause in life's rat race keeps us continually connected to each other in a world that tends to pull us apart, and gives us the time to communicate what has gone right and wrong in our lives and our relationship so that we can try to improve things for the coming year. It's a wonderful tradition that some of our friends and loved ones have adopted as well.

Buying Implications

One of the benefits of maintaining a stable marriage over time is that it creates the opportunity to build long-term financial stability. Partnerships have long been understood to be financially viable ways to make life work effectively—and at a greater profit. And a long-term relationship allows for financial assets to build over a lifetime. However, at various points along a life path, partners in a long-term relationship may have differing needs. For instance, one might want to take a year off to relax and regenerate while another might want to go back to school. These ideas need to be built into long-term financial plans that are updated regularly with a knowledgeable financial planner who knows as much about planning life as evaluating investment strategies.

Another financial benefit of an enduring relationship is that if a household remains intact, there's no need to continually buy basics such as dishes, mattresses, and furniture unless a family's renovating or wants a change. As a result, money can be used for other expenditures, such as luxury items, or saved and invested. Shared and undivided property can also be improved, expanded, and maintained, bringing it greater value. Financially, at least, long-term relationships still make the most sense. So how does one develop and maintain one?

To begin, we'll need to learn and practice relationship training. Yes, that could even mean therapy. It's always amazed me that there are so few easily available training courses in how to make relationships work successfully. We have training courses in everything from how to use computer software to how to invest our 401(k)s, but we're primarily on our own when it comes to making our marriages and family relationships work. There are some religious institutions that offer premarital training programs, but those are usually aimed at the young who are about to marry for the first time, excluding a lot of us. They also don't necessarily take into account the change from a linear to a more cyclic life pattern that creates more complications in sustaining a long-term relationship. Training in relationship-building through books, tapes, and best of all, hands-on, interactive programs can help us learn how to more effectively communicate and relate better, and maybe help our long-term relationships last even longer. In addition, we may want to have annual checkups with a counselor or therapist, even when things are going great, so we can develop tools on an ongoing basis to help us grow in a relationship. This might even be done on a subscription basis so that every six months or so, partners check in together with a counselor to assess how things are going.

At the other end of the spectrum, we need to have tools to help us leave a relationship without forsaking our entire bond with a former spouse. That means exiting with the minimum amount of pain and humiliation and without financial ruin. Simple prenuptial agreements could be a tool not just for the rich but everyone. The divorce process, too, could be made easier and less painful. These legal documents could be available in kits or through arbitrators who are also family counselors. Like wills and insurance policies, dealing with these legal documents is not a pleasant experience, but if we could be upfront about them and create them while we're still in love and want the best for each other, it would minimize the pain and hardship down the cyclic road.

On a brighter note, long-term relationships need punctuation and rejuvenation at regular intervals. To endure, a relationship needs care and feeding. A couple needs time away, just the two of them, from the stress and strain of everyday life. That may mean a candlelit dinner or a romantic weekend getaway. It might mean forming a couples group with friends or within a church or synagogue or attending a couples-only retreat. Resorts, cruise lines, spas, restaurants, and even camping grounds need to create opportunities for couples of all ages to get away without their children.

Long-term success also means keeping the relationship's sexual energies alive. In our world, where sex and death are linked due to AIDS and other STDs, monogamy is definitely in. Everyone from Dr. Ruth to *Playboy* offers consumers advice through books, videos, and software programs. Actress Kim Cattrall, who plays the sexually active Samantha Jones on the HBO series *Sex and the City*, combined her 40-

something character's expertise as a sexual connoisseur with her real-life experience as a married woman to write *Satisfaction: The Art of the Female Orgasm* with her real-life husband, Mark Levinson. She hoped to fill the void by providing valuable information on how a woman's sexual satisfaction can enhance relationships.

Cybersex, too, is alive and thriving. The Internet search engine, Yahoo, lists more than 300 websites that deliver interactive sexually explicit services, described as "phone sex with visuals." Some are just plain porn aimed at single men or women, but others target couples looking to spice up their sex lives. Virtual Dreams, a Las Vegas–based cybersex company, offers virtual strip shows where individuals or couples can not only watch a stripper but also direct him or her for as little at $5.99 per minute. They claim to gross close to $1 million a month.

Forrester Research estimates that in the United States alone online sales of adult merchandise ranging from how-to videos to slinky lingerie make up approximately 10 percent of all products sold online.[6] Obviously, not just long-term marrieds are buying these products. But in the past, everyone assumed long-term marrieds didn't buy any of those products. We know now that they are a viable and motivated market for spicy accoutrements. We've all seen the crowds in Victoria's Secret and noted the impressive prime-time ratings for its televised fashion show. Clearly, erotic and romantic gifts for those in committed, long-term relationships will continue to be a growth market in the cyclic love phases that lie ahead.

CYCLIC MONOGAMISTS

The famed anthropologist Margaret Mead once said, "I've been married three times, and each marriage was successful. The first time was for romance; the second was for family, and the third was for companionship." Mead pointed out that she had gone through several distinct LifeCycles where her needs and priorities were so completely different that no man could have met them all. She said, "I loved each of my husbands for who they were, but realized their limitations and acted accordingly."

As a result of the LifeCycle revolution, many forms of love and romance will appear on the radar screen rather than just the standard model of love-marriage-children. While some of us will still choose to have one soul mate for life, others won't. The same year Ken's parents celebrated 60 years of marriage, my mom celebrated her 10th wedding anniversary in her second marriage while a good friend of ours invited us to his fourth wedding. The groom, John Alexander, was 60 with five kids from previous marriages while the bride was 35, marrying for the first time and looking forward to having children soon.

My mom's first marriage was to her high-school sweetheart, my dad. They were married before either of them had a chance to graduate college, and she was pregnant before she was 20. Right after her first baby came the second. My parents were so busy trying to make ends meet and raise a family that, somewhere along the way, they lost each other. Although they stayed in their marriage until death parted them, their time together was filled with ups and downs. They even separated for several years and found their way back together again. When my dad died, after almost 40 years of marriage, my mother wasn't sure she would ever have another love cycle that was meaningful.

But she did. When she was 61, two years after my dad passed away, she fell passionately in love with Ray. Within months, they married, even though their children—both my brother and me and Ray's five children—disapproved. (We all thought it was too quick.) Ten years later, it's apparent they were meant for each other. They have a loving, stable relationship built on romance and companionship. In fact, they seem like they're soul mates. Like Margaret Mead, my mother would describe both her marriages as successful, but her second one as happier, and less strained by conflicting priorities, raising children, and economic instability. Like my mom, many of us will have relationships in one stage of life—maybe when we're in our 20s, maybe in our 60s—that exceed our expectations.

Others, like my friend John mentioned above, will cycle in and out of multiple relationships that may even bring them back to the LifeCycle of parenting. The percentage of marriages between never-married women and divorced men increased between 1970 and 1990 while the number of men remarrying in their 40s and 50s has also edged upward.[7] Obviously, John has a lot of company. For instance, Berkeley Business School Professor William Sonnenschein and Stanford University economics Professor Martin Carnoy have more than academic careers in common. They're both in second marriages with wives who have never been married before. Both also have second families to go along with their second wives. According to Professor Sonnenschein, "If you asked me 20 years ago, I'd have told you that I wanted to retire at age 50. But, having another child, there's no doubt that I won't retire until she's through college." In the next chapter, *The Virtual Family*, we'll be looking at the phenomenon of second families and blended families in more depth.

One of the biggest changes in our perspective on love cycles is that we no longer accept a bad relationship as a lifelong commitment. In an era when many of us are living longer and are better educated, many women are no longer solely dependent on their husbands economically and socially. These factors combine to give us less reason than ever to stick it out in a bad relationship for security's sake. (See divorce rates around the world in Figure 4.1.)

One result is what author Pamela Paul describes as "the starter marriage" which comes early in life, lasts just a short time, and ends before children arrive.[8] She suggests that some couples spend more time planning the nuptials than remaining married and that as many as 25 percent of first marriages fall into this category, failing within two years. Although young people don't start out planning to have starter marriages according to the survey done in The National Marriage Project, only 6 percent of young people believe they will stay married to the same person for life.[9]

Cyclic monogamy can sometimes mean cycling back into relationships with the same person more than once. We've all seen movie stars like Melanie Griffith and Don Johnson or Liz Taylor and Richard Burton have on-again, off-again relationships in the spotlight of the media. That's not the kind of cycling I mean. I'm talking about real people who may have loved each other once but somehow lost touch in one cycle of life but rediscover each other in another. Marian Fournier and her second husband are a lovely example. They were teenage sweethearts completely in love in prewar Berlin in the 1930s. It was a tumultuous time in Germany then, and her family emigrated to the United States in 1939 while her sweetheart, Guy Hofstein, ended up in France. Both

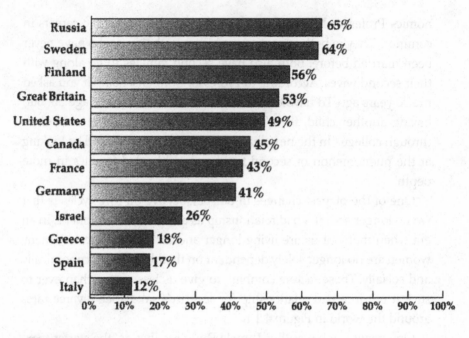

Figure 4.1
Divorce Rates Around the World, 1999
(As a percentage of all marriages)
Source: United States Census Bureau; Divorce Center; CDC; UN, 2000.

went on to live full and happy lives apart. Marian married, had two children, two grandchildren, and two great-grandchildren. She also built a professional career. After decades in their respective happy and monogamous relationships, both Marian and Guy were widowed. More than 50 years after their love affair had ended, they met again in 1992, at a school reunion. Their attraction was immediate and as strong as ever. At age 74, Guy abruptly left his life in France to join Marian in Auburndale, Massachusetts. They married and are creating a life together, undeterred by the 50 years they spent apart.

Not all stories are as happy as Marian's of course. For instance, Emily Morris fell in love with Jake Katz when she was still in college. Together they moved to New York to start their respective careers. For five years, their relationship thrived, but Emily came to realize that Jake was not interested in having the children she yearned for. She left him, still feeling love for him, but knowing she needed to create a relationship with a different man to experience the next cycle of her life, parenting. Emily is still hoping to meet a parenting partner, and Jake remains single.

As Jake's example shows, although marriage and children were always the desired destination for couples in the past, that's not always the case anymore. Recent studies suggest "marital satisfaction drops by 70 percent, in the first few years after the birth of a child."[10] The National Marriage Project at Rutgers University states that only 16 percent of young adults agree that the main purpose of marriage these days is to have children. A clear majority of young men (62 percent) agree that, while it may not be ideal, it's okay for an adult woman to have a child on her own if she has not found the right man to marry.[11]

Some couples opt to have no children or to at least delay childbearing, sometimes until it's too late. When actress Kim Cattrall, in her 40s, happily married and busy working on *Sex and the City*, was interviewed by *Vanity Fair* magazine, one of the questions that came up was What about children? She answered, "It's too late, way too late for that. I think to be a mom you definitely have to give up at least five years of your life. And I'm having a great time. I don't really want to change nappies right now. It's not where I'm at."[12] Kim Cattrall has lots of company; today childless marriages are increasing, with two out of five women having no children.[13]

Of course, different priorities related to bearing children and raising a family aren't the only reason people divorce. Sometimes couples just don't get along. Money has been identified as the number one reason couples divorce. And a variety of studies point to the fact that "by the time many couples say, 'I Do,' the seeds of marital distress and divorce" are already present for those who end up eventually divorcing.[14] It's just one among many indications that changing goals and lifestyles are inherent in the cyclic life. Margaret Mead might have been more of a trailblazer than she realized.

Buying Implications

In 2001, the wedding industry in the United States alone brought in $32 billion, up 230 percent from 1982. When we think about brides, weddings, and honeymoons, however, we tend to think about young people and market those products exclusively to them. That's not necessarily the case anymore. Brides can be 20 or 60, and, in either case, they may choose to elope or have a big wedding with all the trimmings. When my mom remarried at age 61, she had the wedding she always dreamed of rather than the one her parents were willing to pay for. The other difference was, her children and grandchildren were there this time to share the joyous experience. Getting married for the fourth time, John Alexander and his fiancée were registered for wedding gifts just like any young couple might be. He said, "We're starting a household together for the first time. I don't want any of her former life in my face and she certainly doesn't want to look at dishes or furniture that one of my former wives picked out. So we're starting over."

All the purchases we make when we start a household—from sheets to glasses, from couches to blenders—are made in excess when we marry whether we're 28, 42, or 73. Businesses that manufacture furniture, for instance, need to consider the comfort and, oftentimes, more sophisticated tastes of midlife and older couples marrying and starting a home together for the first time. Chances are that the older we are, the more certain of our taste and style we become, and the more willing and able we are to invest in that relationship through purchases. On the other hand, as we get older, we may need more ergonomically appropriate furniture and appliances that can help us manage our households with comfort and ease. And if we divorce and do not remarry, the cupboards will still need to be restocked and new mattresses chosen, this time to our specifications alone.

And for the remarrying type, let's not forget the ring or the honeymoon. Midlife and older couples want all the romance that young couples want and, statistically, they're more willing to spend the money to have their dreams come true. Yet few travel resorts or even jewelry stores market aggressively to this segment. It's a tremendous missed opportunity.

Let's not forget that "money is always among the top three concerns of newly and soon-to-be-married couples," according to research by Synovus Financial Corporation, a banking company based in Columbus, Georgia. Their research has stated that 2.5 million couples get engaged each year, and that most of those couples plan on merging their financial futures, but don't exactly know where to start. To maximize this opportunity, Synovus had even launched a website that provided financial services for The Knot, a wedding-related e-business that attracts about 1 million visitors per month.[15] Their plan was to capture many of the newly married as they embarked on merged lives. They understand that today women are an important part of the financial decision-making team; they understand that many couples are tech savvy and will utilize online banking services for convenience; and they understand that each couple will need to plan their finances in a personalized manner based on the LifeCycle events they expect to be part of. Although Synovus limited their target market to 18- to 45-year-olds exclusively, people of all ages are newly engaged, about to merge their finances as well as their lives, and in dire need of assistance. Companies of all types—from financial services to health care, from realtors to retailers—could miss out on a huge opportunity by limiting their thinking in this way. Love and marriage is a cycle of life, no longer limited by age. If we can internalize this reality, we can greatly increase our target market and better serve consumers of all ages embarking on shared lives.

EMPTY NESTERS: PURCHASING GIANTS

If we look back just a few generations, we'd notice that in the past, few couples lived long enough to become empty nesters. At the beginning of the twentieth century, average life expectancy was only 47, so by the time the children had grown up and started their own families, it was likely that at least one of the parents had died. With extended longevity a demographic fact of life today, most couples who choose to have children and stay together will experience the empty nest.

It is estimated that by the year 2010, there will be 36 million empty nesters. In fact, the average couple can now expect to spend more years *after* parenting than during it. Not surprisingly, this stage of life often tests the resiliency of relationships, but when they last, they often bring forth new roles, new interests, and plenty of purchasing power to go along with them. Empty nesting has emerged as a thriving new cycle of life in which couples once again get the opportunity to focus primarily on their own needs rather than those of their children.

Linda and Keeler Chapman never even had time to figure out what their own needs were until the last of their three children graduated from college and accepted a job in a large city hundreds of miles away. They began emptying their empty nest of its kid-safe furniture and rethinking their home's layout almost immediately. Over the course of just four years, the couple discovered new passions and interests. The basketball hoop came down and a garden went in. Linda found she has a knack for home remodeling and design (practicing first on her own ever-evolving space, of course) and Keeler is indulging his life-long ambition to become an architect. He also plays percussion in the local symphony, a talent he had never before found the time to indulge. They have a list of all the places they'd like to visit and are knocking them off, one by one. Their children are, of course, very concerned that Linda and Keeler will waste away from lack of purpose now that their nest is empty, but the parents themselves are far too busy to worry much about it.

Buying Implications

Empty nesting has become the stage of life blessed by the greatest discretionary time and money. The average empty nester asserts, "I can do what I want when I want to do it." And many are. As the couple I just talked about shows, empty nesters are a potential gold mine for the real estate industry, since that's when most adults renovate their primary home or buy up. A recent survey conducted by the American Furniture Manufacturers Association (AFMA) found that when the kids fly the nest, couples redecorate it. According to the research, nearly half of America's empty nesters will reinvest in their nests by renovating their current home, or purchasing a new house or vacation home.

Yes, many wait until the kids leave to purchase a better home. And *better* does not always mean *bigger*. In fact, more and more empty nesters are moving out of their huge suburban houses to live in cozier, more customized homes. For instance, Renee and Simon Milstein bought a huge brick and stucco home in a spanking new development in the Minneapolis area. Within months of living with "vaulted ceilings and towering banks of windows," they realized they hated it. "When night fell, those windows seemed like big black holes," Simon said. "It was overwhelming." So they sold their home for $470,000 and immediately built a custom home nearby for $650,000. It was 1,000 square feet smaller but more architecturally detailed, with window seats, nooks and built-in bookshelves. Renee, a Spanish teacher whose husband is a physician, said, "This house reflects who we really are."[16]

Although many do start all over with a new home according to the AFMA survey, one out of four couples renovate their current home, with upgrades that include purchasing higher-quality furnishings. More than 78 percent of those surveyed, in fact, plan on adding a dream piece of furniture. The living room is most often targeted first, followed by their children's old rooms. According to the survey, children's bedrooms are most likely to become a library, hobby studio, guestroom, home theater, or office. Other rooms up for a facelift include the master bedroom, dining room, or family room.

Twenty-five percent of empty nesters will buy a new home or vacation home. Many in this group are still years away from the traditional age of retirement and remain at peak earning power. With the children no longer a responsibility, and a first mortgage either paid off or close to it, empty nesters are in a good position to buy second homes.

"Over the past 20 years, the number of second homes in the United States has doubled to 3.6 million in 2000, according to Census 2000. And it no longer is the exclusive domain of the wealthy. The median income of a second-home buyer is $68,800 while the median age is 43, according to the NAR's 1999 biennial survey." The National Association of Realtors (NAR) also reports that the September 11, 2001, terrorist activities and fears of potential threats in the future have fueled the desire for people to have second homes in more remote areas, far away from potential terrorist targets.[17]

And they're filling these homes with all kinds of luxury items designed for smaller, more sophisticated spaces: tiny wine cellars that can be tucked under a stairwell or kitchen counter, smaller Jacuzzi spas that are more fuel and water efficient, compact kitchen tools designed for professional kitchens but scaled down for smaller households. Not surprisingly, most of these homes also have complete home offices and are wired for high-speed Internet access.

Other luxury items register on the empty nester radar screen as well, including boats, exotic or adventure travel, sporty cars, and designer clothes. For some, empty nesting is short-lived, as kids come back after college (which is called boomeranging), stretching marriages in new and often demanding directions yet again. I'll focus on this increasingly prevalent trend in more detail in Chapter 5.

SOLO FLIERS

According to seventeenth-century English common law, women were either married or to be married. It was expected that a woman was a dependent of her father until she married and then a dependent of her husband.[18] In most cultures, that was how it worked.

For most of society, singlehood was a short-lived life passage that preceded marriage. Romance and courting were an essential part of the mix because the goal was to find a mate. Those who remained single too long were considered old maids, spinsters, bachelors, and worse. A widow represented a "crack in social construction and social arrangements" and posed a problem to family, church, and state for she no longer was under the control and protection of a man. Some cultures burned widows alive in their husbands' funeral pyres, while others tried to quietly find a lone male relative to take them in or offer them a life devoted to religion. In medieval Italy, a widow was offered the option of remarriage or "monastic withdrawal." The presence of single women without immediate marital prospects or intentions was seen as a threat to society because there was no clear-cut role for them. Their value to society was less than zero. Their attractiveness as a target market was close to zero. Not anymore.

Today the power of one is very real. Solo fliers are all ages. Many choose to be single for a whole lifetime, happy and resolute on their custom unicycles. Others cycle in and out of singlehood at several intervals throughout their lives. Still more long to be partnered but never find their soul mates. In any case, what is clear is that singlehood is an important cycle in the LifeCycle revolution that presents unprecedented personal and business opportunities.

Most of us will cycle into singlehood at least a few times throughout our lives, judging by the demographic realities alone. With average life expectancy at 77 and rising and with women outliving men by 7 to 10 years, there are only 38 men for every 100 women 85 and older.

But it's not just the numbers that will grow. Our attitude toward singlehood has dramatically improved. No longer is flying solo considered peculiar or shameful, the plight of old maids, bachelors, and widows. With nearly one in three women today a solo flier, it has become a viable stage of life, rich in choices and opportunities.[19] Singlehood will continue to gain power in this LifeCycle revolution.

Many enjoy the solitary lifestyle so much once they rediscover it that they choose not to leave it at all. Ruth Goldman, for instance, had spent much of her adult years married to Marvin. Although they had their ups and downs, they successfully raised two children and survived the empty nest together. Marvin died suddenly when Ruth was 62. She picked up and moved to a new community where she found the perfect house to suit her needs, made a new group of friends, and found her way back to school to finish what she'd never had time for before. When a visiting friend from New Jersey asked if she had met a man so that she could remarry and find real happiness, Ruth laughed and said, "I have found true happiness. No one tells me what to do or when to do it. My life is truly my own for the first time, and I wouldn't trade that for anything."

Like Ruth, Pearl Hedlund of San Antonio, Texas, went through an extended period of grieving after her husband's death. After that, she decided that she had to meet other singles and try to go on with her life. One day, she read an ad in the personals on Yahoo.com that struck a chord. It was placed by George, a man who lived 70 miles away and had been divorced for 18 years. They e-mailed and decided to meet halfway between their homes. Immediately, they hit it off. "George invited me to the mountains of New Mexico for the summer. That's when we decided to get married. Now every morning I tell George how great it is to be alive and enjoy another day with a great person," says Pearl.

Not surprisingly, groups are cropping up all over the world to offer singles a way to make new friends and lovers. Some of them even focus on giving back. For instance, SVDC: Single Volunteers of D.C., founded by software analyst Dana Kressierer, is exactly what it sounds like. Dana started the group in early 1997 after splitting up with her boyfriend. Armed with a master's degree in sociology and inspiration from an article she had read about a singles' volunteer group in Vermont, she and a friend, Catharine Robertson, logged onto the Internet and gathered 30 volunteers for the launch meeting. Her friend, Catharine, actually fell in love at that first meeting. She says, "SVDC provides a chance for people to do something good and feel good about themselves. And it offers a huge pool of intelligent, caring people looking for friends or partners." SVDC is growing and now boasts more than 2,500 volunteers who mix socializing with acts of kindness like building homes for the disadvantaged, cleaning trash for Trash Force, or sprucing up a cemetery.[20]

Today there is choice; no longer is a single the odd man—or woman—out. The largest group of singles in our country is older women, often on their own for the very first time in their adult lives. At their extremes, they're the wealthiest and healthiest as well as the poorest and frailest of any LifeCycle segment. Many older women today enjoy traveling together, investing together, and socializing together. The next generation of single adults, still in their 40s and 50s, will definitely bring new attitudes and expectations to this LifeCycle and might even spur a resurgence of '70s-style communal housing arrangements.

Buying Implications

There are 43 million single women in the United States alone, yet it took a long time for young and midlife women to get on the radar screen of business. Now it's a known fact that woman are a target worth pursuing. Older women, however, are still invisible to most marketers. Yet this population is "low-hanging fruit," eagerly looking for opportunities to buy products that help them look good, feel good, and maybe even live out some of their dreams. They are an untapped market for everything from mutual funds and home remodeling to spa treatments and video game purchases for their grandchildren. Any company savvy enough to reach out and touch them will reap tremendous rewards.

Single women are also impacting the U.S. housing market more now than at any other time in history. Single women in all stages of life—

divorced, widowed, or never married—have dramatically increased their share in the national home-buying market from 13 percent in 1989 to 18 percent in 1999, according to a study by the National Association of Realtors. This outpaces the 9 percent share single men have held in the market since 1989.

Debra Purvis, president of DesignHouse, a home-design firm based in Wiggins, Mississippi, attributes the increasing presence of women in the housing market to changing lives and roles. "Women are just not waiting for Mr. Right to come along and take care of them. They're going out and doing it for themselves."

Purvis profiles her typical single woman client as over 50, widowed or divorced, with a moderate to high income. "They tend to ask for not very large homes—maybe 1,800 square feet or under—with a lot of light and glass, tall ceilings, a feeling of open air. And at least one walk-in closet! They want to be able to see into the Great Room from the kitchen so they don't feel stuck there when entertaining. Low-maintenance is also key. Some single women have asked for duplexes. I've gotten a lot of requests from people with aging parents who want an attached dwelling—a suite with its own kitchen and exit—that is integrated with the house so their parents can come to live with them."

Michael Noonan, vice president of Rottland Homes' Minnesota Division, characterizes single women home-buyers as "more independent, more financially well-heeled, and more knowledgeable about the market—and demanding consumers," and credits this profile to an increase in women in the professional world. His company has also noticed the trend toward attached housing choices in this demographic. "The town homes we build really seem to appeal to single women because they offer a maintenance-free lifestyle, and the proximity of neighbors gives them a sense of intimacy and security."

While buying low-maintenance attached housing may be the predominant choice of single women, it's not a choice that suits them all. Many women are choosing instead to build their dream homes.

"I decided to buy a home because I knew I needed to invest in something," says Diane Koschak, 37, a divorced teacher and singer from St. Paul, Minnesota. "I was paying the same in rent that I am now in a mortgage, but now I'm building equity."[21]

Products designed for singles in general will be a flourishing market. Single-serving food and snacks have been around for a while, but look beyond the obvious and you'll see products beginning to appear that specifically meet the needs of just one individual. For example, members of ClubTable.net, an Amsterdam-based service, can pay an annual fee of $50 and be provided with dining partners in a variety of cities throughout the world. It's really aimed at business travelers, especially women, who usually dine on room service alone rather than enjoy the ambiance of the city they're visiting. ClubTable.net puts together groups of four to eight diners for dining only companionship. However, we can easily see how this might be a relevant service for singles beyond the business traveler.[22]

And customized products, described in Chapter 2 in detail, are particularly relevant to singles. As the lifecycle revolution puts the spotlight on personal choice and individuality, life gets easier and more comfortable for singles.

CONCLUSION

In the cyclic life, love and romance will no longer be activities exclusively designed for young people with the clear-cut goal of marriage and family. The LifeCycle revolution breathes new life into these traditional concepts, offering us a variety of paths to take in terms of our love cycles. Yes, many of us will marry young and have children, but that will be just one of many socially acceptable paths we might travel down, including staying single, gay and lesbian marriage, cohabitation without marriage, delaying marriage and parenthood until later in life, and serial monogamy.

Some of us will fall in love just once and find unique ways to make that love grow throughout a lifetime while others might experience cyclic monogamy with love blossoming several times during different LifeCycles and with different partners. Some might not discover love until their 40s, 50s, or even 70s while others may experience it in short, quick relationships throughout their lives. And there will be those of us who opt to fly solo throughout our life spans. In any case, the choice will be ours as the menu of available options vastly increases.

None of the choices will be made based on age alone. Even the wedding industry will no longer aim its diamonds and honeymoons at only the young. Segmenting an industry by age no longer makes sense. And new household formation will be a cyclic event for many based on changing relationships rather than age. The one thing we can count on is that the LifeCycle revolution will change the way we think about love, romance, and marriage forever with a huge impact on business.

THE VIRTUAL FAMILY

In the linear life arrangement, the traditional nuclear family prevailed, creating the now familiar images of a young mom and dad, two or more kids, a dog, a cat, and a station wagon. It was *Ozzie and Harriet* and *Leave It to Beaver*. Most children were born into a family with two parents and a clear-cut, gender-specific division of labor. Dad was the hunter/gatherer, working in the outside world to bring home the bread. Mom was the nurturer, minding hearth and home, and baking that bread. Child rearing was the main purpose of that family. Anything outside of this ubiquitous model seemed odd.

As a result of this prime-time homogeneity, young families became the much-coveted bull's-eye for American business. Mom, Dad, and the kids were the people product manufacturers had in mind when they designed, marketed, and sold everything from blue jeans to electric ranges. Adults in this youthful lifestage, usually defined as being from 18 to 34, became the center of gravity for most businesses. The era of age-focused, demographic target marketing was born. With the dual belief that most consumer behavior could be easily slotted into predictable age-based stages of life *and* most consumers formed brand preferences when they were young and kept them for the rest of their lives, this kind of mass market myopia made perfect sense at the time. Not anymore.

Due to increased longevity, rising median age, worldwide low-fertility rates, and changing attitudes and values pioneered by boomers, we're seeing the very concept of family morph in response to the LifeCycle revolution. Fifty years ago, you'd have been hard-pressed to find a neighborhood block whose white-picket fences contained anything other than a traditional, nuclear family at some clearly defined point along its prescribed linear path. Today, around that same block, the challenge would be to find more than a few examples of the intact, male breadwinner, female stay-at-home-caretaker, nuclear household. Variety is now the norm, and among our friends and neighbors all of us can count many different types of families that are embarked on any number of LifeCycles. *Ozzie and Harriet* might live next door to contemporary television's *Will and Grace* or *Judging Amy*'s large, extended family.

As a result, no longer can the traditional bull's-eye of American business neatly be pinpointed at the center of a large and clearly defined target. In some cases, it's broader than ever, but its edges are murky at best and, in almost every case, the bull's-eye is in constant motion. To complicate the picture even more, no longer can business count on consumers remaining loyal to the product and brand choices of their youth. Today's consumers change brand and product allegiances just as comfortably as they move from one LifeCycle to another. In fact, many are becoming more and more comfortable with change and, given the opportunity, they embrace it.

NOT JUST THE CLEAVERS LIVE HERE ANYMORE

To show how the old model has changed, we could look at five virtual families, all in the same socioeconomic bracket, even in the same lifestage—parenthood—but with little else in common. One could be a traditional young couple in their late 20s with two children, a dog, and an SUV (to replace the station wagon). However, this June and Ward never married, and she is the breadwinner while he keeps the house tidy and watches the kids. Her elderly mother lives in an assisted living facility nearby, but is in poor health and requires more and more help from this young, overextended family.

The second couple could be recently married, in their 40s, with two toddlers from their union and two college students from prior marriages. The wife is taking a sabbatical from work to spend time with her young children. The husband is working harder than ever at a company that provides the health coverage they need for their expanding brood.

The third couple have two children—one from his first marriage and one from hers. In their 50s, they've both worked full-time since they married. One of their children just graduated college and is pregnant, making them soon-to-be grandparents. She's dropping hints about returning home for a few months until she's recovered from childbirth and can establish herself in a new job and apartment. Her stepbrother, meanwhile, is about to leave for college, giving the couple their first glimpse of an empty nest in years, for however long or short a period that LifeCycle might last.

The fourth couple, in their mid-30s, is eagerly awaiting the arrival of a new baby. The expectant mother and her female partner used artificial insemination to give them the chance to parent together. The two career women have long been accustomed to spending their considerable discretionary income on luxuries like travel and entertainment. Now they spend their weekends choosing nursery colors and high-end rocking chairs, and delight in the change.

The final couple are actually roommates, long-time friends, and business partners who went through divorces within a few years of each other. Both edging toward 40, they've pooled their resources to provide a bright and lively—though unconventional—home for their five children and pets, sharing grocery bills, car pools, and baby-sitting duties, but remaining romantically separate and even hopeful of remarrying others and moving on sometime soon.

These families are all in the same parenthood LifeCycle and their income brackets are nearly identical. Yet their family life is dramatically different, not based on age or socioeconomics, but on their family structure. Their family life might change several more times; they might circle back into another cycle of life they've already experienced or embark on entirely new configurations of family, complete with empty nests that become full again, parents of adult children who opt to have another baby, creative shared custody arrangements, and the blending of home life and work. The options are no longer restricted by social conformity to the linear-life pattern of what family life ought to be, and how families ought to live their lives. And they're no longer the clear-cut, age-defined bull's-eye for the world of business.

THE NEW CYCLIC FAMILY

While the family remains alive and well, young families with children are no longer the primary household type. Adult-centered families have taken over. As Matilda White Riley, former president of the American Sociological Association, points out, "As four or even five generations of many families are now alive at the same time, we can no longer concentrate primary attention on nuclear families of young parents and their children."

In addition, as women have become an important part of the work-force in all types of industries, at all levels, families can no longer rely on a full-time, gender-defined household manager. According to a recent report, "The Emerging 21st Century American Family," from the National Opinion Research Center at the University of Chicago, "households will move further away from the family-structure model of stay-at-home mother, working father, and children."[1] Tom W. Smith, director of the General Social Survey and author of this report, said, "People marry later and divorce and cohabitate more. A growing proportion of children have been born outside of marriage. Even within marriage the changes have been profound as more and more women have entered the labor force and gender roles have become more homogenous between husbands and wives. A majority of families rearing children will probably not include the children's original two parents. Moreover, most households will not include children."

Divorce has further fragmented today's family. As it has become an accepted reality, single parent families have shown up on the radar screen, representing nearly 25 percent of all households with children; so have single individual and same sex partner households. And the definition of family has expanded to include close personal friends, often taking on the roles once reserved for blood relatives and even referred to as aunt or uncle by the children in the family. What quickly becomes obvious is that the concept of family has become less rigid,

more flexible. One size definitely doesn't fit all. Nor does one age segment predominate.

The fact is, this new cyclic family is not limited to the United States.
Most of the westernized world is contending with similar changes. It is
truly a global phenomenon.

The cyclic family is a make your own sundae smorgasbord, diverse in
options, not limiting in its structure. It's also become more vertical than
horizontal, often including many generations alive at once, but with
fewer literal aunts, uncles, and cousins living close to one another. As a
result, the supporting fabric of family life has changed dramatically.

Midwives may support laboring mothers, rather than sisters or aunts.
Nannies care for the children of dual-income parents instead of Aunt
Susie or Grandma Joan. When family members are under the weather,
they're less likely to have home-cooked meals delivered by a phalanx of
relatives and more likely to order in. The advice of a Home Depot expert
might replace the expertise and toolbox of your brother-in-law. And, in
the event of today's emergencies, a complex web of backup systems is
activated to replace the traditional reliance on the well-rooted and
always available family tree. Very few schools insist that a relative pick
up a sick child when the parent is out of town; most names on the "In
Case of Emergency" list are members of the virtual family instead.

While these differences may prompt a certain wistfulness for the
beauty of days gone by, the emerging virtual family system has arisen in
response to and achieves admirable parity with the horizontal extended
family organization. Friends and exes step in to fill the shoes of distant
relatives. Employees and roommates fill other gaps. Book clubs and e-
mail buddy groups replace long-term over-the-fence neighbors and
coffee klatches. Stepparents, half-siblings, parenting grandparents, and
live-in partners fulfill our communal need for shared intimacy, without
necessarily sharing the same gene pool.

It's imperative that we remember, however, that all of these
diverse family structures are purchasing products and services for
themselves and for each other. The target market known as *family* is
as strong as ever, it's just changed forms and can no longer be
defined simply as adults 18 to 34. Good-bye, demographic bull's-eye;
hello moving target.

EXPANDED PARENTING

In the cyclic family, parenting takes on both an expanded definition and an expanded age bracket. Traditionally, parenting started young and was about your own or, sometimes, your adopted children. Today the definition is clearly being stretched: parenting children at age 25, 35, 45, and sometimes even 55 or 65; parenting stepchildren or even grandchildren; parenting elderly parents, grandparents, spouses, or other ill relatives; and parenting the boomerang adult child who needs a helping hand.

In the cyclic life, one of the biggest changes we're witnessing is that women feel the freedom to have children at a variety of ages. In the linear life, childbearing was the domain of young women exclusively. According to Stephanie Ventura, a research statistician with the federal National Center for Health Statistics, women started delaying childbirth in the late 1970s when boomer women began entering the workforce. By 1995, the number of births more than tripled for women 30 to 35 years old and quadrupled for women 35 to 39.[2]

Obviously, no longer is conceiving and raising children an activity limited to young people. A few years back, a 63-year-old woman lied about her age, so that she could undergo in vitro fertilization with a donated egg. She and her husband (also in his 60s) gave birth to their first child, a baby girl. This is definitely pushing the envelope, but there's no doubt that the trend toward older motherhood and parenting is here to stay.

Designer Nicole Miller says, "All the girls I went to high school with were having kids, and I thought, that's such a grown-up thing to do." Although Miller did lots of other grown-up things like start her own successful designer label of clothing, she didn't get married and have children until she was 44 years old. In fact, she was already eight months pregnant when she walked down the aisle. And, for her, the timing couldn't have been better. "This is the perfect time to have kids," she says. "If I were younger, I would have had a harder time dealing with it. I'd have been more upset about the body changes. This is like a new lease on life. When it's, 'Should we go to a movie or stay home with the baby?' we stay home."[3]

Buying Implications

With so many women over 35 eager to have children, conceiving them has become big business. Over the last 20 years, first-time births of women age 35 to 39 have jumped 80 percent and almost 50 percent for women age 40 to 44. And since one in six American couples have trouble conceiving, most over the age of 35, a lucrative fertility industry with an entire treatment spectrum that includes everything from drugs and surgery to sperm washing and in vitro fertilization has risen in response.

The adoption business has also proliferated as couples face the realities of the female biologic clock. Often after spending years chasing fertility, couples choose adoption as an alternate course. This, too, can be a process that takes a lot of time and money involving lawyers, adoption specialists, and even foreign governments.

It can also take some interesting turns, creating unusual extended families. Putting ethical issues to the side for a moment, families can extend through embryo adoption, already a reality. Couples who have created more frozen embryos than they need through in vitro fertilization can donate an embryo to another couple. It's already happening. ABC News' *Primetime* featured one such story in August 2002 involving Bob and Susanne Gray and Greg and Cara Vest.

The Grays had four children—fertility drugs helped them conceive their first child, in vitro brought them twins, and a traditional pregnancy brought them the fourth. Although they felt they had the perfect family they also faced a dilemna—what to do with the 23 frozen embryos in storage from their fertility treatments. The Grays believed that life begins at conception—and that each of the 23 embryos preserved was a human being. Bob Gray told *Primetime* that there's really no difference between letting the embryos die and aborting a pregnancy. "We wanted to give them the best possible life and the best possible future," Susanne Gray said. "And that meant finding the right family for them."

Via the Internet, the Grays found the Christian-run Snowflake Embryo Adoption Program that promises to help genetic parents find a suitable home for their "preborn children," giving them "some control over their destiny." The program put the Grays in touch with a Virginia couple, Greg and Cara Vest. The Vests had spent five years trying to get pregnant, but not even in vitro fertilization worked, so they had signed up with the Snowflake program.

The couples arranged to meet at Bob and Susanne Gray's home. "It was like walking into family," said Cara Vest, who played with the four Gray children and at one point had all of them on her lap. By the end of the weekend, the Gray children were calling the Vests Uncle Greg and Aunt Cara. The couples decided to go ahead with the adoption, signing a contract in which the Grays gave up all parental rights, but were guaranteed at least a yearly update on the child's progress.

In May 2002, Cara Vest gave birth to a baby boy named Jonah. Three months later, the two families had a reunion at the beach in Ocean Isles, N.C. Cara Vest said that Jonah would grow up with two families who had both made allowances for him to have a good life: The Grays gave up their embryo so the Vests could have a child, and the Vests are allowing the Grays to be a part of his life.[4]

On another note, think what midlife parenting means for maternity fashions and other avenues of the big baby business. Older parents generally have more financial resources to buy top-of-the-line strollers, cribs, and baby monitors. Older parents are also better educated and more safety-conscious than their younger predecessors. Today's moms, dads, and other caregivers insist on safety belts that adjust to each weight range, research and purchase mobiles and rattles designed to stimulate infant brains, know precisely how many inches to allow between the bars of a crib. *Consumer Reports* rates every car seat, and each maternity ward must certify that they're inserted properly before baby can even go home. The walkers, cribs, and playpens of the past have been found wanting and been replaced. Nanny cams and fingerprinting services are available to any parent who wants to take an extra safety measure and many do. There's *Bach for Baby*, massage for preemies, sheepskin diaper pad covers, breathing monitors, and gymnastics and yoga classes for babies and their adults. Baby food has gone gourmet and organic. And of course, there are diaper genies to eliminate any odors the precious ones might leave behind.

It doesn't stop there. For highly educated older parents with generally more financial resources, there are private schools and, for some, advisors to hold their hands as they walk through the entry process, which is often cutthroat. As the kids get older, soccer, karate, and a whole retinue of competitive sports—most of which are private and pricey—replace yoga for babies.

For example, club volleyball is a popular sport with middle school and high school girls. There are clubs throughout the United States with programs that are generally six months long and cost around $1,500 plus travel. To stay competitive for a high school varsity team, these programs are often viewed as mandatory. Some clubs even offer scholarships to talented players who can't afford them. The so-called supplemental arts and science programs are popular with parents keen on giving their children every advantage along the path to adulthood. From Shakespeare to "mad science," these programs are offered after school and as summer programs. Often affiliated with museums, theatres, or universities, they are designed to spark interest from kids who might not be exposed to the subject at school or who have a burning desire to increase their knowledge.

Summer camps and learning programs are not only popular but also sometimes difficult to get into. Many learning programs offered at universities combine sports and other recreational activities with learning. For instance, my daughter attended a three-week acting camp at University of California, Berkeley, last summer. There she attended classes for four hours a day on playwriting, voice mechanics, scene study, and costume design. In the evening, they saw Shakespeare in the Park, a repertoire theatre performance in San Francisco, a performance art experience, and took part in play readings. At the same time, UC had dozens of other educational programs, including a group of teenage boys from Italy, there to learn English. (This was a definite plus, according to my daughter, who was ready and willing to tutor.)

The process of college admissions is laden with stress and teams of professionals anxious to help pave the path to success. And college itself may end up costing more than a home. The point is that parents who are slightly older and better educated seem more willing to reach into their pockets to pay for their children to have every advantage, especially if they're well-educated, dual-income families.

DUAL-INCOME FAMILIES

As we cycle in and out of different moments of parenting, many of us are working simultaneously. Today, 62 percent of all women work while 80 percent of all boomer women work.[5] In stark contrast, in 1950 around 32 percent of women worked. In less than a generation, American women moved from the home to the workplace.[6]

Boomer women have been the trendsetters in the dual-income arena, combining work and family on their own, with few role models to follow. Fifty-three percent of the female Harvard Business School class of 1973 moved along the cyclic path to be mothers without giving up income, and 70 percent of the women of HBS's class of 1983 did the same.[7] University of Maryland sociology professor Suzanne Bianchi says, "I can remember in the '70s, being in graduate school, you wouldn't signal anything but being on the straight and narrow toward getting that degree." Women, in an effort to be taken seriously on the linear path of upward mobility in the world of work, did everything they could to appear focused exclusively on building successful careers.

Interestingly, the cyclic life may help to reverse this trend slightly to offer us more balance, if we choose it. In the workforce the percentage of women with infants has been falling since the year 2000, signaling a shift that can be viewed as an acknowledgment of the emerging cyclic life pattern. In October 2001, the U.S. Census Bureau reported that 55 percent of mothers with children under one year were working, down from 59 percent in 1998. That was the first statistically significant decline since the government began compiling statistics on working mothers in 1976.

Experts agree that the new data doesn't forecast a mass retreat of women from the workplace at all. Instead, it reflects the strong sense among many women that their place in the workforce is here to stay and that they can leave temporarily without losing out professionally. Instead of frantically trying to have and do it all simultaneously, they will be cycling in and out of work as their family responsibilities ebb and flow. Bianchi says, "Women being here to stay in the [labor] market is more of a given in 2001 than it was 30 years ago."[8]

For instance, Sandy Chambers, of Chevy Chase, Maryland, the

mother of two boys younger than 3, quit her job as a human resources manager at age 40 to raise her children. She'd been in the workforce long enough to realize work will always be there, but those "firsts" of raising a child, she felt, could never be recaptured. She added, "I feel completely confident that I can go back into the workforce. I don't think the stigma is there from employers."[9]

Overall and overwhelmingly, male and female boomers have taught their children that women are a definite part of the landscape of work. Their daughters have played dress-up with briefcases and laptops. Some have even seen their mother work full-time while their dads stay home as the primary caregivers.

According to the U.S. Census Bureau, in families where both spouses work, wives earn more than husbands about 25 percent of the time. In recognition of this fact, we're beginning to see more men take on the role of nurturers while their wives focus on career advancement. For instance, Frederik Hellqvist changed his last name from Hellqvist to Nilsmark. He adopted his wife, Catrin Nilsmark's last name because, as he said, he became "Catrin's wife." In 1996, Frederik was a well-regarded sports broadcaster on Sweden's sports channel. He interviewed a Swedish golf star, Catrin Nilsmark, who was playing in the 1996 Women's British Open. When they met, it was love at first sight. Within a year, his life underwent a 180-degree transformation. Frederik and Catrin married, had a baby, and moved to the United States, so she could pursue her career with more focus. Frederik left his job to help keep his wife's on track. His main job now is caring for their baby girl, Tuva. He says, "I feel fortunate just to have so much time with my daughter, to watch her grow and learn. So many men are caught up with earning the money and being, 'the man of the family' that they miss seeing their kids getting older."[10] Chances are high that Frederik will cycle back into a career chapter of his life, but, for now, he's happy as a homemaker.

For the last 10 years we've lived next door to a family with three kids just a little bit older than ours. Both parents are Stanford Business School graduates. Gary was a senior executive at his company for years while Nina was an investment banker. When his company reorganized, Gary left the company and tried his hand at an entrepreneurial venture, which quickly went public. When he again found himself free of work responsibilities, Nina had become busier than ever. They decided the most practical solution was for Gary to be a stay-at-home dad, caring for the three boys. Last year he was the football coach for his son's freshman team while overseeing a renovation project at their home. He told me it was sometimes frustrating but, overall, a valuable experience that has created a deep bond between him and his three sons.

Today, many fathers of all ages want to be more involved in raising their children for the very reason Sandy Chambers gives—they don't want to miss out on all the precious firsts. Work will always be there, but kids grow up fast. Larry Kelly, formerly Intel's manager of work/life effectiveness, believes "It's not macho to say, 'I want to do something family-related,' but more dads are . . . being explicit about it in the work environment and they're not viewed negatively at all" anymore.[11] This is the cyclic life in action.

Buying Implications

Working women have created demand for both convenience and luxury products and services unlike anything that has come before. Controlling close to 80 percent of household spending, working women buy better clothes, makeup, and jewelry for themselves and their children, utilize household help, eat out more often, and have fueled the day care industry, home care for children, and education programs and services. They have even impacted federal law requiring employers to provide unpaid family leave.

Working women also have dramatically changed the beauty and fashion industry with their demands for attractive work clothes and low-maintenance beauty care. First, women wore pricey suits that looked prim and buttoned up to fit in with and resemble their male counterparts. They even wore ties for a while. This was great for the fashion industry, because it was predictable, and the clothes included jackets, which made them far more expensive. Over the years, fashion touches like color and different details were added to motivate women to keep buying. Today women dress more casually at work, enjoy looking feminine, and feel it's their obligation to look professional and attractive. That means more expensive clothing, haircuts, manicures, massages, facials, and more. They also often feel the right to splurge on their children, buying them luxury items as a matter of course. Most importantly, it has empowered many women, who otherwise might not feel the freedom to do so, to leave marriages that were either abusive or just not working.

At the same time, men are more often taking on some of the responsibilities of household management. Even those who work often share some household duties such as shopping, carpooling, and cooking. Product manufacturers can no longer ignore the fact that men are buying laundry detergents, vacuum cleaners, and baby foods while women are buying briefcases, office supplies, and high-technology products.

BLENDED FAMILIES

With the divorce rate hovering at around 50 percent, remarriage involving the blending of families is a growing reality in the cyclic life. One-third of all Americans belong to stepfamilies. Everyone, for instance, knows someone who has more than one set of children from more than one marriage.

For example, Tim Berns, a Washington D.C.–based entrepreneur, married young, right after he graduated from medical school. He followed the traditional path prescribed by society. As he worked his way through internship and residency, he fathered two daughters. But the Berns didn't live happily ever after, and both Tim and his wife opted to move on to create fresh starts for themselves. They divorced when their daughters were ages 17 and 19 and heading off to college. It wasn't too long before Tim changed careers and remarried, fully aware of the fact that his second wife wanted children. Jan was already over 40 when she gave birth to two beautiful children, Max and Kelsey, within a few years. Tim was 50 when his son was born and 54 when his daughter entered the world. Tim laughs when he recounts how someone once stopped him as he was walking down the street with Max and Kelsey to tell him how cute his grandchildren were. Tim and Jan take particular pleasure in watching Max and Kelsey play with Tim's older children. Although the older girls are away at college most of the time, when the four get together, they are very close.

We all know people like Tim. But 15 years ago, such behavior was considered offbeat. It was not the norm in the linear life. In the cyclic-life, it's one of several paths that have been pioneered, opening the door for a new consumer target for businesses that once catered exclusively to the 18–34 demographic.

Blended families abound as do divorced parents with joint custody arrangements. For example, Jay and Lori Norris were married for more than 15 years when they decided to call it quits. With three children ranging in age from 14 to 7, Jay fought hard to share custody. What he really wanted to do was leave his marriage, but not his family. He wanted to be with his kids all the time, just like he always had. But that wasn't possible. Instead, he found himself sharing custody and setting up a household of his own in the same suburban community as his ex-wife so the kids weren't disrupted too much in their school and friend-ship routines. It also meant negotiating with his ex-wife continuously over things they used to take for granted, like overnight work trips, dinners with clients, and purchases for the kids. Jay and Lori learned to work together to re-form their family into a new configuration. They started to realize that even though they were no longer married, they were still part of the same virtual family. And they often are put in the position of making consumer purchases as a family even though they live in separate homes.

Buying Implications
Blended families are a new consumer target, ripe with duplicate buying implications. Consider a blended family in which a teenage daughter comes to live with her new baby stepbrother, dad, and stepmom. This arrangement might be for weekends only, for an extended period of time, or as part of a joint custody arrangement. In any case, she'll need her own phone, a computer with modem hookup, bedspread, pillows, furniture, makeup and hair accessories, clothes, coats, shoes, and luggage. She'll have to have a similar setup at the home of her mother. She may even need a special pet that makes each house feel like home. The baby, in turn, needs everything from crib to formula. If the example features a pair of younger children, figure in sports equipment, a basketball hoop and bicycle, ballet clothes, handheld games, and videos. Make the

example child a little older and you can throw in a car, and the insurance that goes with it. Don't forget medical insurance and the convenient network of pediatricians, dentists, and orthodontists that works for everyone. And, in all likelihood, when the family blends, it will make an overt effort at a fresh start. That means new dishes and silverware, artwork, furniture, books, and plants.

It also means potential conflicts and accommodations over holidays and LifeCycle punctuation points such as birthdays, graduations, and weddings. Several years ago we attended a wedding where the bride had two mothers and two fathers present. She walked down the aisle with both her birth father and stepfather, arm in arm in arm, everyone in a festive mood filled with love. But that's not always the case. Blended families often have to contend with relatives boycotting events due to conflicts with other family members. We attended another wedding where a few close relatives weren't able to be there in person, so they sent their good wishes to the couple via a videotape message that was shown to the entire wedding party. Not so dissimilarly, soon after the September 11, 2001, debacle, Circuit City stores invited people to tape 30-second video messages for the troops in Afghanistan over the Christmas holidays at participating Circuit City stores. Chances are that this idea and others like it will become treasured gifts for family members separated over the holidays or to punctuate an important family event they can't attend. This concept might even be transformed into multimedia holiday cards, sent for a price via e-mail or even snail mail.

A question that often arises is who pays for college education in a blended family? When families blend, the need for financial advice and planning increases significantly, requiring the cooperation of sometimes-hostile parties. A good financial planner (who doubles as a psychologist at times) can help blended families better prepare for the financial burden of private schools, summer camps, supplemental education needs, and indispensable and often pricey college educations.

FRIENDS AS FAMILY

In the linear-life arrangement, family was distinct from friends. Family was usually considered the more important of the two because it was assumed family would last forever. In the cyclic life, that's often not the case. Family is often physically spread throughout the globe; family ties can be torn by divorce, custody battles, inheritance feuds, or even resentment over who takes on the burden of caring for a frail or dying parent. At the same time, friendships often can last a lifetime. Even if they wane for a while, they can often be stoked back up when friends are in need of each other. The bonds of friendships, like family, can be cyclic and sometimes stronger than blood.

The acceptance of friends as family is becoming more ingrained in our culture. In the last couple of years, for example, *urban tribes* have become an identified trend. Ethan Watters, author of an article on this phenomenon in the *New York Times* magazine, describes urban tribes as never-marrieds between age 20 and 29, living in urban areas that form tight groups based on bonds of friendship. These groups function similarly to a family with their own hierarchies, roles, and relationships within the group. They help each other during periods of crisis and celebrate holidays and moments of joy. Just like most families, urban tribes usually have their own set of family values as well.[12] The ensemble of characters on TV's *Friends* function as a mainstream example of an urban tribe, for instance, as do the complex set of relationships evident on other hit series like *Will and Grace* and *Sex and the City* and the perennial favorite, *Golden Girls*.

If we look around, we would probably begin to realize that urban tribes are all around us in real life as well. They are not limited to never-marrieds, urban areas, or adults 20 to 29. For instance, Sandy West became part of a such a tribe when her husband died. Feeling lost and alone with her family spread out all over the country, she attended a support group for widows. Long after the formal support group ended, she was still meeting regularly with three women and four men from that group. They would go to movies and concerts together. When one of the men had a heart attack, members of his urban tribe took turns standing vigil at his hospital bed. When he went home, they cooked him healthy meals and supported him on his exercise program by starting a similar program themselves. They laugh together, cry together, hug each other, and even argue, just like a family.

Like all family relationships, friends bonding as family members are not limited to people in the same age group or lifestage. It offers an opportunity to bridge generation and lifestage gaps just as blood-related families do. Almost 80 years ago, Joan Watson had the good fortune to be born next door to the Layman family. An only child, Joan lost her father when she was a baby. She and her mother were enveloped and nurtured by their next-door neighbors. Joan's mother and her fiancé died within a few years of each other in the 1940s; Joan never married. But she was far from alone. One of the Layman children, Corabelle, adopted Joan, who was present at all the weddings and showers and for the births of Corabelle's five children and ten grandchildren. Over the years, the fact that Joan was not a blood relative became irrelevant. Today, she's Aunt Joan, presiding over the holiday gatherings of her extended family. She never forgets a birthday, nor does hers ever pass without a celebration, and she has an impressive array of nephews to call when she needs a picture hung. She reminisces with her photo albums and shares her life story with members of her family, who are as intrinsically hers as they would have been had Joan been born a Layman herself.

Buying Implications
Virtual family members often are not bonded by blood but by love, compassion, and deep-rooted companionship; they need to be recognized as an important part of the family. In response to this, greeting card companies, for example, will have the opportunity to create cards aimed at virtual family members. Come the holidays, retailers ought to capture the opportunity of friends buying gifts for each other that are beyond mere tokens but an expression of close ties once reserved for the gene pool.

If a friend is going through any phase of illness, recovery, or death, friends often are taking on a role once exclusively delegated to family members. The health care and legal establishment needs to acknowledge this and help make this difficult role easier to fulfill. Doctors and lawyers usually defer to a family member before a friend, which may not always be in the best interest of a sick or dying person. We will increasingly turn to attorneys or packaged kits to create documents that empower our friends to take on these roles once exclusively limited to family.

A durable power of attorney ensures that a trusted person of our choice will be able to manage finances and health care on our behalf. Advance directives, including medical power of attorney and living wills, ensure that our health care preferences will be respected. A medical power of attorney allows another person to make medical decisions on our behalf while a living will states our wishes for the medical care we would like provided or withheld.[13] Some companies have recognized that many of us don't have the financial resources or inclination to have an attorney prepare these documents. They can now be purchased in kits that help us to create our own paper trail.

Even visiting hours for the very ill in hospitals and critical care units are often limited to family members which could exclude the very people who could offer emotional support to those who need it. Insurance companies often deal only with a family member while recovery, which might include rehabilitation and a variety of therapeutic treatments involving insurance reimbursement, is often coordinated by a close personal friend who may not only arrange for these things but also can provide the personal care and companionship so necessary for recovery. These are the realities of the cyclic family that we ought to recognize.

BEYOND THE FEATHERED NEST

As I mentioned in Chapter 4, just a few generations ago few couples lived long enough to become empty nesters. That's no longer the case. In Chapter 4, I focused attention on this important new life phase; however, a few additional things bear mentioning.

Today empty nesting has emerged as a new LifeCycle when both partners often look to fulfill the personal goals they've put off to raise their children. It's a time of new beginnings: starting new careers, going back to school, taking a break from work for the first time. The options are limited only by our imaginations.

While empty nesters do tend to gratify their delayed desires for toys, travel, and tonier living spaces, as I described in detail in Chapter 4, many are fortunate enough to be able to forge another loving relationship with a child—this time without the responsibilities, obligations, and exhaustion attached. These lucky empty nesters are among our country's growing legion of grandparents.

They've always been loving and indulgent, but today's grandparents are also wealthier, healthier, and more numerous than ever before. The increase in the divorce rate has stretched grandparenting to produce yet another identifiable trend: multiple grandparents. In the past, a child was lucky to have several living grandparents. With increased longevity, children often have all four natural grandparents alive. If a couple with children divorces, and each remarries, then eight grandparents compete for the grandchildren's affections. Another divorce and suddenly the lucky kids have 10 or even 12 grandparents. This figure may sound extreme, but studies have shown that as many as 33 percent of all adults over 65 are stepgrandparents.[14]

Buying Implications

Studies have shown that the highly emotional relationship between grandparents and grandchildren, including stepchildren, translates directly into purchasing. The grandparent industry is estimated to spend some $30 billion a year on the kids they're connected with.[15] An AARP study revealed, "The median amount spent by individual grandparents—both genders combined—is $489 per year."[16] Stores report that purchases by grandparents account for one-third of total purchases for kid gear, a 20 percent increase in the last five years.

The older generation, however, can be confused and unsure about what exactly to get their grandchildren. A few upscale toy stores have taken note and created services to help grandparents purchase age-appropriate toys and games. At Imaginarium, for example, expert "toy-ologists" are always available with specific, kid-tested suggestions to fit every child's unique personality, but far more is needed.

Grandparents and stepgrandparents travel with the kids to bond over new adventures. This also gives the parents a break! A few travel companies have responded by creating intergenerational trips catering to the young and old. The trips have itineraries that appeal to everyone and often have special counselors who create activities for the young-sters. Elderhostel organizes intergenerational trips in the United States and abroad, creating comfortable, all-inclusive trips with an educational focus. The trips also feature adult and child counselors to ensure that all participants have a good time.

Another industry that could build off the strong desire of grandparents to purchase for their grandchildren is financial services. Often what grandparents are attempting to do through gifting is to create a bond or even leave a legacy of things to be remembered by with their grandchildren. What better way to do that then through financial gifting? Creating financial gifts in the form of trusts or investments that can later be used to finance further education, a home, a sabbatical from work, or some other dream that becomes tied to a memory of a grandparent could be the direct fulfillment of this kind of desire.

Boomerang Kids

For some, empty nesting is changing again, with boomerang kids moving back after college or another LifeCycle transition, stretching marriages and family in new and often demanding directions once more.

Since the 1970s, the number of adult children moving back in with their parents has been steadily rising, reversing the trend in the first two-thirds of the twentieth century where each generation was more likely to leave home at a *younger* age than their parents. In 2001, 56 percent of current college students reported that after graduation they planned to live with their parents for some time.[17]

More than 18 million young adults (ages 20–34) live with their parents; that's 38 percent of all young adult singles. But it's not just college graduates who return home. Kids of all ages feel like it's a viable option to regroup and figure out their future after a transformative cycle of life. Whether it's due to a job transition, a failed marriage, completion of a cycle of education, or any combination of these factors, it's not seen as a loss of independence or as a permanent move. According to Joe Fisher, a Northeastern University graduate who moved home after five years of college, boomeranging just made sense; "No rent, no money spent on food, the luxury of a washer and dryer."

Another benefit is that young adults who may be having difficulty with a cyclic transition receive much-needed support from the safety net of parents and a stable home life. Frances Goldscheider, a family demographer, Brown University professor, and coeditor (with Calvin Goldscheider) of *The Changing Transition to Adulthood: Leaving and Returning Home*, says, "Not only can young adults return home, it has increasingly become normative to do so. "With a nod to the cyclic life, she adds, "The leaving home transition has become more renewable, less of a one-way street and more like a circular migration."[18]

Whether it's for one day or one year, today's parents, often boomers, seem comfortable with letting grown-up kids boomerang back home to help guide them through a cyclic career transition or through a bump in the road, wherever it may occur. According to Amanda Freeman, director of research and trends at Youth Intelligence, a market research consulting firm, "Parents have smartened up. They want to guide their children, not just point out problems, but also help them find solutions. They want their children to pursue their passion, not simply track down the highest paying job possible."[19]

Suzanna Zisker married young and had children right away. Before she knew it, she was the mother of three wonderful children, including a set of twins. She had her hands full and never even considered work as a viable option. But her husband was struggling, too. The pressures of marriage and a quickly growing family became too much for him. He descended into alcoholism and was often so hung over that it was hard for him to keep a job. The downward spiral continued until Suzanna couldn't take it any longer. She and the kids moved back to her parents' house where she had grown up. Her parents provided the stability and emotional support Suzanna and her children needed. They helped her think through what careers she might pursue now that it was clear that she needed to work. While she was going back to school, her parents not only provided a stable home for her and the kids but took care of the kids as well. Once she started work, they helped keep the kids safe, both emotionally and physically, during the transition period. After Suzanna was back in the workforce, her parents invited her and the kids to stay indefinitely. She insists on contributing financially to household expenses, which her parents appreciate now that they are living on a fixed income. She even put a down payment on an RV for them, one of their lifelong dreams. And, they have grown so close to the kids, they feel it has helped keep them young by interacting with many generations instead of just people their own age. Boomeranging worked well for this family.

Buying Implications

Although some might view this phenomenon as a sign of financial weakness, it's often quite the opposite. Young adults often move home to take responsibility for their finances. Many are paying off student loans while saving to invest in real estate and their own financial future. The concept of long-term savings is more concrete for them than in past generations of young adults. They're seeing long-lived relatives and friends all around them and realize they need to plan well financially, which is more easily started when mom and dad handle the basics like food and shelter. Gina Doynow, a Citibank vice president and college business manager, says, "Far from the myth of college grads being unable to manage their finances, all of our studies and data indicate that in recent years they've been among our best customers as managers of credit and personal finance."[20]

At the same time, the discretionary income of boomerang adult children rises dramatically. Often they pay little or nothing for rent and food, which frees them up to save and to spend. They need new clothes for job interviews and, ultimately, new jobs. They want that new sound system and the big screen TV they've always dreamed about. A new laptop is probably on their wish list as well. And, of course, they have to buy decent wheels to get them to work in style. They may also be paying for a health club membership, health care insurance, and maybe even graduate school. Of course, entertainment probably becomes even more important when living with mom and dad. They still have to escape to dinner, the movies, skiing, river rafting, or any other activity that involves friends and spending their hard-earned cash. The point being that boomerang kids are a viable market for a variety of products and services.

They buy products not just for themselves, but often for their parents. Intergenerational purchasing—parents buying for children and children buying for parents—is far more likely to take place when children live close to parents and interact with them on a regular basis. And there is nothing closer than their parents' home. Like Suzanna

Zisker, who showed her appreciation for her parents' generosity by helping them purchase the RV of their dreams, many adult children want to make gestures of appreciation to their parents in the form of purchases. Maybe they'll buy them a romantic weekend getaway (with the added bonus of getting the house to themselves for the weekend) or tickets to a football or basketball game they might not spring for on their own. They might even take them to a Rolling Stones or Santana concert so they can share some time together. Whatever it might be, boomerang children appreciate their parents and demonstrate it by purchasing gifts.

THE VERTICAL FAMILY

As we watch life expectancy continue to rise, families can now consist of four or five, and maybe even six generations alive at once. That means that each of us will have more years to cycle in and out of different lifestage events that define our needs, and significantly, so will our other family members. Some of us will even cycle in and out of different families. This means that the complexity of family relationships will increase exponentially. So could family obligations.

In 2001, the *New York Times* carried a photo of the Knaus family that showed six generations. At the head of the clan was Sara Knaus, 118 years old; her daughter was 95; her grandson was 73; her great-grand-daughter was 49; her great-great-granddaughter was 27; her great-great-great-grandson was 3. Clearly, there wasn't just one adult in the middle, there were four. It may be that the Knaus family is a portrait of what is in our collective future.

With the average family consisting of far more elderly parents than young children, the extended family is taking on increased significance, time, and attention. An estimated 22 million American households are already caring for aging parents. Within the next two decades, the number is expected to double. One-third of all working adults have some kind of elder care issue to deal with. It's become such a prevalent issue that sociologists have coined a phrase to describe people caught between the job of parenting children and parenting elderly family members: the *sandwich generation*.

Caregiving for elders is one of the curves in the road we're just beginning to encounter as we see families similar to the Knauses emerge. Multiple generations in need of potential care from one or more healthy younger family members, probably somewhere between 20 and 65, will become more and more common. Now it's true that many older adults won't need any care. In fact when my grandmother was in her 80s, she volunteered her time to work in a nursing home with what she called the old folks. However, with life expectancy rising, experts like Joshua Wiener of the Urban Institute of Washington, D.C., predict, "While caring for multiple elders won't be the majority experience, it will certainly become a lot less rare."[21]

Although more and more men are involved with caregiving, it typically will continue to be a cycle of life that women face. Seventy-three percent of elder care providers are women. In the past, this made perfect sense. In 1950, for instance, few of these care providers were in the workforce. Today, an estimated 64 percent of sandwich care providers work, and more than half of those work full-time. Today the average caregiver can be an executive, manager, professional, or in any other type of job they don't plan on quitting to attend to full-time caregiving responsibilities. In addition, more than 40 percent of these women juggle their elder care responsibilities with parenting children under 18.[22] Many of these women are involved in at least three lifestages simultaneously and are seriously busy. Needless to say, most are in need of some nurturing themselves.

The prevalence of the sandwich generation depends on more than demographic trends alone. Like every aspect of the cyclic life pattern, the function and form for adult children caring for both aging parents and children emerges, in part, from the influence of the boomer generation. "In the Middle," a recent study commissioned by AARP, suggests that the parents of boomers were very smart to feed their boomer children the message "You're special" when they were growing up. Although many of those parents felt that it manifested as narcissism when boomers were teens and young adults, earning them the label the Me Generation, it has morphed into self-reliance and a take-charge attitude in midlife which is now earning them a new label, the Us Generation. Couple this quality with the love and respect they genuinely feel for their parents, and you'll find that most boomers are comfortable caring for their elderly parents even though it's a time-consuming and stress-inducing process. Nearly half of boomers 45–55 have children at home and parents who are still living. Nearly 25 percent are caring for those elders. Almost half—48 percent—wish they could be doing even more for their parents. It's revealing to note that while more than 80 percent report providing some type of care for those parents, many don't even identify themselves as caregivers.[23] For them, caregiving is simply an accepted part of life.

The vertical family and the elder care those sandwiched in the middle provide promises to be an issue that lands front and center in the near future impacting our lives, work, and the social infrastructure of our society. One ramification is easily seen in the workplace: According to a survey by the Metropolitan Life Insurance Company, loss of employee productivity due to family-care responsibilities is "conservatively estimated at $11.4 billion annually."[24] Thus, some corporate benefit packages are beginning to acknowledge the changing personal needs of their employees.

Just as employees demanded comprehensive child care in the '70s and '80s, they will increasingly demand elder care from employers and the private sector in the coming decade. Women, leaders in breaking with the status quo to make life on the job more humane, convinced many employers to provide child day care back in the '80s. With one-third of all workers having some type of adult caregiving responsibilities, they will create a similar revolution in elder care. Boomers, especially women, will demand elder care when it is required for their parents. The companies that want to keep employees happy and working productively will support elder care either directly or indirectly through benefits and program recommendations. This will create business opportunities for the savvy entrepreneur.

Buying Implications
Sandwich caregivers will not only seek help in balancing work responsibilities but also in stretching their dollars and handling the stress of caring for an elder. Commercial enterprise will offer exciting new products and services to meet the growing demands of elder care as well. Everything from an Internet-based nationwide elder care referral

network to brick-and-mortar services such as adult day care, home health services, and assisted-living facilities will thrive from this boom.

Intergenerational marketing—a reality with boomerang kids living at home—is becoming a viable way to sell products meant for elderly adults to elders and their adult children. It has existed in the children's market for decades, with many ads urging children to get their parents to buy a product. In the coming decades, everything from banking and investment products to real estate purchases and health care insurance aimed at elderly adults will need to be positioned to appeal to multiple adult generations of the elderly.

In a multigenerational world, most of us will want to live on our own for as long as possible. This means that architects, home designers, and builders will need to consider universal design elements in their work. Universal design means that the design is user-friendly for people of all ages, abilities, and disabilities. It's meant to look attractive and be ergonomic at the same time. Moving furniture, bringing in the groceries, or preparing a meal becomes less of a burden in a home with larger doorways, a standard universal design feature. At the same time, it helps create better flow from room to room, a definite aesthetic benefit. Lever-style door handles make it easier to open doors whether someone has arthritis or not; they're also very attractive. No-sill entries reduce the possibility of tripping when coming into the house for people of all ages. Closets designed to allow people with disabilities to access items stored in them reduce stressful lifting for anyone. Pull-down cabinets reduce stress in the kitchen.

As we live in more multigenerational families, universal design encourages us to live at home longer and with more independence. It may also be a wise investment. A universal designed home may have an aesthetic and functional advantage over a similar home lacking universal design features.[25]

Linked directly with the elderly living at home independently is the explosive growth of the home health care industry. The number of home health care aides is expected to increase 138 percent between 1992 and 2005, according to the National Association for Home Care. The U.S. Bureau of Labor Statistics has honed in on this job as one of the fastest-growing job opportunities.

If the adult children of an elderly parent believe their parent can no longer manage at home, they are often crucial in the search for and choice of alternative housing. Whether they choose an assisted living community, senior residence, a retirement community, or continuing care retirement community, elderly parents usually want their adult children to help make this critical decision.

Wherever the frail elderly might live, their adult children will be worrying about their well-being and the quality of care they'll be receiving. Some high-technology tools are beginning to appear that can help ease some of these concerns. For example, just like many overnight camps let us access photos of our kids' activities while they're away at camp via the Internet, some assisted-living facilities are installing video cameras and surveillance equipment in public areas such as dining rooms and recreational areas so we can monitor our elderly relatives' activities via the Internet. It's usually not intrusive, but it does help create a connection and can get family members more involved in caregiving decisions.

Oatfield Estates, an assisted-living facility in Milwaukie, Oregon, uses high technology to complement their homey environment filled with plants and pets. It enables them to both care more effectively for their elderly residents and offer them more freedom of movement. Besides using video monitoring equipment, wall sensors track the movements of residents while transponders worn by residents function as location monitors, alarms, and room keys. Almost every room has a computer so that residents can easily communicate with family members or just surf the Net.[26] We can see how high technology tools can easily be adapted to use in elderly patients' homes so nurses or family members can monitor them more readily.

Keep in mind, this is not a challenge limited to North America or the United States. From Japan to France, this issue is taking on increased importance. (See Figure 5.1.) In Japan, for instance, the elderly population is growing faster than any other. By 2005, adults over 65 will account for 20 percent of the population. Many fear the rising cost of elder care and funding corporate pension plans, as well as caring for the elderly in a society so quickly changing. Others see this phenomenon as a tremendous business opportunity.

In 1999, the Minister of Health and Welfare assured the Japanese that the government would help defray the cost of caring for the elderly by picking up the tab for aides, called home helpers. They also encouraged private companies to enter the marketplace to provide this care. According to Nippon Life Insurance Company's NLI Research Institute, the market for nursing the elderly is estimated to be $80 billion. They project that by the year 2010, the market could hit $106 billion. In response, entrepreneurs have begun to enter the marketplace. Masahiro Origuchi, a former owner of some of the biggest nightclubs and discos in Japan, started Community Medical System & Network, Inc. (Comsn—a subsidiary of Goodwill Group, Inc.) to provide home nursing for the elderly.[27] His stock price more than tripled on the first day of trading after its initial public offering in July 1999.

Other products will be purchased by multiple generations of one

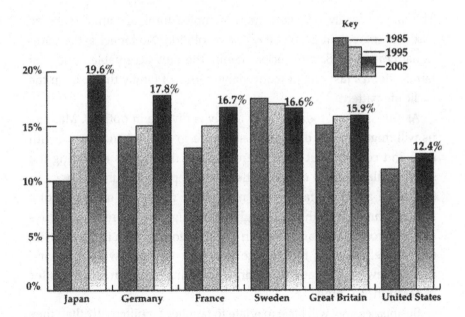

Figure 5.1
International Challenge
(65+ People as a Percentage of Population)
Source: Government statistics, 2000.

family, including respite care services, consumer goods for themselves and those that they care for, and solid multigenerational financial planning.

For example, extended-family vacations are a relatively new concept. But, since 1995, three-generation trips have increased 25 percent.[28] With families geographically spread out, it's a natural bonding time. In the summer of 2002, my stepfather celebrated his 80th birthday. To punctuate the event, he gathered his seven children (which includes two stepchildren), eleven grandchildren, and three great grandchildren in Fort Collins, Colorado, for four days of bonding time. There were events and dinners scheduled, each sponsored by different family members, including horseback riding, river rafting, and a blowout party. (Yes, my 80-year-old stepfather took part in all of it.)

CONCLUSION

The virtual family is a new, more complex form of family that's an essential ingredient in the LifeCycle revolution. No longer is the traditional *Leave It to Beaver* nuclear family the only acceptable option for family life. It's just one of many viable forms of family that exist in the cyclic life pattern.

As this implies, today's cyclic family is diverse in options. Many of us will migrate from one family structure to another, maybe not with ease and comfort, but with the realization that others are facing the same challenges and opportunities. At one point in our lives, we can be part of a nuclear family; the next phase might see us as part of a blended family; and the next might see us juggling the responsibilities of caring for parents and children simultaneously. With few successful role models of how to navigate this new territory, we are carving rugged new paths that will continue to define family in new ways for generations to come.

Businesses, too, will have to relate to families far differently than they have in the past. The beauty of the linear life was that family had a neat, clean, age-defined definition. This made it easy for businesses to position their products. It allowed for a homogenous message to resonate with the masses. Not anymore.

Today business has a much more complex task. The cyclic life gives the definition of family greater depth and breath. It is no longer simply age defined by a female household manager between ages 18 and 34; it is no longer primarily involved with raising children; it is no longer just nuclear. The challenge is for business to look far closer at the needs of diverse forms of family to better understand their needs and desires as they cycle through various LifeCycle events. It's a more complex assignment, but an interesting one with greater opportunities as well.

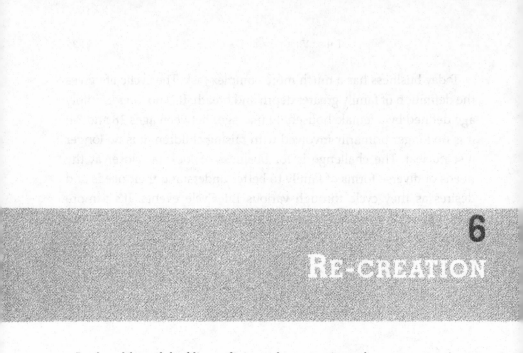

6
RE-CREATION

In the old model of linear living, play was given the most attention at the beginning and end of life. Primarily a phase designated for kids and the retired, we needed it when we were young and offered it as a gift to the elderly before they died. However, with almost 30 extra years added to our life expectancy in the past century, and imminent biotechnology breakthroughs promising to raise that number, this model no longer fits.

Not surprisingly, boomers are leading the charge toward reinventing recreation for the cyclic life. The next generation to reach what has traditionally been considered mass retirement from mainstream life, most boomers won't be retiring in any traditional sense of the word. Most won't be able to afford to. And since many boomers get much of their identity from work, they won't want to give up their influential roles in mainstream society or the freedom to spend as they want. They may work less hard and put in fewer hours, but they still will want and need that connection to work.

Boomers also want the freedom to enjoy life *now*. Unlike older generations, they seek immediate gratification. They don't want to put off the fun until their later years. Leisure has always represented freedom, and boomers want more of that now.

Instead of retiring en masse at 65, boomers will gradually shift the balance between work and play in their lives. They will weave recreation and leisure in throughout their lives in larger and larger doses as they get older. Since many will avoid traditional retirement until well after age 65, they will avoid living on a fixed income. As a result, they will feel the freedom to experiment with vacation time and indulge themselves periodically. The travel and leisure industry will reap the rewards. In the process, they will change the perception—for all generations—of what re-creation means.

This is good news for the travel and leisure industry, a growth sector in our economy until the September 11, 2001, terrorism. After that tragic event, the travel and leisure industry has suffered more than any other sector. Although there will be a gradual recovery here, boomers will help speed it up as they search for moments of respite, relaxation, and, yes, even fun.

CYCLIC RECREATION

The notion that vacations from work should be two or three weeks a year is a remnant from the old linear-life arrangement when life had a rigid sense of order. That's not the case anymore. As we break out of the linear life mold, we are finding ways to escape in short spurts such as weekend vacations or recreation nearer to home. We're even beginning to see examples of some who enjoy extended vacations or experiment with sabbaticals that last anywhere from three months to one year. In the more cyclic approach to life, we will determine our own work-to-play ratios. These will be based on our personal needs, interests, and our financial planning.

As recreation time becomes more flexible and the family becomes more virtual, the new cyclic life frees us to re-create differently. Not only are we looking for more than the annual vacation, we're beginning to gain comfort re-creating solo, with a close friend, just one family member, or even complete strangers.

Vacations traditionally meant family vacation. If you had kids, they came along. At the very least, you spent vacation time with a significant other. That's beginning to change. I recently went to the Esalen Institute, famous as the center of the human potential movement in the '60s and '70s, for a weekend getaway. Although no longer famous, it still offers a complete menu of programs. It's also one of the most beautiful spots on the earth, perched high on the cliffs over the ocean in Big Sur, California. At dinner one night, I met Steve, a lawyer living and working in the Silicon Valley. He had never before gone away just by himself, especially to do a yoga workshop. He had never even practiced yoga before. But he felt like he needed to get some time to himself to remember who he was. He said his wife and son were surprised by his desire to take a weekend away; they were a very close family. Yet, they supported his need to have some time to rediscover who he is and why he's doing what he's doing. He wasn't interested in a resort or even a spa where the emphasis is on exercise and pampering. He was looking for time to look inside himself, and he thought Esalen was a good place to do that.

That same weekend, the owner of Esalen, Michael Murphy, was also there. We had a chance to talk, and I asked him to define his customer. He said, "It's a great place for people to visit when they are transitioning. Whether it's going from being single to married or married to single, leaving a career or taking on a new career, becoming a new parent or a caregiver to an elderly parent. . . . Whenever someone redefines an aspect of who they are or what they do, time alone is needed to integrate that change. Esalen is the perfect place for that process to take place."

Whatever the length of our escape routes, with whom we choose to escape, or the direction those escapes take us, re-creation in the cyclic life will take on added vitality, novelty, and importance for consumers of all ages, professions, and incomes.

FANTASY FUN

In the cyclic life arrangement, many people will want to "be more than one person in their lives." For some, that will mean having different careers; for others it might mean living in different family arrangements; for still others it might mean living in exotic locales. Some adults, however, will yearn to take on a role that has always been a life dream, but will never manifest into reality. The cyclic life—together with commercial ingenuity—is opening up that possibility. The travel and leisure industry is at the early stages of providing a venue in which to actively explore fantasy environments and roles that we could only dream of exploring in our real lives.

At the grassroots level, we're seeing a few entrepreneurs develop programs targeted to adults where we can take on roles not available to us in real life. We can pretend we're someone else—a major league ballplayer, a rock 'n' roll star, a gourmet chef, an actor, an astronaut, a detective, or even a heroic fireman.

Skip Maggiorra owns a music store in Sacramento, California. He loves music and has always enjoyed teaching it. Not too long ago, he began to notice that a growing number of his music students were not kids, but rather, adults who still fantasized about becoming rock stars. They'd come in dressed in business suits with a buttoned-up business attitude, but would quickly change into their jeans and T-shirts and take on a whole new aura. He decided it would be great fun to help them realize their fantasy of part-time rock 'n' roller. So he started Weekend Warriors, a music camp that provides adults with a chance to live out their dreams for only $75. He provides weekend warriors with the instruments they choose, four or five fellow band members, a coach, rehearsals, and one gig. "This is instant gratification for anyone who used to play as a kid but decided they couldn't make a living at it," Maggiorra comments. Already more than 1,000 people have gone through his program, which is now available in 125 locations throughout the United States and Canada. (This is also a fantasy for Maggiorra who always dreamed of doing more than just teaching music in his music store.)[1]

Similarly, sports fantasy camps have been cropping up to help adults realize the sports fantasy of their choice. Pick a sport—basketball, baseball, hockey—any sport. Suit up, get the equipment, and hire retired players to take on the role of personal trainers, coaches, and teammates and suddenly the playing field is filled with grown-up kids who would usually be found cheering in the stands. Melinda Hayes sent her husband to Magic Johnson's Basketball Fantasy Camp in Hawaii for his birthday. It set her back $6,000, she said, but even though it was so pricey, "It was totally worth the money. It was so much fun, we're doing it again this year."[2] It's also a great gig for retired players.

Even just being a kid again is now a fantasy-come-true for many overworked adults in search of some re-creation. Several overnight camps designed for kids realized this when parents would come up to visit. Camp management would hear comments from parents like, "If only I could spend a week like this," and "I'd do anything to go to camp again." In response, some camps are beginning to devote a few weeks a year to grown-up campers.

Camp Winnarainbow, owned and operated by Wavy Gravy, has designed just such a program for grown-ups who feel like they've forgotten how to lighten up and let loose. For those who aren't aware of Wavy Gravy's rightful place in history, he was the emcee of the ultimate boomer bash back in the '70s, Woodstock. Ben & Jerry's even named an ice cream in his honor. Now in his 60s, every year for one week he turns his camp over to grown-up campers who want to play but might have forgotten how. Wavy believes "adults need to play to get back in touch with themselves, and then they can let their spirits rise into rainbows of joy."

Getaways and resorts designed to help us experience another time or place have increasingly become popular with those seeking a release from their everyday life. Disney and Las Vegas Resorts are the obvious mass-market examples of this. Prior to the September 11, 2001, terrorist attack Las Vegas attracted more than 30 million tourists a year, and it is still the ultimate embodiment of leisure.

The next generation of fantasy resorts consumers will, in all likelihood, move beyond the Disney and Las Vegas concept of fantasy. Rather than being just a unique environment to observe, they will offer the chance to jump on a time machine moving to another era. The experience would change from a more passive to a more active one. What if we had a chance to be a Knight of the Round Table, or an art apprentice for Da Vinci, or have a drink at the Star Wars Bar? What about visiting an old steel mill to get a firsthand experience of what the industrial era was really like by doing rather than just observing? Or, attending a Hollywood premiere on the arm of a famous movie star (who is really just a look-alike)? The resorts of the future might combine fantasy locales with exciting moments in history or once-in-a-lifetime experiences.

Fantasy Lifestyles

Some people may even choose to spend a significant chunk of one of our LifeCyles in a fantasy environment. Some real estate developers have sensed that possibility and have begun to create back-to-the-future environments for blending the best of the past with the best of today.

For instance, there's Celebration, Florida. This built-from-scratch town has many of the features we associate with small towns in a bygone era merged with the latest technologic innovations for easy living. Located near Orlando, Florida, the vision was to create a town with a strong sense of community that provides residents with the opportunity to enjoy life on a daily basis without the hassles of traffic and congestion, on the one hand, or the blandness of suburban living, on the other. The developers wanted to create a place where community and fun were strong components of everyday life. The feel of a sleepy, southeastern town with pre-1940s architecture inspires the design of the entire town. Most of the homes have big, old-fashioned front porches to encourage residents to interact with their neighbors. Shopping is all within walking distance and stores are designed to charm as well as offer the best products. Lots of restaurants, a movie theatre, a post office, and promenades dot Main Street to further encourage people to mingle and fun events to take place. A town hall designed by famed architect Phillip Johnson is in the center of town. The school, too, is in the center of the community; as is an office park, doctors' offices, and a hospital. Blended with the old-fashioned mood and tempos, on the contemporary side, we see walking paths, nature trails, a fitness center, a golf course, and a network of advanced telecommunications and information systems connecting all parts of the whole. The community even has its own Intranet.[3]

The town of Celebration represents a fantasy LifeCycle many of us might find appealing. However, name another era or a theme and it, too, might hold appeal as a fantasy-living community. For instance, if sports is the theme, a housing development could be created around that passion. It could have a state-of-the-art fitness center; pool; biking; walking and running paths; tennis and golf, but go further still to include climbing walls, an in-line skating park, and well-stocked fishing ponds. The restaurants could serve high-performance food and peak performance would be the goal of most residents. Regular tournaments would be held which would culminate in Olympic Games. Alexander Garvin, an adjunct professor of urban planning and management at Yale University, sees this as a future development and says, "We're going to have to start looking at the world in which there's a lot of competition for scarce leisure time, and where people want to spend that time trying to maintain their health."

Living year-round on a luxury cruise ship that travels around the world may soon be a reality for a few lucky—and super wealthy—people. For $1 million plus, anyone can now buy a condominium aboard *The World,* a ship that combines luxury cruising with luxury living. It's got all the pleasures found on the world's most beautiful yachts combined with the communal activities so popular on commercial cruise lines such as entertainment, learning experiences, and exciting excursions into the most beautiful ports throughout the world. Although some of the prospective buyers are older retirees, many are not. Airline and shipping magnate Polys Haji-Ioannu says, "I will probably spend three or four hours a day on the phone to various business associates. The rest of the time, I'll be swimming or playing tennis."[4]

Knut Kloster, Jr., the developer of this project, acknowledges that his project caters only to the rich, but believes that floating real estate developments will soon cater to people of all incomes and taste levels. Since the ties that bind us to a locale have been loosening up gradually and the definition of work and leisure are shifting, the cyclic life offers interesting possibilities of new ways to live, work, and play.

Children, too, might take a yearlong sabbatical from school just the way their parents might from work. This will become more common with home schooling a viable option, especially since each new living experience holds tremendous potential as a vital learning tool.

Where we choose to live at different LifeCycles will be strongly influenced by our fantasies. As added years combined with technologic innovations give us the freedom to pursue our fantasies in the real world, whether it be for a short break or a longer interval, more and more of us will be living our dreams and being more than one person in our cyclic approach to life.

Interactive *Virtual* Delights

As games become more interactive and complex, we see more and more adults playing them. Seventy percent of all computer and video games players are now over age 18, according to the Interactive Digital Software Association. The U.S. electronic games industry—software and hardware combined—is growing so quickly that it's already larger than the movie business. In 1999, revenue for the game industry was $8.9 billion compared to $7.3 billion in box-office receipts. At this writing, there are more than 10,000 game sites listed on the Internet.[5]

One reason for its popularity is that gaming software has gotten far more sophisticated. It goes well beyond great graphics and animation. No longer does the speedy eye-hand coordination of kids rule. Many games use artificial intelligence to create sophisticated behavior, requiring brainpower and life experience. This not only holds great appeal for many young people but also gains the adult player as a new audience searching for an easily available escape from the everyday stresses of life.

Everquest, an online 3D fantasy role-playing game, was the most popular group game with more than 400,000 players in 2002. With its own virtual environment including diverse species, economic systems, alliances, and politics, players can customize their characters and begin their quests alone or in larger parties. Up to 60,000 people have been known to play simultaneously.

Virtual reality will bring these experiences closer to feeling like the real deal. Created through the magic of technology, it allows us to experience different environments through a combination of sensory stimuli and technology without actually traveling anywhere in the physical world. In the not too distant future, as the technology improves, virtual reality will become commercially viable. People might get the chance to fully immerse themselves in a new experience or environment while never leaving a virtual reality site. Full immersion virtual reality or *mysting*, as it's been called, will give the recreation consumer the chance to visit another planet, climb Mt. Everest, or watch Picasso paint without ever leaving an armchair.

Such virtual experiences are sure to be a hot commercial attraction for adults and children alike. Interactive video arcades are at the earliest

stages of development. The Sony Metreon in San Francisco is an interactive playground with everything from virtual bowling to an IMAX
Theatre. It also is a high-tech mall where the shopping is truly a corol-
lary to the entertainment. The first of its kind, with smaller versions
under construction in Tokyo and Berlin, the term *Metreon* is a combination of metropolis and eon, a Greek word meaning gathering place. All
generations are there, enjoying themselves together. Two attractions are
geared toward families, one based on Maurice Sendak's *Where the Wild
Things Are*, and another based on David Macaulay's *How Things Work.*
One of the most popular elements of the Metreon is *The Airtight
Garage*, a cutting-edge techno-entertainment center with early stage
virtual reality, interactive games such as *Quaternia, Badlands,* and *Hyper-
Bowl.* These games are all based on the science fiction and fantasy
designs of French graphic novelist Jean "Mobius" Giraud. *HyperBowl* is
the most popular game there and is basically interactive virtual bowling
where four players have the option of bowling down the city streets of
San Francisco, a pirate's ship, or ancient Rome using what looks like
bowling balls but responds like a computer mouse. A prototype for
entertainment that includes large elements of interactive, virtual reality,
Metreon clones could be available everywhere in the near future.[6]

Interactive *Real* Delights

Interactive games that merge real-life experiences with Internet experiences are also at the pioneering stage, but will catch on with consumers
of all ages and LifeCycles. The first to appear is *RealityRun.com,* a live
Internet game show that takes place both online and in major cities of
the world. Conceived in Berlin, it is reminiscent of the game Michael
Douglas played in the movie, *The Game.* Recruiting players in each city
where it takes place, the game is basically a bounty hunt. A *Reality Runner* is chased by *Reality Hunters.* The challenge of the Reality Runner is
to stay hidden for seven days armed with nothing more than a small
allowance and a microphone which broadcasts every move live on the
Internet. If the Reality Runner can remain undetected for seven days, he
or she wins $10,000 and becomes eligible to compete for the grand
prize for $100,000 to take place in New York. The hunter who finds the
runner wins the $10,000 but must split it with any Internet players who

provided helpful clues. The entire game is covered live on the Internet, enabling the audience to influence and alter its course through voting and direct contact with the game characters.[7]

Even our average night out can combine a fantasy experience with an interactive one. Karaoke bars, for example, offer each of us the chance to cut loose, have fun, and be a star (or a jerk) for at least one song. Music producer Linda Goldstein has been organizing singing tours for singer Bobby McFerrin for several years. She was fascinated when the interest in karaoke took off in this country, and rather than dying out after a year or two, spread like wild fire. She sensed that audiences wanted the chance to get involved with a performance and even create a sense of community with the performer and other audience members. She decided to give them that chance at a McFerrin concert. I attended a concert in San Francisco with my kids where Bobby McFerrin took on the role of conductor of the audience that became his instruments. It was a magical experience where everyone had a chance to sing along, performing a sophisticated harmony together. Not only did everyone have a great time, but we all felt a little more connected to each other by the end of the shared experience. It also created a bond with the performer and made it far more likely that audience members would be back next time McFerrin is in town.[8]

The desire for participatory fun that creates connection among those taking part will cause interactivity to spread through the arts. Participation in the arts has often been considered an elitist activity. It's true that it's strongly tied to higher education, but, as Chapter 2 tells us, boomers are the most highly educated population of all time, creating a generation of children that are hypereducated. They enjoy the arts, both fine and experimental, and are open to the chance to interact more closely with them. They work hard to create these experiences with their children to make the arts more accessible and fun.

We'll seek the chance to be involved in concerts, theatre productions, and even art exhibits. For at least a decade, interactive exhibits in the arts, science, history, and technology have begun to sprout in museums aimed at children. Hands-on exhibits have long been thought to inspire the young, but why do that only with children? Why not carry that concept further to include a general audience? Artists could help make their art more accessible if they could create hands-on art. Experiments in this kind of interactive creativity have seeped into our culture already. Consider the long running off-Broadway show *Tony 'n' Tina's Wedding*. It has played in all sorts of venues including a church. Audience members take on the role of invited guests at a wedding. Just like in an interactive video game, when the audience makes a specific choice, the production changes to accommodate that choice. In fact, at one point in the production, the audience splits, half going to one potential outcome while the other goes a different route.

Interactive performance can even be integrated into passive media like film. Anyone who has ever participated in a midnight screening of *The Rocky Horror Picture Show* will attest to the interactive fun of such an experience. The audience interacting with the movie is where the real fun lies. If this trend continues, we might someday attend the theatre or a movie and be given a script at the door with a choice of characters we can play and costumes we can wear to be an active part of the production.

Consumers will demand a whole new breed of activities that help stimulate creativity and develop a bond between performers and audience. Along the way, it will also link with other forms of entertainment to create hybrid brands of play for every age and income.

CHASING ACTION AND ADVENTURE

Many of us want to go well beyond an active lifestyle to bring more action and adventure into our lives with the adult twist of safety and comfort. Whether for one day or one year, these thrill rides for adults are gaining popularity with all generations. They take many forms from exotic travel to almost-impossible-to-get-to destinations to one-day immersion experiences such as flying a jet fighter or riding tandem on a professional bobsled course. Some are free while others are very expensive, giving rise to an entire subsegment of the travel and leisure industry.

Customized tours to meet every income, taste, and activity level will be the rage in the next decade. For instance, Daniel Mann wanted to tour Alaska in a nonpolluting way but at the same time to get to places off the beaten path. He was not interested in a big cruise or an organized tour, but neither was he interested in coming face-to-face with a bear all by himself or setting up camp and cooking solo every night. So he organized a group of seven friends, hired a guide via an adventure travel company, and custom-designed a moderate-priced kayaking trip along the Alaska coast that was adventurous yet safe and environmentally conscious. The experienced guide, who was local to the area, had tremendous firsthand knowledge that he eagerly shared with the group. Plus he was a great cook and expert at putting the campsite together quickly and efficiently each night.

Activist vacations are gaining popularity for those anxious to both contribute their time and energy for a cause they care about deeply and to experience remote locations. Some programs emphasize social and even environmental responsibility. They will, for example, use kayaks rather than motorized boats, bikes and horses rather than cars or buses. If they're hiking, they'll stay on marked trails to avoid disrupting the fragile environment of the region.

Earthwatch is one organization that organizes activist vacations. The personal watchdog for more than 161 global sites, this group sent volunteers—more than 40,000 to date—to observe and chart ecologic sites and conditions that require love and care. Volunteers of all ages pay huge sums of money to be part of excursions to sites such as the French Alps to survey the glaciers or Alaska to chart the mating behavior of Caribou. Once there, they donate their time to maintain and clean up the environment. Many of those who take these trips come home to live more environmentally aware LifeCycles and even teach these ideas in their local community.

Another twist on adventure travel is extreme vacations, designed for those looking for a heavy endorphin rush. Introduced in 1997, extreme vacations have grown tremendously in popularity—up 44 percent in the last year alone. This upward trend will continue through the decade. Based on the idea that rest and relaxation are for the meek, these are meant to push people to their limits so there's no time left to stress out over the issues of contemporary life. Lisa Didus of Active Journeys, an extreme vacation company, says, "By having a physical purpose, our clients have time to relax mentally. If they're sitting on a beach, all they can think about is the work they left behind. But if the challenge is to get over the next hill, there's no time to think about what's waiting back on their desks." One of the trips Active Journeys offers includes a 10-day, 300-mile bike ride between the Atlantic and Caribbean coasts of the Dominican Republic. "Not only is it a hard trip physically, it's challenging mentally."[9]

Whether they last one day or one month, these packaged and often customized adventures offer travel agents a chance to redefine their role and their profession. The old model of travel agencies, bringing in fees from booking airline and hotel reservations, has been destroyed with airlines cutting commissions drastically and online reservation booking promising to erode airline and hotel business even further. And since so many Americans are worried about safety and security since the September 11, 2001, terrorist attacks, we need a good reason to get on a plane. Re-creation has to be more than just traveling.

In response, some innovative travel agents have discovered a new revenue source to attract clients willing to pay higher fees for specialized information on unique travel spots or new ways of seeing the familiar. They prefer the title *travel consultant* to travel agent and see themselves selling inside information on fabulous travel destinations. Travel consultant Sally Watkins of Austin, Texas, contrasts the two: "There's a real difference between a travel agent and a travel consultant. An agent can run a computer but may not have traveled that much." She goes on to point out the ways each professional sells their services: Travel agents say, "We're free, we're free," while travel consultants say, "We're smart, we're smart."[10]

A travel consultant usually has firsthand knowledge about traveling to a particular place and can plan trips that include information from direct experience rather than from brochures. Sally Watkins limits her advice to Australia and Switzerland where she can arrange custom-designed trips that combine her extensive knowledge of the location with the personal needs and interests of each client. She charges as much as $500 per trip for her fee. McNair Travel Management in Alexandria, Virginia, caters to overseas honeymoons and weddings while Ker & Downey offers safaris to Africa complete with traditional tented camps. With such value-added services in demand, many of us will choose an expert who has the know-how to meet our every desire. Niche travel advice assures us that our next experience is fantastic.[11]

At different points in the cycle of life, most of us will choose to add a little more adventure to our every day routine. Many savvy companies and enterprising individuals will seize this hook as a way to create new products or to cater to the needs of new customers.

SPORTS FRENZY

Just as the cyclic life offers up a potpourri of fantasy, interactive, and adventure experiences for adults of all ages, an assortment of participatory sports programs are emerging targeted to adults.

Parental involvement with kids' sports has spawned recreational sports leagues for adults. Adult leagues at many different levels of competition are cropping up everywhere. At the community center in my town, they have recently started a basketball league, a racquetball league, and a volleyball league, all aimed at adults.

Like many things in the brave new world of LifeCycles, the leagues are not divided up based on age as they are for children but on ability. (They do have separate leagues for men and women.) In the coming decades, this relatively new way of segmenting—based on ability rather than just age—will be routinely applied to far more than just sports leagues. It will be a core feature of the cyclic life that will help eliminate age discrimination.

Adults of all ages are beginning to participate in traveling club sports just like their children do. Designed for the more experienced athlete, club sports are just starting to show up for adults. Forty-two-year-old Paul Akin plays basketball in such a league. When he was growing up, sports were a high priority. They were the basis for many of his lifelong friendships and even helped him get into college. The thought of giving them up entirely as an adult didn't hold much appeal. After he married and had children, he thought that coaching any possible sport his kids might play would be the practical outlet for his sports interest. Coaching sports was fun but full of frustrations. So he joined a basketball league sponsored by his fitness club. While playing there, he got drafted to play in a more competitive league that participates in tournaments throughout the Northwest. On weekends, he travels with eight other men throughout the United States to play amateur competitive basketball. Suddenly his kids are cheering him on almost as much as he cheers them on. His participation in team sports has grown, rather than waned, as he has gotten older.

Paul's not alone. Men and women of all ages are seeking re-creation opportunities in organized sports, both team and individual in nature. Just because we're adult, doesn't mean we don't want to still play team sports. Just as many communities have strong high school football or basketball teams with devoted fans, adult leagues will begin springing up throughout the country with devoted fans of their own.

For adults who want to improve their sports skills, business has already begun to respond. Nike, for instance, has golf camps for adults, just as they do for children. Scuba diving schools are often found on the premises of tropical resorts offering the opportunity to get certified as well as escape to enjoy the surreal underwater beauty that scuba diving opens up. Ski schools that used to be primarily for kids now offer a variety of programs for all levels of skiers, no matter what age they might be. Schools and clinics across the country have created successful small businesses to serve sports enthusiasts under the age of 18. Now they have an opportunity to increase their business by expanding their consumer base to include adults.

Beyond group programs, millions of affluent adults are ready to splurge with a personal trainer right on the golf course, ski slope, or in the gym to gain instant skill without hurting themselves. Bill Burk, while taking a weekend break with his wife, was playing a frustrating round of golf. He just couldn't get it right, because he never had enough time in his work/travel schedule to get lessons on a regular basis. So he hired a golf pro that very weekend to play a round with him. The golf pro gave him tips that he was able to immediately integrate into his game, and he found that his game improved dramatically in just one day.

One of the great aspects of sports is that they're a way to share time with friends and family. As a result, highly manicured ski resorts like Deer Valley, Utah, will see continued growth in the coming decade. With groomed runs and valet ski-carrying service that remove some of the hassles and provide added comfort and safety to the experience of skiing, Deer Valley attracts skiers of all ages and experience levels. Similarly, campgrounds with valets to help set up equipment and get dinner going in remote locations will have great appeal. River rafting trips where participants do some but not all the work, stop for gourmet meals, and even stay at lodges along the riverbanks are proliferating as many generations choose to take part in active sports in safety and comfort.

Several sports camps are designed for a parent and child to attend together. Last year Phil Pollen decided he wanted to do something special with his 10-year-old son, Justin. They spent days reading through brochures on resorts, campgrounds, and adventure tours all over the globe. Nothing seemed to fit right. Finally, Justin said, "Dad, what I really want to do is go back to the basketball camp I went to last year. Maybe you can come watch everyday." Phil mentioned this to a friend over lunch who had a solution. He said, "You're not going to believe this, but Stanford University has a father-son basketball camp where kids and their fathers can attend together. They even share a dorm room." Although staying in a college dormitory didn't sound all that great to Phil, he immediately signed Justin and himself up for basketball camp at Stanford. He hadn't played basketball since he was in his teens, but Phil had the best time with Justin and the other fathers and sons. Although the dorm food was as bad as expected, it freed them to order out pizzas at night, play music and games and, most importantly, bond big time. Phil even got better at basketball and learned some simple techniques to help improve Justin's game as well. Justin thought it was the most fun they ever had together and already wants to sign up again for next year.

Some sports that have been around for decades are morphing into new forms. As adults refine their skills over decades, they might decide to experiment with the rules of the game and invent new games in the process. For instance, in Palo Alto, California, a few adult renegades have begun to experiment with their own form of golf, "radical golf" as they call it. No carts allowed. Slip a few clubs into your backpack, and walk the entire course. The goal is to see who can finish first with the fewest strokes. This speed game is a completely different approach from the one traditionally played. It's a convergence of skills that we see in other newly emerging sports such as wave boarding, roller hockey, and freestyle skiing. The hugely popular X Games have given us all the freedom to explore the boundaries of games we're highly proficient at. But Xtreme has come to mean dangerous. Less dangerous combinations will emerge that emphasize more adult capabilities like skill and endurance.

Take diggling. Inventor Rob Fruechtenicht thought it would be fun if he could safely skateboard or surf down the Mount Tamalpais bike trail near his home in Marin County, California. In 1996 he began to build something that might fit his needs. Without a seat, it looks like a BMX bike that's been extended to make room for a scooter-like foot deck between the two wheels, and it's perfect for surfing mountain trails. "We were spitting out terminology for catching air, ripping turns, digging, grinding, sliding," says Fruechtenicht of the naming process. Diggler was the end result. Not surprisingly, ski resorts anxious for activities for summer visitors are beginning to buy digglers. By midsummer 2002, 50 resorts were renting them to kids and adults alike.[12]

As more and more adults of all ages actively participate in a wide range of sports, tremendous consumer opportunities will arise for business. Adults of all ages, some with testy backs, shoulders, or knees, participate in sports and demand the best in equipment. They are willing to upgrade that equipment often. Titanium golf clubs, bats, and tennis racquets, often oversized to make swinging easier, have replaced older graphite models. Mercedes-Benz has designed the ultimate in mountain bikes. And skis now come in all sizes and shapes, designed in different ways for different terrain and conditions. Many adults have two and three pairs.

Many also have other shoes and clothing that accompany sports participation, even on a casual basis. Ben, a 40-year-old real estate broker, is also a weekend athlete. He plays basketball and tennis, hikes and skis. He has a different pair of athletic shoes for each sport as well as specialized clothing.

The increasing demand by adults for sports means that the grassroots programs—camps, leagues, and schools—will grow by expanding their customer base to include adults of all ages. And experienced athletes who want to apply their skill to teaching other adults can develop their own personal coaching business.

SHOPPER-TAINMENT

As shopping and entertainment inch closer toward each other, shopping will be more and more about fun. Although e-tailing hasn't yet lived up to its potential, it has awakened fear in the hearts of many retailers and mall developers who realize they need to work hard to keep consumers coming back for more. Their goal is to help mold consumers into destination shoppers, keen on coming back for fun and to purchase products.

This is not a new concept. For years, movie theatres have been essential entertainment elements of malls. Niketown has created a fun environment unlike that seen in stores in the past. But it's a new twist to the concept. The Niketown example is a passive environment. Active entertainment will begin to merge with square footage and magnet stores.

Mark J. Rivers, executive vice-president and chief strategic officer at Mills Corporation, believes, "The long-term players in our business should be in the 'out-of-home' entertainment business. We see ourselves more as a Disney-type venture than a mall. Vans Skatepark is to Ontario Mills what Space Mountain is to Disneyland."

Rivers is referring to Ontario Mills Mall, a mall his company owns near Los Angeles, where Vans, a Los Angeles–based sporting goods retailer, built a 60,000 square foot skate park and off-road bicycle track. The idea was that not many people buy a tennis racquet or golf clubs or even roller blades every year let alone every day, so Vans needed to sell an experience that would both increase profits and drive people into the store on a more regular basis to make smaller purchases.

Vans isn't the only retailer that has caught the shopper-tainment bug. Bass Pro Shops, a chain of outdoor-sports equipment stores based in Springfield, Missouri, fills their stores with giant aquariums, waterfalls, trout ponds, archery and rifle ranges, putting greens, and classes in the unusual such as ice fishing. Gibson Musical Instruments' Guitar Showcase at Opryland Mills Mall in Nashville, Tennessee, invites customers to watch while their instruments are being made. Wizards of the Coast is a retail chain of stores known for fantasy games and collectibles. At Wiz-ards, the game room is where the action is. Filled with tables for card trading, tournaments, and banks of computers where kids can play video games with one another, parents often drop their kids here to play—with supervision—while they shop. The video games are $7 an hour, and most kids usually want to buy things before they leave.[13]

Similarly, 10-year-old The Mall of America, in the Minneapolis sub-urb of Bloomington, successfully combines retail, entertainment, and community. Most of the entertainment, including an indoor amuse-ment park and a Lego Imagination Center, is aimed at keeping the kids occupied so mom and dad can shop. But, there is also a wedding chapel, a radio station, a high school, a university, and a medical clinic. Shopper-tainment now needs to go much further than movie theatres and entertaining the kids; it's got to be a destination of choice for adults seeking fun and re-creation.

Xscape is an example of what the future could look like in terms of multigenerational shopper-tainment. Xscape, a 4.7-million-square-foot shopper-tainment complex in Milton Keynes, England, is billed as the ultimate in entertainment with Europe's largest "real" snow slope; a health and fitness club; indoor soccer and basketball; two rock climbing walls and a climbing boulder; ten pin bowling; a multiplex cinema; and trendy bars, restaurants, and nightclubs. It is *the* place to go in Milton Keynes. The developers are planning another Xscape in Yorkshire, En-gland, and the Ruhr Valley, Germany. It won't be long before American developers will build shopper-tainment centers as well.[14]

Event shopping will gain popularity. Some stores have successfully experimented with this notion, but it will take off in the coming decade. Both big events like concerts featuring stars performing live and simul-taneously video-cast into large chain stores and more intimate book readings at local Barnes & Noble or Borders Books will be destinations that combine purchasing with enjoyable experiences.

Personal stylists and shoppers have long been at the service of the rich and famous. Michelle Pfeiffer, Jennifer Aniston, and Geena Davis rely on them to select the right clothes for the right occasion. This cus-tomized service will go mainstream with savvy retailers noting the direct link between personalized services and increased sales.

If the retail industry is to succeed, stores must provide far more than goods and services at a price. This will mean that brick-and-mortar businesses will need to offer online services for commodity items that are easy to select online and easy and cheap to ship. Beyond that, retailers need to think of themselves as being in the *experience industry* with varied options available for adults and children alike. They will need to serve many generations at once. Many midlife adults will be shopping not only for themselves but also for elderly parents as well as children. Impeccable service will have to be built into the process to make this manageable. Personalized attention with shopping assistants will be expected. Many forms of leisure and re-creation will be integrated into the shopping experience to create a new form of entertainment—shopper-tainment.

FACE ENTERTAINMENT

The restaurant industry has been getting more and more competitive. Price-Waterhouse reports that the number of restaurants in the United States is growing twice as fast as it did five years ago. With this in mind, restaurants do what they can to stand out from the crowd and offer a unique experience. Sushi Samba in New York City takes the freshness of sushi to new extremes serving a lobster sashimi so fresh that its pincers are still waving. Another one of their specialties is silver-dollar-sized crabs served live and designed to be eaten claws and all.

Culinary extremes as entertainment experiences are not just happening in New York. Café Atlantico in Washington, D.C., serves an appetizer of sea urchin sprinkled with Altoids and a celery-root soup accompanied by a spray bottle of white-truffle oil. Waiters instruct diners to spray the white truffle oil in their mouths twice before eating their soup. One of Café Atlantico's most popular desserts during summer 2001 was a dessert margarita with "Pop Rocks" candy sprinkled on top. Yes, more than one customer has been hit with a Pop Rock. Even Paris, long the haven of serious gourmet dining, is home to a restaurant, Le Chipper, which serves deep-fried Mars and Snicker Bars topped with whipped cream and strawberry coulis.[15]

Extreme cuisine, as this has been called, is catching on with those who get their kicks from being ahead of the curve with trends. Even the Food Channel is getting in on the act. They have a show airing on Saturday nights, called *Extreme Cuisine* that has gotten so popular it's seen a 58 percent rate increase since its debut.

As adults crave more interactive entertainment, fantasy will merge with food to create new forms of re-creation. Entros, a restaurant in Seattle, successfully combines the leading edge in innovative interactive games with great fusion food. My husband, Ken and I, went to a 40th birthday party at Entros and wanted to return with our kids. Maneuver-A-Ball was an interactive experience that required six to eight players to work together. Everyone stands on a floating platform encircling a cylinder that looks like a pinball game. By shifting weight together, players try to move the ball into the center of the pinball while avoiding a variety of trapdoors. There's also a specially designed game show room where restaurant diners who want to take part are transformed into game show contestants. Everyone divides into teams and competes to answer silly questions. The host is very funny and gets everyone interacting quickly. One of the founders, Stephen Brown, says, "We want to inject something into the middle of a group of people who may have known each other for years that allows them to rediscover what they liked about each other in the first place."[16]

Entros defines a new direction that some restaurant dining experiences will begin to embrace: offering an evening of fun and recreation rather than just an evening of fun or recreation. And games are just one example. What about an open mike at a restaurant? Max's Opera Café in San Francisco and neighboring suburbs is a deli-style restaurant popular for big desserts and talented waiters and waitresses. They take turns singing at the open mike accompanied by a pianist. Why not extend the invitation to diners? Or dinner theatre where you get a role in the show. Now, I'm not saying we won't still want evenings devoted to good food and conversation, but we'll also seek live, experiential entertainment. It's the revival, remix, repackaging, and update of the dinner theatre model, but with a more modern, interactive spin.

At the other end of the spectrum, the slow food movement has taken root. It began in Italy, where fast food was never that popular. Only 5 percent of all food eaten out of the home in Italy is fast food while in the

United States, that number is 50 percent. However, since the 1999 opening of their New York office, the slow food movement has been catching on, even in the United States.

Slow food is the opposite of fast food with a manifesto that states, "May suitable doses of guaranteed sensual pleasure and slow, long-lasting enjoyment preserve us from the contagion of the multitude who mistake frenzy for efficiency." That's quite a mouthful! The group was founded in 1989 in Rome by Carlo Petrini who was trying to organize a protest against the first McDonald's being built in Rome. Today the organization has grown to more than 60,000 members in more than 42 countries. Dedicated to preserving fresh and regional food, they believe that eating should be a joyous experience to be savored, not rushed, with friends and loved ones in beautiful surroundings. Alice Waters of Chez Panisse Restaurant is one of the world's most famous chefs and has been involved with this movement. She has helped create eating groups called *convivia* which sponsor meals, lectures, and trips to farms and other regional producers. There are more than 30 convivia organized already throughout the United States with more certain to come in the future.[17]

Some restaurants devoted to fine dining may begin to include food preparation in the dining experience. In the '80s, we saw a lot of restaurants appear with open kitchens that allowed diners to watch the chefs in action. In the near future, we may see restaurants allow diners to help prepare dessert or appetizers or even go out to the garden to select lettuce for their own salads. Wild About Mushrooms organizes mushroom hunting trips followed by gourmet dining using the mushrooms picked that day to create scrumptious meals.

A few of the more innovative kitchen stores such as Home Chef now include cooking schools as an essential way to gain more customers and added revenue. Some are even beginning to offer the services of their chefs to organize in-home parties and special events. This trend of making food an experience to be shared over an evening rather than just nutrition to be grabbed on the run will grow over the coming decade. Some restaurants will cater to this need. In addition, the demand for local chefs to cook at small dinner parties will rise and break out of the stereotype of "just for the rich." Some may even take on the role of camp counselor as well as chef, organizing guests to help out in the kitchen.

Others may take it further and provide a full spectrum of services, including subscription food. Already some well-known nutritionists who cater to the rich and famous have successfully experimented with this model. The idea is to create flash frozen foods that are nutritious, home-cooked, and delivered fresh to your freezer's door to be microwaved to perfection as needed. It takes the concept of frozen foods to a whole new level.

SPIRIT SEEKERS

The boomers have always been spirit seekers, just not in the traditional sense of the word. Boomers were the first generation to be open to a new, more multicultural, and often mystical brand of spirituality. This has been one of their defining characteristics since their teen years. Many are passing this attitude on to their children with the credo: I am a spiritual person, but not necessarily a religious one.

According to a Roper Survey on boomers, there is near total agreement that deep inner values, including being true to yourself, having control of your life, finding satisfaction within yourself, and having inner peace are key elements of the American Dream. This mind-set is impacting traditional forms of religion as well as creating new spiritual highways for people to travel, especially post 9-11. The so-called experience industry is already a multibillion dollar industry that will grow in new ways as we seek new paths to re-creation.

Spiritual retreats as vacations have been slowly gaining popularity with adults of all ages. The New Camaldoli Hermitage is a Benedictine Monastery in Big Sur, California, where vacationers opt for a stark room, a modest bowl of bean soup, and the chance to catch up with themselves. The Omega Institute for Holistic Studies in Rhinebeck, New York, offers a catalog of over 250 retreats and wellness vacations. They bill themselves as a "peaceful oasis in which to nurture body, mind, and spirit."

In the heart of New York City, Gabrielle Roth offers classes called "Sweat Your Prayers" where God can be experienced through dance. At Jivamukti Yoga Center in the East Village, Roth tries to bring illumination, radiance, and enlightenment or what the Hindus call *Samadi* to students. Writer Trish Deitch Rohrer attended a session and wrote in *New York* magazine, "I feel a gale force coming up from the place where my most creative work resides and from where I love my daughter. I feel the same force coming from my fellow dancers." To experience this in a one-hour dance class in the middle of Manhattan is truly remarkable.[18]

Evangelical churches have long offered uplifting prayer and song to create the feeling of joy, the spirit of connection, and the strength for personal re-creation. A wonderful example of a church creating a spiritual opening is Glide Memorial Church, located in one of the poorest parts of San Francisco, the Tenderloin. Well-known nationwide for their active community role in caring for the poor and neglected, the church attracts a wide cross section of people from all walks of life from the down-and-out to Sharon Stone to average people.

My daughter, Casey, got the chance to attend services and work in the soup kitchen at Glide Memorial with her religious school class. Sixteen preteen boys and girls from suburban San Francisco took the B.A.R.T. train into the heart of the Tenderloin early one Sunday morning to make ham sandwiches before church services began. They worked side-by-side with homeless people from the Tenderloin who helped prepare food that they would ultimately be eating. After work came re-creation in the form of services. People line up around the block to get into the Sunday services known as Celebrations where the choir, the Glide Ensemble, sing gospel, rock, and freedom songs. A six-piece rock/soul/jazz band accompanies the Ensemble. The church used to have a traditional wooden cross at its pulpit; that's been replaced with a multimedia light show which flashes colors and patterns focusing on human-experience symbols that are relevant and immediate.

Lisa Morris from Plano, Texas, always considered herself a seeker of the more spiritual side of life. Active in her church throughout her adult life, she also was not inspired by the routine offerings of worship and raising funds for the poor whom she never got to meet. When her church decided to experiment with a program that would give a group of congregants the chance to give more than money to the poor, she signed up right away. Her church regularly gave money and aid to a sister church in Honduras. Through this relationship, they organized a trip to Honduras to offer hands-on help to the rural community that the church served. Lisa and some of her fellow parishioners lived right in the community for two weeks.

Lisa served as a nurse's aide for a clinic that helped malnourished children. "Most of the children in the community were malnourished," reported Lisa. "The hard part was that we would have the children for about two weeks, and then they'd be forced to go right back to the conditions that created the problem in the first place." She never saw such dire need, and it tugged at her heartstrings. For the first time in her life, she had a direct experience of what poverty really was, and it changed her life. She knew she would have to go back annually to give more to these people; she also knew she could actively raise funds for them in a way she never could have without the direct experience.

Nonprofits of all kinds could broaden their appeal by realizing that we're all seeking emotional and spiritual connection to causes. If they could find ways to offer that experience, chances are they could increase their appeal to the public. For instance, fund-raising events, usually dinners with entertainment or a speaker, are commonly organized by nonprofits trying to raise money. Everything from the National Cancer League to the Democratic Party to Battered Women's Alternative plan these events and depend on them to meet their budgetary objectives. But what if the National Cancer League, for instance, could organize a visit for donors to a cancer hospital to serve lunch to and visit with the patients. Or the Battered Women's Alternative could, similar to Habitat for Humanity, organize a renovation event where donors gave time and money to rehabilitating a building that would house women and children who use these services. Chances are that more donors would surface and be more committed to giving large amounts if they felt a firsthand connection with the real people that a particular cause served.

In a long-lived culture where technology is one of the holy grails and terrorism is a grim reality, humans will seek humane ways to relate to one another at home, in the community, and at work. Spiritual renewal will be a growing mode of re-creation. Since evidence throughout time proves that money doesn't improve happiness, many will be spending their hard-earned cash in pursuit of inner happiness and peace that can stay with them throughout their LifeCycles.

CONCLUSION

Re-creation will be an integral part of the cyclic life. Whether it's a day at the spa or a monthlong trek in the Himalayas, we will be seeking a variety of experiences that take us out of our daily routines to give us time to relax, regenerate, have fun, give back, and connect with family, friends, and ourselves. As we move along the cyclic life path, there will be times where recreation will dominate; at other times it will take a backseat to other activities. Re-creation will come in many forms, serve many purposes, and have different durations. What they will all share is the opportunity for us to cycle away from our normal routines, even if it's just for an hour. And it offers the travel and leisure industry new opportunities in serving the diverse needs of LifeCyclers craving a wide variety of experiences.

RECOVERERS AND REJUVENATORS

One of the most predictable aspects of life in the traditional linear arrangement was that the older we became, the more likely we'd be to get sick and die. In our minds, we've linked aging so closely with illness, disability, and dependency that most of us have dreaded getting older, likening it to a slow death sentence. Not anymore.

The cyclic life makes chronological age just a number, not a definition of who we are or how we live. Fifty once signaled that the best years were behind us, that we were over-the-hill. Today, it can signal new beginnings and reinvention, a chance to try new things we've never done before. As Robert Butler, founding director of the National Institute on Aging, says, "What was old in the last century is not old anymore."

AGELESS AGING

More research and resources have been deployed to battle aging in the past 10 years than in the previous 10 centuries. This has given us insight into what is disease, what is aging, and where the two intersect. Today, many of the diseases and disabilities once assumed to be symptoms of aging—including physical decline, decreased mobility, and memory loss—can actually be slowed or stopped. In fact, researchers at the Scripps Research Institute in California and at the University of Illinois–Chicago theorize that the physical ravages of aging are not inevitable at all and that aging itself might be curable.[1]

In the cyclic life arrangement, many of us will count on this. We will want to maintain our health and vitality for as long as possible to give us the freedom to cycle in and out of whatever LifeCycle events we choose. If we want to run a marathon at 60, start a new career at 45, or fall in love at 80, we won't want anything to stand in the way.

This is not to suggest that those of us embarked on a cyclic life path are now magically immune to accident or disease. Regardless of any leaps of progress in medical science or personal behavior, we remain human beings, with our vulnerabilities intact. The difference is that those vulnerabilities will no longer be at the helm of our life's journey. Whereas travelers along the linear-life path were resigned to the inevitability of decline leading to death, those of us on the cyclic path will recognize that periods of poorer health might represent a temporary detour, not a destination.

In other words, we will be less resigned at the onset of illness, and more hopeful of recovery and rejuvenation. These two strategies are absolutely critical to success on the cyclic life path and can even be seen as related poles along a continuum of self-awareness and empowerment. Recoverers are often shocked into their own empowerment by the disruptive onset of disease. Rejuvenators come to a gentler appreciation of their own personal power to heal and improve through a reflective evaluation of their health status and where they would like it to be.

RECOVERERS

Until the (imminent) arrival of some amazing and actionable breakthroughs in medical science, many of us will do serious battle with a killer disease, maybe even coming close to death, at various points along the life path. Worldwide, over 1 million people wage war on cancer each year. In the United States, that translates to 4 in 10 Americans with the risk increasing with age. Approximately one out of every two American men and one out of every three American women will have some type of cancer at some point during their lifetimes. An estimated 194,000 women fought breast cancer while a slightly larger number of men—198,000—fought prostate cancer in 2001. Anyone can get cancer at any age; however, about 80 percent of all cancers occur in people over the age of 55.[2]

Cancer is the second leading cause of death in the United States, exceeded only by heart disease. Some 7 million Americans suffer from coronary heart disease (CHD), the most common form of heart disease. CHD is the number one killer of both men and women in the United States.[3]

Keep in mind that medical science has already made tremendous inroads in the battles against these and other diseases. Until President Dwight Eisenhower had a heart attack during his first term of office, cardiovascular disease was seen as an automatic death sentence preceded by a sedentary life. He changed all that with his robust recovery and decision to run for a second term in office. "That to me was a key turning point for the attitudes of both patients and physicians," says Dr. Robert Myerburg, director of cardiology at the University of Miami.[4]

But even more important are the empowered attitudes toward a catastrophic diagnosis now embraced by patients themselves. When someone of our grandparents' era was given a sentence of cancer, he or she resolutely began to prepare for the end, clearly and inevitably in sight. That kind of immediate surrender is far from the norm today. "The attitude now is rehabilitation rather than stagnation," says Dr. Myerburg.

For Ardith Rodale, CEO of Rodale Publishing, publisher of *Prevention Magazine* and other health-related titles, the lifestage of illness and recovery started with a routine visit to her gynecologist. The doctor noticed a dimple in one of her breasts—one of the warning signs of cancer. "I was so surprised—I honestly thought that dimple was there because I had been trying to lose some weight."

She got a mammogram that revealed a tumor. It was cancer, localized in her breast. Along with her husband and doctor, Ardith decided on a lumpectomy as the best course of action.

Ardie then took a detour into her first recovery mode. Surgery was followed by weeks of daily radiation therapy. She didn't rush getting back to work even though she was at the helm of a large publishing company. "I was on the telephone, but I was generally able to take it easy because I have a good team. I went back when I felt I was ready, not when the doctor said I was ready. There's a big difference." The thought of surrender never crossed her mind.

After weeks of radiation therapy, Ardie went back to work and the whirlwind of her life. Her recovery cycle was complete. But, four years later, the second bout with breast cancer came. "I was having some breast pain, and I knew something was wrong." It was in the same exact spot. This time Ardie had a mastectomy. After months in recovery mode this time, Ardith slowly moved back to work.

Today Ardie is cancer-free and busier than ever as chairman of the board and chief executive officer of Rodale, Inc. She writes, speaks, and is involved in a variety of charitable endeavors. She's taken the lifestage of illness away from the end of her life's continuum and redefined it as a cyclic detour, centered on recovery.

With illness and recovery becoming recognizable lifestage events rather than signals that the end is here, the health care system becomes a valuable resource to navigate and access as we choose. Cycles of illness and recovery might happen at 20 or 80; they could happen just once or several times. Chances are good, though, that we will conquer the enemy and bounce back to full recovery, offering us the opportunity to again enjoy work, play, and any other activities we choose to be part of with energy, vitality, and even added resilience and strength of purpose.

Lance Armstrong, the famed bike racer, for example, takes an incredibly positive approach to his battle with testicular cancer, describing it as an "unexpected gift" that changed his priorities and his entire approach to racing. He didn't win the Tour de France until after his long, grueling battle with cancer, and feels like he might not have accomplished this victory without the complex experience of coping with a disease that almost killed him. He sums up the change this way: "It's ironic, I used to ride my bike to make a living. Now I just want to live so that I can ride."[5]

REJUVENATORS

Those of us who are spared the unexpected gift of life-changing illness will not be left out of the picture of renewed health in our cyclic life plans. More years and better health will instead afford us the opportunity to repeatedly assess our bodies, minds, and spirits, and to devote our energy to obtaining goals related to them.

These *rejuvenators* among us will experiment with emerging techniques and products that promise to halt or even reverse the aging process. Rejuvenators will try to push the envelope and transform the concept of aging by either slowing or eliminating many of the effects of aging, adding years to our lives and allowing us to cycle in and out of the lifestyle experiences we value most.

Barbara Black of Corvallis, Oregon, found herself in bad physical shape at age 74. Bending over was painful and she could barely lift herself out of a chair. She wasn't overweight, but she said her body was mostly "flab and mush." She heard about a study taking place at Oregon State University, right in her hometown, on the relationship between exercise and bone density in women over 50. She enrolled in the study and, over five years, has reversed her health remarkably. Her bone density alone has increased 15 percent. "Before I started the program, my bone density was below average. To actually gain bone density is really fantastic." She adds, "You don't have to go downhill. This shows you can go uphill, too."

Like Barbara's, some rejuvenative therapies may require putting aside days, weeks, or months in hopes of increasing our health span. Longevity centers are already beginning to appear throughout the world. Some of these are basically spas upgraded to include longevity measurement devices that can diagnose vulnerabilities and customize megavitamin or hormone treatments. Others, however, include a Chinese menu of antiaging remedies ranging from megavitamins to HGH treatments, from herbal remedies to exercise techniques, even surgical procedures requiring recuperative stays of a week or more. They even can include strong educational components so that we can bring our wellness techniques back home for the benefit of our families and ourselves.

Some spas, too, such as Canyon Ranch walk the line between *spa* and *health center,* with physicians an essential part of their staffs. They often insist on at least a one- or two-week stay and can provide personalized nutrition and exercise counseling that includes the appropriate recommendations for the right pharmaceuticals, nutraceutical supplements, and an exercise regimen for each client.

Building on the cycles theme, Dr. Michael Roizen, author of the bestseller, *The RealAge Diet*, has organized a rejuvenative RealAge Cruise "to help you grow younger, and to give you proven health tips that will help you to continue to grow younger after you get home."[6] These cruises emphasize how a getaway itself can reduce stress for longer life and offer practical advice on how to eat to increase health and vitality. Other rejuvenation options that offer a time-out from real life will appear on the horizon, especially during times when the economy is bad and people feel a need to focus on their own health and happiness for a time.

DEMOGRAPHIC FORCES AT WORK

Two of the demographic forces propelling us into other aspects of the cyclic life are at work making recovery and rejuvenation a priority. Increased longevity and the pioneering attitudes of boomers will improve the likelihood that health and vitality will be an integral part of every cycle of our lives.

Increased Longevity

Life expectancy is on the rise, and with it, a welcome public interest in *prolonging health expectancy* as well. The reasons for this are overwhelming, obvious, and inescapable. More than half of all people who have ever turned 65 are alive today and those who make it to 65 can expect to live on average, another 17 years.[7]

According to Dr. James Fries, professor of medicine at Stanford University Medical School, as we see large segments of the population living longer, it becomes essential to the overall good of society to "compress morbidity" or to "live long, live healthy, die fast." He says, "a life that is vigorous and vital until shortly before its natural close" is the ideal.

We've got a long way to go to reach that ideal, though, and it's time for us to step up to the plate. So far, there has been little national emphasis on linking longer life spans with longer health spans. If we as a society continue to elevate life expectancy without fostering healthy aging, many of our less fortunate members will still live for decades with disease, growing disabilities, and pain.

Our current health care system is not designed to encourage the lengthening of our health spans—and the habits of our citizens in the upper age ranges show it. In the United States, Medicare, the national health reimbursement program for older adults, doesn't even reimburse for health promotion or disease prevention. Tragically, two-thirds of the elderly don't exercise, over half don't wear seat belts, and 75 percent don't even take their medications as prescribed.

This is a reflection of how entrenched in the traditional paradigm—where life was short and disease was acute, fast acting, and largely out of our personal control—we still are. This defeatist attitude is a dangerous relic that demands change. For example, technically my grandmother died last year at age 94; but we all knew she had really died more than nine years before when she was diagnosed with dementia. My children had never really met the real Frieda Gordet, only the body she once inhabited. Her doctors offered us no hope, no cure. They told us dementia was an inevitable symptom of aging that was out of anyone's control. But, recent research is beginning to question that theory, and suggests that there are preventative measures that can either delay or halt the onset of dementia. You can bet that my mother and I will monitor the science and take the necessary preventative measures to postpone or avoid living through the hell of my grandmother's last years.

In that same mode, we as a country need to aggressively develop a model of health care designed for a long-lived population battling chronic, degenerative disease, loss of cognitive ability, and decreasing physical strength. Long life without health could be like a prison sentence. Maintaining health and vitality for as long as possible should be the new goals of the health care system.[8]

The Boomer Effect

Count on the boomers to help reshape our relationship with health, health care professionals, and the symptoms of aging as they cope with their own aging and the aging of their parents. They already are. According to a *Newsweek* Poll of Americans 45 to 65, most people in this age group feel positive about the way they look and feel and are likely to be physically and mentally active, pursuing a broad range of personal and professional interests. These ages don't equate with winding down anymore. Instead, they can be opportunities to cycle into new lifestage events.

One of the most obvious differences boomers demonstrate from generations before them is their rebellious nature and inherent need to question authority. The older adults of today have traditionally placed physicians on a pedestal, like gods who were not to be questioned or second-guessed. In contrast, most boomers recognize that physicians are just one component of the health care system rather than its sum. And boomers will be the first to tell you that doctors, like the rest of us, are human and fallible. The pedestals are gone and, in terms of intellect and ability, aging boomer patients and their doctors stand on level ground.

As David Eisenberg, Harvard Medical School assistant professor, points out, "Boomers questioned a lot of establishments when we were younger and still don't accept that there's only one way to do things."[9] He says this boomer propensity has created growing interest in less mainstream medicine like acupuncture, massage, and homeopathy. And younger people are following the boomers' lead with enthusiasm. Already, according to a November 1998 study published in the *Journal of the American Medical Association*, "Americans are more likely to visit an alternative medicine practitioner than a primary care physician."[10]

EMPOWERED PATIENTS

Most boomers will consider maintaining health and vitality as the minimum acceptable level of commitment in their cyclic lives. Pushing the envelope to bring youth with them to their middle and later years will ultimately be their goal. This will propel them to explore a spectrum of options to recover and rejuvenate health and bring back physical vitality, energy, muscle mass, smooth skin, better functioning organs, and more.

So how will they get from here to there? Through an empowering twist on an ancient dictum to physicians: Patient, help heal thyself.

Thomas Edison once predicted, "The doctor of the future will give no medicine, but will interest patients in the maintenance of the human frame, in diet and in the prevention of disease." Edison was always a man ahead of his time. More than 200 years later, the Centers for Disease Control report that, "more than 50 percent of our potential for life-long health is determined by our personal behaviors." Recoverers and rejuvenators alike can make tremendous strides in increasing their health spans, just by practicing good self-care and disease prevention tactics.

There's no question that exercise and healthy eating—along with staying socially and mentally active and avoiding cigarette smoke— result in longer health spans. Tragically, however, awareness—and motivation to take action—are not what they should be. "There's a huge percentage of the public for whom good nutrition and exercise don't even appear on the radar screen," says Wotjek J. Chodzko-Zajko of the University of Illinois, president of the International Society for Aging and Physical Activity.[11]

According to Dr. Gerald Fletcher of the American Heart Association, "The problem is that people don't understand the important of exercise until they are lying in a cardiac care unit." The seminal MacArthur Foundation Study of Successful Aging confirms that regular exercise, above all else, is the single most important ingredient to stave off disease and keep the body from declining physically. It is the first step toward effective self-care. The Framingham Heart Study proved that if we were to walk about an hour each day and burn 2,000 calories a week, we could increase our life expectancy by two years. The 1996 Surgeon General's Report on Physical Activity and Health is more specific, stating that exercise can benefit almost every organ and system in the body.[12]

There's so much good information on exercise out there I don't need to go into it in detail here. Suffice it to say that regularly participating in exercise in its three key forms—cardiovascular, strength-training, and flexibility—will improve the quality and increase the quantity of your entire LifeCycle. Without question. End of story.

Even regular exercise can't make up for diets lacking in vital nutrients, and abundant in empty calories. As Americans, we are a nation obsessed with food, its value, and its intake. Yet obesity and malnutrition are at their highest levels ever. Healthy eating has somehow become a complex web of confusion. However, it really can be simple to eat a diet that promotes a longer, healthful life. Start with the idea of eating foods high in nutrients and low in calories. This will lead directly to a diet that includes lots of fruits, vegetables, whole grains, fish, nuts, and low-fat dairy with very small amounts of lean meat. This is the diet that studies consistently point to as one that promotes long life and health, and it will make a difference. Melanie Polk, director of nutrition education at the American Institute of Cancer Research, says, "If everyone ate at least five servings of fruits and vegetables daily, that alone would reduce incidence of cancer by as much as 20 percent." How much clearer can that prescription be? And what better way for empowered patients to take the lead in increasing their health cycles?

But, as I've mentioned, even the most empowered and healthy of us will occasionally need to take detours through the medical system as we cycle through periods of rejuvenation and recovery. When we do, the onus will be on the individual to navigate and evaluate the tremendous options in our health care system, and to keep up-to-date on the most current options.

To do this well, obviously, we'll first need to have a thorough understanding of our baseline health status. Before we can improve anything—from a golf score to a salary to a household budget—we've got to get a grip on where things stand. That's especially true when dealing with our own bodies.

A spectrum of new health risk assessment tools is already available that can let us know what our health risks are and how we might improve our health. First, they measure lifestyle, genetic factors, and medical history, and then feed back personalized advice and information. Craig Fourde of Well-Med, a health-information company in Portland, Oregon, says, "We're generally able to uncover risk factors you may not be aware of like diabetes or hypertension."[13] From highly sophisticated to rather simple, assessment tools like these help us figure out the best health care choices we can make from what to eat, how to exercise, and even what kind of health care professionals best meet our own needs. All based on where we stand, healthwise, right now.

The very best risk assessments go far beyond collecting medical history and genetic predispositions. Today we can assess our health through full body scans. The Electron Beam Tomography scanner provides painless, noninvasive full body scanning in 10 minutes. We can have our heart, lungs, abdomen, pelvis, bone density, and even our brain scanned. Holistica Hawaii has performed more than 5,000 scans at this writing and has found the most common problem to be hardening of the arteries.

Don Mankin, author and business consultant, found that to be the case. "This test probably saved my life," he said, referring to the Electron Beam Tomography test he took in the form of a heart scan. "With a family history of heart disease and a love of good food, I took it routinely on my own initiative. I had no symptoms of heart disease, but the test clearly showed blockage in one of my coronary arteries. This led to another test that led directly to an angioplasty. I had been planning a backpacking trip scheduled for a few weeks later and, without this test and subsequent angioplasty, I would have opened myself up to the possibility of cardiac arrest in the wilderness where no one could help me."

As we recognize that prevention and self-care will have to be strong components of the health care system of the future, the annual 15-minute checkup by a busy, overscheduled doctor will morph into a high-tech, preventative health care exam that includes a strong educational component. A nurse practitioner or an osteopath might administer it instead of the time-pressed physician. The choice will be ours.

For the well-to-do, companies that specialize in comprehensive physicals such as the Mayo Clinic and Executive Health Group will proliferate, offering both high-tech and high-touch wellness visits and a chance for us to take preventative steps to monitor health. They will also provide copious instruction so we can continue to improve our personal wellness knowledge base and activities.

Similarly, for those willing to pay extra, subscription-based premium health care is beginning to appear in progressive communities such as Seattle, Washington, and south Florida. By paying a subscription price of about $5,000 annually on top of regular health care insurance, a patient receives the kind of care we used to expect from physicians but that no longer exists (until now). Everything from doctors making house calls and giving out their personal cell phone numbers with the advice, "Call me anytime of day or night" to doctors accompanying patients to scary medical tests to hold their hands. For example, Jill Day of Poulsbo, Washington, subscribes to such a service and reported, "On Thursday night, I was just writhing with pain in my colon. I didn't know what it was. I just knew that I could call early in the morning. So at seven o'clock, I called Dr. Nietsche. He answered the phone and said, 'Come on down. Let's see what's going on.' That was a great relief to me."[14]

Jill Day's family pays for this kind of attention. As premium members of the Virginia Mason Medical Center in Seattle, they have a primary care physician with only 300 patients rather than the typical urban physician who might handle as many as 3,000 patients. Virginia Mason Medical Center's Chief of Medicine Robert Mecklenburg says, "What patients want is more self-determination, and control, and choice over their health care. They want to see their doc where and when they want to. They want the convenience they had enjoyed years ago."

The Internet, although not personalized, can offer tremendous convenience and act as a critical partner in providing patients with research, information, and education. In some instances, it can also help us assess our own health care options for little or no cost at all. Although few websites are designed to dispense medicine or make specific diagnoses, many health-related sites do offer in-depth information, answer questions, and can even refer information to the appropriate health professional in a secure, password-protected environment for subscribers.

When Andy Grove, former CEO of Intel, was diagnosed with prostate cancer, he used the Internet as a key partner in figuring out the right path to take. Rather than just following his doctor's orders, he dealt with his illness with the same determination he applied to overcoming a business challenge. He spent weeks doing research on the Internet. He charted all potential treatments that were available, from the experimental to the widely accepted. He contacted the leaders in the field to gain further insight on the most promising therapies and surgical procedures. Finally, he chose what he considered to be the best solution. It wasn't the solution his doctor had suggested, but Grove felt confident it was the right choice for him. He won his battle against cancer, acting as his own commander-in-chief. His revolutionary attitude toward coping with a life-threatening illness landed him on the cover of *Fortune* magazine. The headline read, "Taking on Prostate Cancer." In and of itself, the concept that we can "take on" a deadly disease and win is a new and totally empowering idea.

Health plans will soon offer practical health promotion education classes online, empowering members to proactively take responsibility for their own health care. Participants who pass the test could then be eligible for health plan discounts and other freebies such as at-home diagnostic tests as incentives for self-care and prevention.

Easily available at-home diagnostics and screening tests will more and more replace expensive physician-ordered lab tests. Already these products that detect pregnancy, urinary-tract infections, HIV, sugar levels for diabetics, bone density, drugs and blood in the stool, and even hormone levels are gaining popularity and are widely available on websites and in retail stores. Soon to come will be tests measuring cholesterol levels; other tests will detect yeast infections and sexually transmitted diseases.

At-home gadgets that track health will soon be as common as kitchen appliances. Some already are: for years we've been able to take our temperature, weigh ourselves, and take our heart rate and blood pressure at home. Biofeedback machines that help us regulate our vital signs, for example, might become valuable tools in the fight against heart disease and high blood pressure. The LifeShirt system, already available, monitors 40 health indicators, which can be downloaded through a PDA and then passed on to *www.lifeshirt.com* which, in turn, can pass the information on to our own doctors. Soon digital cameras working with our computers will monitor our skin for melanomas. Sensors on toothbrushes will check saliva to monitor a laundry list of diseases.

In Japan, where the population is aging faster than in many other parts of the world, they are already working hard to come up with home health monitoring systems. In the Warp Square HII House built by Matsushita in Tokyo, sensors in the toilet check body weight, body fat percentages, and urine sugar levels. A health monitoring box takes pulse rate, temperature, and blood pressure. All of this information can be downloaded and transmitted via computer to a personal physician.[15]

An Expanded Spectrum of Health Care

In our new cyclic scenario, in the spirit of *rejuvenation*, the first line of defense in health care will shift from primarily managing disease after it's occurred to preventing or delaying its occurrence. When there is a need for intervention beyond self-care, we will insist on accessing a broader range of mainstream and alternative health care options to promote a complete *recovery*. What all health care options will have in common is Dr. Fries's philosophy to"live long, live healthy, die fast."

Health care professionals of all colors and stripes will need to increase their understanding of how the body and mind change with aging and know how to extend health and vitality as long as possible. The Alliance for Aging Research estimates that the United States alone will need"no fewer than 37,000 geriatricians, four times more than the 8,800 practicing now."[16] Today only 11 out of 125 schools of medicine nationwide even offer courses in this subspecialty, and most primary care physicians have little to no continuing education training in geriatrics. The effect that has on our aging population is chilling: Fully half of all Americans over 65 report that no doctor has ever told them to exercise, let alone which type of exercise might benefit them most. Nurses, pharmacists, and other allied health professionals also lack specific training in the health care needs of people in their second half of life. Medical and nursing schools nationwide as well as continuing education programs will need to offer more courses in geriatric medicine, nutrition, and life extension, including recuperative and rejuvenative medicine.

In the coming years, patient demand coupled with greater mainstream acceptance will bring the development of more health centers that combine the best of the traditional with the best of alternative therapies in an environment that promotes education, health, and emotional support. For instance, the Mind*Body*Spirit Clinic is a unique partnership between the University of Minnesota's Academic Health Center and Fairview Health Services. It offers patients and their families an opportunity to choose the exact kind of health care solution they want, from the traditional to alternative wellness services like yoga, massage, energy balance, meditation, and dream decoding. The focus of all the programs is to "promote interdisciplinary patient care, education, and research that integrates biomedical, complementary, cross-cultural, and spiritual aspects of care." In other words, it's designed to reach patients wherever they might be on the recovery–rejuvenation continuum.

Dr. Dean Ornish and his Preventative Medicine Research Institute have been pioneers on the forefront of recovery from and even reversal of heart disease through a combination of traditional and alternative medical techniques and lifestyle management. In 1983, he began a study, "The Lifestyle Heart Trial," the first of its kind to "demonstrate that heart disease is often reversible by making comprehensive changes in diet and lifestyle." In 1998, he reported the results of a five-year study that "demonstrated even more reversal of heart disease after five years than after one year." The study also found that "almost 80 percent of patients who were eligible for bypass surgery or angioplasty were able to avoid it by changing diet and lifestyle." Mutual of Omaha calculated an average savings of $29,529 per patient. Dr. Ornish turned his study into a self-health lifestyle center affiliated directly with several hospitals in the United States where patients can come not only to take charge of their health, but to reverse their negative health condition. Since he was able to show empirical evidence in terms of health condition reversal and cost savings, several insurance companies have begun to pay for their members' participation, a prime example of how illness and recovery are beginning to be linked in the public eye.

ON THE HORIZON

In the Robert Heinlein novel, *Time Enough for Love*, members of the Howard family were genetically gifted and, by the year 2136, could live at least 150 years. Some were eliminated from the family for the unforgivable sin of "dying of old age too young." Every 40 years or so, they took advantage of rejuvenation therapies to defy the physical signs of aging while still accruing life experience to make them wise. Each family member had a "rejuvenated age" as well as a calendar age.

Obviously the Howards live only in a science fiction novel, but the concept of living long without encountering old age may be a path in the cyclic life that some of us choose to take. There are really many divergent paths to extending our health span and youthfulness quo-tient. Some of them are proven and many are not. Some look familiar: pharmaceutical products such as Lipitor to lower cholesterol and Evista to prevent bone density loss and osteoporosis. Some are verified and straightforward: regular exercise and a nutritionally dense diet. Others are controversial: caloric restriction or human growth hormone injec-tions. Everything from cosmetic surgery to renovate the face and body to heart surgery to renovate an internal organ is now available. These are just the early experiments on the horizon of *ageless aging* and we are the pioneers. Some of the landmarks we encounter on this new frontier could include developing options like these:

- Super nutrition
- Pharmaceutical solutions
- Hormone manipulation
- Bionics and regenerative medicine
- Cosmeceuticals

Super Nutrition
Caloric restriction is a radical but proven rejuvenative method to stay younger longer. The key is to eat a nutritionally dense diet while restricting calories, not an easy feat. Dr. Roy Walford, a 79-year-old UCLA pathologist, is a living experiment in this area. He's lived on 1,200 calories a day for years and looks about 20 years younger than his actual age. Animal studies seem to support the theory that caloric restriction can maintain bone mass, skin thickness, brain function, and immune function. The only trick is making this lifetime commitment to a difficult and still hypothetical path.

In our quest to increase our health spans through recovery and reju-venation strategies, we will avidly experiment with super nutrition products. There will be a merging of food with supplements of all kinds including vitamins, minerals, herbs, and drugs to both fight disease and boost health and vitality. Kurt Landgraf, executive vice-president of Du Pont and director of life science there, predicts, "As we enter 2000 and beyond, we'll see massive changes in the way mankind deals with disease and nutrition. It will include biotech, but also food processing and medicinal claims for supplements and foods like soy which can be proven through clinical trials."[17]

Dr. Stephen Felice, one of the pioneers in super nutrition, coined the phrase *nutraceuticals* defining them as "any substance that may be considered a food or part of a food that provides medical or health benefits, including the prevention and treatment of disease."

Dr. Eric Rimm, one of the authors of a Harvard study on vitamin E and heart disease, is such a believer in this that he has said, "The risk for not taking vitamin E is equivalent to the risk of smoking." The evidence on vitamin E is more mired these days, but this kind of thinking is driving more and more of us to dabble with nutraceuticals of all kinds, mixing and matching at our whim. Forty-five percent of the U.S. population now takes some type of vitamin, mineral, or herbal supplement on their own for increased physical stamina, relaxation, or even to help alleviate aches and pains, according to General Nutrition Centers. (See Figures 7.1 and 7.2.) Ginkgo biloba has been linked with improved memory; ginseng with increased stamina; St. John's Wort fends off depression; and echinacea helps prevent colds and flu. (See Figure 7.3.) A casual walk down the supplements aisle of my local Whole Foods Market reveals thousands of nutraceutical options, available in almost any combination, to combat almost any imaginable ill. Keep in mind, side effects from some of these are beginning to emerge in the research literature. This is new territory.

Supplements are not just taken on their own but are making their way into foods, beverages, and even bottled water for specific health values. (See Figure 7.4.) These are called *functional* or *smart foods*. Clare Hasler, executive director of an interdisciplinary functional-foods program at the University of Illinois, says functional foods are about "removing the bad and enhancing the good." Calcium-enriched orange and cranberry juice and vitamin-fortified cereals have been common for years, but only small doses of essential nutrients have been added to them to prevent acute diseases from striking. Now the goal is broadening to include products that provide us with more energy and vitality and even slow the onset of diseases such as heart disease and diabetes.

Vitamin Type	What It's Good For
Vitamin A Beta-carotene	Helps with growth and repair of tissues, boosts immunity against infection, and improves night vision.
Vitamin B-1 Thiamine	Needed to process fats, proteins, and carbohydrates. Helps form the fuel your body needs to function.
Vitamin B-2 Riboflavin	Processes amino acids and fats. Also activates vitamin B-6 and folic acid.
Vitamin B-3 Niacin	Releases energy from carbohydrates and processes alcohol.
Vitamin B-5 Pantothenic Acid	Converts nutrients into energy. Also essential for processing fats.
Vitamin B-6 Pyridoxine	The principle vitamin for processing amino acids. Also helps convert nutrients into energy.
Vitamin B-12 Cyanocobalamin	Maintains healthy nervous system and assists with blood cell formation.
Folic Acid B Complex	Assists in normal development of cells, especially during pregnancy. Also protects body from amino acids linked to heart disease and stroke.
Vitamin C Ascorbic Acid	Helps heal wounds, strengthen blood vessels, and build resistance to infections.
Vitamin D Calciferol	Strengthens bones and teeth.
Vitamin E Tocopherol	Helps maintain healthy skin. Also shown to reduce risk of heart disease.

Figure 7.1
Common Vitamins
Source: www.bcbsnc.com/html/wellvitasupp.htm

Many believe the nutraceutical industry will be transformed by research into phytochemicals or plant chemicals. There are only 44 nutrients currently known to be essential for health but there are thousands of phytochemicals, some with properties we've yet to discover. Phytochemicals occur naturally in plants and could be the key to halting specific diseases such as breast cancer or heart disease. Cauliflower, for instance, has thousands of phytochemicals, but one in particular—indole-3-carbinol—has been linked to reducing the risk of breast can-

Mineral	What It's Good For
Calcium	Assists development of strong bones, teeth, and muscle tissue. Also regulates heartbeat, muscle action, and nerve function.
Iron	Helps get you the energy needed to function.
Magnesium	Used by the body to form bones, proteins, and fatty acids. Also needed to make new cells, relax muscles, and for blood clotting.
Potassium	Helps body regulate water balance, blood pressure, and nerve-muscle function.
Selenium	Boosts immune system and helps protect against cancer.
Zinc	Helps repair wounds, boosts immunity, maintains fertility. Also shown to shorten the duration of colds.

Figure 7.2
Common Minerals
Source: www.bcbsnc.com/html/wellvitasupp.htm

cer. Sulphoraphane, a phytochemical found in broccoli, has been linked to preventing cancer in laboratory animals. As we discover these phytochemicals and link them with their health benefit, they will begin to appear in foods of all kinds to boost our immune systems and add health and vitality to our lives.

Pharmaceutical Solutions

Traditionally, most pharmaceutical research was devoted to curing acute, fast-acting, infectious diseases. Now our disease model has shifted to a more chronic, degenerative one that requires lifestyle management. Drugs are being designed that help us manage and even recover from some chronic degenerative conditions like high cholesterol, osteoporosis, arthritis pain, memory loss, incontinence, anxiety, weight control, and more. The potential for these drugs to improve our health spans—both as individuals and as a society—is staggering. According to *Business Week*, "Ultimately, the new lifestyle drugs could turn the pharmaceutical industry into an engine of growth for the entire economy."[18]

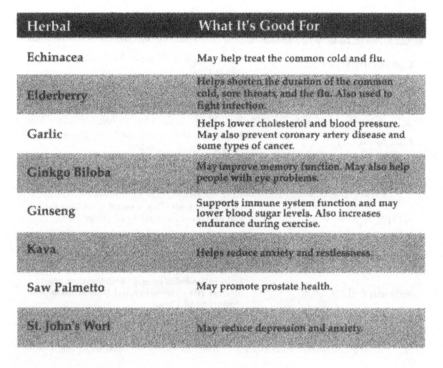

Herbal	What It's Good For
Echinacea	May help treat the common cold and flu.
Elderberry	Helps shorten the duration of the common cold, sore throats, and the flu. Also used to fight infection.
Garlic	Helps lower cholesterol and blood pressure. May also prevent coronary artery disease and some types of cancer.
Ginkgo Biloba	May improve memory function. May also help people with eye problems.
Ginseng	Supports immune system function and may lower blood sugar levels. Also increases endurance during exercise.
Kava	Helps reduce anxiety and restlessness.
Saw Palmetto	May promote prostate health.
St. John's Wort	May reduce depression and anxiety.

Figure 7.3
Common Herbs
Source: www.bcbsnc.com/html/wellvitasupp.htm

For instance, cholesterol-lowering drugs used to be given to only those with very high cholesterol over 250. However, they have had such a positive effect with so few side effects that doctors now recommend them to patients with cholesterol counts as low as 180. That means a large, built-in, long-term market demand for pharmaceutical manufacturers. And one of the benefits for consumers is that it just might provide them with a silver bullet to recover from some specific chronic, degenerative diseases.

What works well for one person may have little or an undesirable impact on another. Charles Cantor, Ph.D., founder of the Human Genome Project and professor of biomedical engineering and pharmacology at Boston University, predicts that personalized medicine using gene analysis to tailor drugs for individuals will soon be developed. Custom-designed drugs that take into account age, genetics, back-

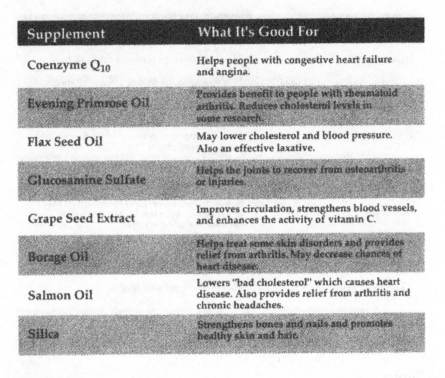

Supplement	What It's Good For
Coenzyme Q_{10}	Helps people with congestive heart failure and angina.
Evening Primrose Oil	Provides benefit to people with rheumatoid arthritis. Reduces cholesterol levels in some research.
Flax Seed Oil	May lower cholesterol and blood pressure. Also an effective laxative.
Glucosamine Sulfate	Helps the joints to recover from osteoarthritis or injuries.
Grape Seed Extract	Improves circulation, strengthens blood vessels, and enhances the activity of vitamin C.
Borage Oil	Helps treat some skin disorders and provides relief from arthritis. May decrease chances of heart disease.
Salmon Oil	Lowers "bad cholesterol" which causes heart disease. Also provides relief from arthritis and chronic headaches.
Silica	Strengthens bones and nails and promotes healthy skin and hair.

Figure 7.4
Common Supplements
Source: www.bcbsnc.com/html/wellvitasupp.htm

ground, and personal concerns will rid us of many of the negative side effects of drugs and even improve the efficacy of others.

Someday gene therapy may replace pharmaceutical solutions to provide more permanent solutions. For instance, Trinity Bivalacqua of Tulane University has successful experiments already underway using gene therapy to restore virility to older men. Research has shown that a specific enzyme that declines with age is needed for erections to occur. Using a weakened virus to deliver extra copies of the gene that creates that enzyme in the body, Bivalacqua and his colleagues were able to increase that enzyme level threefold in aged rats. Someday soon, the rejuvenation drug Viagra could be replaced by annual or biannual gene therapy injections. According to Bivalacqua, "Obviously, that's where the future is."[19]

Hormone Manipulation

Estrogen, progesterone, testosterone, human growth hormone (HGH), DHEA, and melatonin are naturally-occurring hormones linked with youthfulness. As the years pass, the natural levels of these hormones decrease. If we can raise the levels artificially, we can perhaps improve health and well-being. Some claim the whole process of aging seems to be stopped in its tracks and even to reverse itself, taking the concepts of recovery and rejuvenation to an entirely new level. Each of these hormones represents a potential bonanza to manufacturers and perhaps an answer to the antiaging puzzle. On the other hand, hormone manipulation is an area that's in its infancy, still highly experimental, and mired in controversy.

Although hormone replacement has demonstrated tremendous antiaging benefits, there are also huge potential risks linked with these therapies. HGH is considered the "master hormone" by Dr. Ronald Klatz, one of the founders of the American Academy of Anti-Aging Medicine and author of *Grow Young with HGH:* "It transforms itself into new hormones, stimulates others, and dispatches them to do their duty—squirted out in tiny pulses by the pituitary gland while we sleep."[20] His theory is that HGH levels begin to lower while we're still in our thirties. As a result, muscle tone, bone strength, sex drive, and feelings of vitality decline. Klatz believes HGH supplements could not only make us look and feel better but also help ward off chronic disease and even extend the human life span. Klatz says, "HGH treatments are like upgrading your microprocessor from a 286 to a Pentium chip."

Despite strong concerns about possible side effects, thousands of doctors now prescribe HGH as an antiaging therapy. Yet it is unapproved by the FDA for this purpose. It's also very pricey. None of this seems to deter those who swear by its effect on the way they look and feel.

Estrogen replacement through herbs or pharmaceuticals or some combination is more common but more controversial than ever. Many have believed that replacing estrogen can protect against heart disease, osteoporosis, and even Alzheimer's disease while rejuvenating skin, bone, and muscle. However, estrogen therapy seems to increase the risk of breast cancer and even blood clots which can cause strokes. That, however, may be just the tip of the iceberg. On July 9, 2002, the

National Institutes of Health chose to halt a major study because of alarming results. They announced publicly that the long-term use of estrogen and progestin seemed to significantly increase the risk of not only invasive breast cancer and blood clots but also heart attacks. These findings suggested that just a yearlong use of estrogen and progestin increased an otherwise healthy woman's risk of a heart attack by 29 percent, breast cancer by 24 percent, and stroke by 41 percent. Although a number of previous studies have linked hormone use with a decreased risk of heart disease, the current analysis suggests that other variables may have been responsible for these positive results. Even the benefits of hormone replacement therapy on osteoporosis have been called into question. Clearly, we are still confused about the best course of action for women about to go through menopause to take. And, there are 38 million boomer women who are, or soon will be, going through menopause, looking for solutions of some kind.

Just as women lose estrogen as they age, the testosterone levels of men drop about 10 percent per decade. Testosterone patches or gels can increase muscle strength, bone-mineral density, and libido; the downside is that it increases the risk of prostate cancer, heart attack, and stroke.

Another androgen, or male hormone, with promising antiaging potential is DHEA (dehydroepiandrosterone). Its touted benefits include increased energy and sex drive for both sexes, and an enhanced ability to lose fat and gain lean muscle mass. Its long-term effects, however, are unknown as are the potential side effects of megadoses.

The final hormone in the antiaging mix, melatonin, is produced naturally in the pineal gland. A derivative of the amino acid tryptophan, melatonin supplements promote regular sleep cycles and reportedly hasten recovery from jet lag. To date, studies on melatonin show few dangerous side effects, but, again, long-term effects are simply not known.

Bionics and Regenerative Medicine
A heart pacemaker to extend life, a hip replacement to restore mobility, or contact lenses to enhance sight or change the color of eyes—these are all bionic devices we've taken advantage of for decades. And each

helps us to extend the number of years we're actively engaged in life; each has also been improving with technologic advances. New breakthroughs such as retinal implants, bionic limbs, and artificial hearing are about to enter the marketplace.

Technology will continue to be a key tool to repair our broken or tired parts in the recovery stages we cycle through. However, someday, bionic parts may be seen in the same light as iron lungs. Many scientists theorize that we are at the forefront of a new type of medicine, tissue engineering or regenerative medicine, that may make our bionic parts seem like remnants of the past. William A. Haseltine, a leading genetic scientist and chief executive of Human Genome Sciences in Rockville, Maryland, believes, "We are at the dawn of a profound revolution in medicine. The chemical era of medicine may, in retrospect, appear to be a clumsy effort to patch rather than permanently repair broken bodies. Cellular replacement may keep us young and healthy forever."

The future of medicine may rely heavily on tissue engineering to replace or regenerate living body parts that are diseased or degenerated through the aging process. Haseltine foresees a time when rather than getting an organ transplant, doctors transplant the precursor seeds instead. "In the future, rather than cutting open the body to provide it with a new heart, we might grow a new heart right inside the body."[21]

We may be edging closer to that ideal recovery scenario that Haseltine describes. To date, the best approach to advanced heart disease has been a heart transplant. However, few hearts are available for transplants, it's expensive, and it can be a very risky procedure. For the past 30 years or more, scientists have been researching methods to regenerate heart tissue without success. Recently Bioheart, Inc., a Fort Lauderdale, Florida, company, successfully regenerated damaged hearts by implanting cells taken from the thigh.

Regenerated or lab grown bone, cartilage, blood vessels, and skin are being tested as well. The FDA has already approved living skin, Apligraf, to treat leg ulcers. A product already exists that regrows knee cartilage. Bones to create new jaws or limbs can be grown from stem cells inserted into a porous material and cut to specific shapes for specific needs—jaws, arms, or legs. Cartilage is being developed that can replace the urethra.[22]

Bladders, breasts, hearts, fingers, and the pancreas are taking shape in laboratories. Doctors at Children's Hospital in Boston have grown bladders from skin cells and implanted them in sheep. Dr. Anthony Atala of Children's Hospital in Boston plans to grow a bladder from stem cells and implant them into humans. Cells that manufacture insulin are being encapsulated and injected into the abdomen to replace the pancreas. This has already been successfully tested on animals and could be in human trials soon.

Tissue engineering is still in its infancy. Yet, it may offer us all an opportunity to rejuvenate our broken body parts just like the Howard family in *Time Enough for Love*. Then suddenly chronologic age may really lose its relevancy entirely.

Cosmeceuticals

As we cycle through the various lifestages, we may discover ways to increase our health span effectively and feel more youthful. Some of us will also choose to go further down the rejuvenation path to *look* younger as well.

Most women today think nothing of shaving or waxing their legs; they also use coloring, highlighting, or even hair extensions to lengthen or thicken their hair. It's a long time since anyone asked or cared, "Does she or doesn't she?" Everyone today assumes she does. The question is: How far will we go to artificially appear more youthful in a long-lived society?

More than half of all adults say they are concerned with looking good. A recent Roper Starch Worldwide Survey showed that at least 80 percent of women in all age groups feel that maintaining an attractive physical appearance is either essential or important.[23] More than half say they are more than willing to incorporate products into their daily maintenance routines that help them reverse the signs of aging. And they already are. For example, more than half of those 35 and older use hair coloring to hide gray hair.

Over the last several years, the antiaging cosmeceutical industry has grown exponentially. In 1998, Americans spent $548 million on over-the-counter antiaging products. Industry analysts expect that number to go as high as $835 million by 2003, according to the Freedonia Group, a Cleveland market research firm.[24] Daily maintenance cosmeceuticals like vitamins and antioxidants will be the prime antiaging option for many. Available in topical creams and lotions, vitamin C is used to improve the tone and texture of the skin. Renova and Retin A are the only FDA-approved prescription drugs for wrinkle reduction. These two creams are vitamin A derivatives used to improve pigmentation and stimulate the deposit of new collagen and elastic tissue in the dermis to even skin tone and reduce wrinkles. Alpha-hydroxy acids available in a variety of products have been proven to help the skin shed dead cells for a smoother, younger-looking appearance. Also popular are teeth whitening systems that help older, yellowing teeth gain back a more youthful shade of white.

Temporary rejuvenative procedures that can be done in the comfort of a doctor's or aesthetician's office with no downtime are also becoming widely accepted. More than 30 percent of women ages 30 to 50 think it's fine for people to utilize procedures that help them look younger, but believe having cosmetic surgery is going too far. According to Dr. Harold Brody, a dermatological surgeon based in Atlanta, Georgia, "People don't really want the *done* look of a full face-lift that was so popular 10 years ago. For this generation, it's too plastic."[25]

With this information in mind, more and more procedures are being done as lunchtime maintenance sessions rather than big procedures that keep us out of commission for a week or more. For instance, instead of going for trichloroacetic acid peels that require 10 days of downtime, we're opting for alpha-hydroxy acid peels that don't require any downtime at all. The effects aren't as radical, but they can be done as often as we like. Even more popular are the laser peels that require no downtime but are done once a month for five or six months and help develop new collagen that can result in plumper and smoother looking skin. And injectables like collagen and Botox to erase wrinkles temporarily are becoming more common as well. The pipeline of available products to inject will keep increasing and improving. The next generation of these products will probably have less risk and more benefit, maybe even last longer. Just as we once saw tanning salons proliferate, expect to see day spas, salons, health clubs, and clinics that offer a menu of procedures—from botox shots to cold laser treatments, from hair replacement to collagen injections—gain popularity.

CONCLUSION

"Live long, live healthy, die fast" will be one of our mantras in the cyclic life, put in action through a lifetime commitment to recovery and rejuvenation. We will work hard to maintain our health and vitality for as long as possible so that we can continue to cycle in and out of LifeCycle events throughout our long lives rather than succumb to illness and a sedentary existence until death.

Self-responsibility and personal empowerment will become watchwords of health care. Physicians and the health care system will be our allies and advisors rather than our health care decision makers. The spectrum of traditional and alternative health care options will increase and be ours to access and select at our discretion. Recovering from serious illness to live long, healthy lives rather than sedentary existences will become the norm. Rejuvenation medicine including experimentation with supernutrition, pharmaceutical solutions, hormone manipulation, bionics, and regenerative medicines as well as cosmeceuticals and many options not yet available will become common. We are the pioneers who will help pave the path toward bringing the feeling of youth with us into the middle and later years of our long, cyclic lives.

METAMORPHOSIS: RETIRING RETIREMENT

In the last century, retirement became accepted as the final life passage in the linear life. When the U.S. national retirement program, Social Security, was implemented in the 1930s, it provided a brief respite from work and mainstream life to rest, reflect, and prepare for the end of life. Social Security enabled people to live Webster's definition of retirement: "To withdraw, recede, disappear; to take out of circulation."

Today, retirement has evolved into several decades of downtime, spent in leisure, adventure, or boredom, depending on circumstances. What retirement means in the cyclic life will likely be yet another incarnation, with myriad options that will include some form of work for most of us. But before we dare predict where the institution of retirement is going, we need to understand how it originally came to be.

A RUDE AWAKENING

Even in the linear life, retirement has only briefly—and lately—been the status quo. At its core, the institution of retirement was founded on the twin beliefs that the older members of society must be removed from the workforce to make room for the young, and that aging itself was a disability that rendered older people incapable of working to support themselves. Each prong of the argument squarely pointed retirees out of the mainstream of society, into a state of relative isolation.

By contrast, throughout most of history, our ancestors worked until they were physically unable to do so any longer. Elders were an essential part of everyday life, a link between generations, passing on history, tradition, and life skills. Wise old sage was the role of most older adults. Thomas Jefferson, for example, embraced this point of view when he wrote that he "wished to be able, in the winter nights of old age, to recount to those around him what he has heard and learned in the heroic age" he had lived through.[1]

This reverential perception of the elderly began to change in the mid-1800s due primarily to a religious and social movement of the time known as the Second Great Awakening led by the evangelist, Charles Grandison Finney, founder of Oberlin College. Though little remembered today, it may be the genesis of society's current dismissive attitude toward older adults and their value to society.

The Second Great Awakening preached that the old had their chance to improve the world, had failed to some degree, and were thus responsible for society's problems. Youth, on the other hand, represented 100 percent of society's opportunity to advance and improve. *They* held the promise of the future while the old represented the mistakes of the past. *Old* equaled deterioration; *youth* equaled hope for the future.

It's no coincidence that about the same time the westernized world was transitioning to a more industrialized world. Many were leaving the rural farms to seek their fortune in the city. For example, at the beginning of the nineteenth century there were scarcely two dozen cities in Europe with a population of 100,000, but by 1900 there were more than 150 cities of this size. The new class of industrial workers included men, women, and children laboring in the textile mills, pottery works, and mines. And brute strength was often recognized as an asset to this new way of life.

Suddenly aging was no longer seen as the natural progression of life, with maturity a stage of wisdom and power. Instead, it was an incurable disease. I. L. Nascher, the physician who developed the modern field of geriatric medicine, described the old as inferior, a burden: "The old man does not know what is best for him . . . he cannot accommodate himself to new conditions brought about by the progress of civilization."

As this negative attitude took hold, the old began to lose respect and status. By the late 1800s, society increasingly defined them as a *problem*. People tried to hide the appearance of being old, concealing such physical manifestations as graying hair or false teeth. Physicians advised elders to "lead an absolutely quiet and uneventful life." Dr. William Osler, a prominent physician of the time, even suggested it would be an"incalculable benefit . . . in commercial, political and professional life if, as a matter of course, men stopped work at *that* age."[2] That age was 60.

The concept of retirement was born. It was designed to rid society of the burden of the old, albeit in a socially responsible, benevolent manner. In so doing, society could make room for its young, valuable members in the modern age.

BENEVOLENT SOLUTION

By 1875 the influence of the Second Great Awakening had spread throughout Europe. That year, Otto von Bismarck confronted the dilemma of an aging Prussian army. His "benevolent solution" was the world's first large-scale pension plan—a precursor to most retirement systems today—intended to rid the army of older soldiers to make room for young recruits.

Chancellor Bismarck could have chosen any number of specific disabilities to help define eligibility, but he chose *age* as the single criterion. At the time, average life expectancy in Germany was only in the mid-30s (worldwide, it was age 47). Bismarck's plan was to create a program that would appear generous but never pay out much in benefits; he chose 65 as the retirement age. And so, he arbitrarily defined old age for all of us, linking retirement directly with chronologic age, and the notion of old age with disability and the end of usefulness.

A kind of human planned obsolescence began to take shape. Bismarck's demarcation point of age 65 took hold, becoming the designated age for removal from an active, productive work life in both the public and private sectors.

In less than a century, the elderly had transformed from powerful, respected contributors to society to vulnerable dependents whose very subsistence was tied closely to the goodwill of their families and communities. Once retired, they were no longer encouraged to contribute to society or even their own families.

The Great Depression cemented the sinking position of elders in postindustrial society. Families that had helped provide for their elderly relatives were barely able to make ends meet themselves and needed economic relief. At the same time, American business desperately needed to cut costs and rid itself of its oldest, highest paid workers while getting younger men into the workforce and off the streets.

As a result, in the 1930s, the Social Security Act was passed in the United States. Emerging from the trauma of the Great Depression, Social Security was established, according to President Franklin Delano Roosevelt, to "prevent a poverty-ridden old age." Like Bismarck, Roosevelt defined old age as 65. That year, life expectancy in the United States was not quite 63.

Mass retirement, unheard of a short time before, soon became the new status quo. Until Bismarck's time, more than 75 percent of men 65+ remained in the workforce. By 1900 that number dropped to 63 percent; by 1950, fewer than half worked. At the start of the new millennium, fewer than 20 percent of 65+ men were gainfully employed. (See Figure 8.1.)

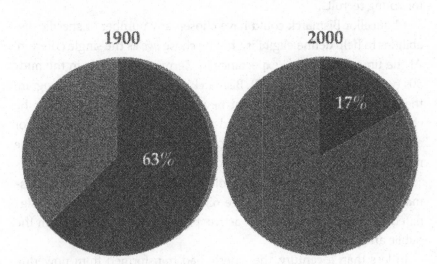

Figure 8.1
Men 65+ in the U.S. Labor Force
Source: United States Bureau of the Census, 2000.

THE DOUBLE-EDGED SWORD

At its inception, Social Security was a tremendous relief to aging Americans in the wake of the Great Depression. The elderly could now be far less dependent on the goodwill of their families or community. The fear of an old age filled with abject poverty subsided as older workers willingly stepped aside to make way for the young.

But the Social Security system sliced through America's post-depression fear of poverty with a double-edged sword. On one edge, there was more federally supported economic security for the elderly than ever before. But on the other, *old* was now defined in chronological terms, beginning at age 65 when physical and mental deterioration officially took hold and rendered us no longer valuable. Suddenly, whatever status or importance men and women had earned through a lifetime of hard work simply vanished. Boston gerontologist Natalie Cabot describes it this way, "Nobody ever suddenly becomes Negro or Jewish, but people do suddenly become 'retired.'" She adds that within three weeks of retirement, a retiree would realize, "he is no longer anything at all." A retired factory foreman of the day explains, "I can't think of anything useful I can do anymore."[3]

We had collectively made a bargain to support the old, partly to make room for the young who needed to work to support their families, and partly because we believed the elderly were no longer capable of supporting themselves. If ill-conceived, this was at least fiscally manageable. At that time, there were 40 workers for each retiree.

An Enforced Vacation

Ironically, just as mass retirement became the status quo, modern medicine made great strides to help us live longer in better health. During the 1950s, the elderly population had grown twice as fast as the population at large. By 1960, the elderly were identified as the fastest growing minority group in America and the cost of subsidizing them was beginning to be seen as a potential problem.

Always on high alert to new opportunity, the business community spotted this growing conundrum and, in response, invented *the leisure lifestyle of the golden years.* In 1951 the Corning Corporation hosted a conference on the relationship between leisure and retirement. The conference defined retirement as the stage of life when there is an "absence of ideas about what to do with oneself." They recommended a national educational effort aimed at everyone over age 50 to alter the image of retirement and introduce soon-to-be elders to the joys of leisure for leisure's sake. The conference chairman, Lynn White Jr., president of Mills College in Oakland, California, described America as on the brink of a new frontier of leisure and consumption. He suggested a national campaign to "glamorize leisure."[4]

This public relations campaign worked. It wasn't long before real estate developers began to see the opportunity to create living enclaves designed specifically for the elderly—together, but separate from mainstream society. Del Webb, the developer of Sun City, one of the first and most well-known retirement communities, invented the phrase *the golden years*. His strategy was to create a new kind of retirement that would be a haven away from the hustle and bustle of mainstream life. Aimed at middle-class retirees, Webb's vision offered retirees the opportunity to move to warm climates, like the rich, but in affordable communities exclusively designed for them. No children or young people were allowed. Age segregation was positioned as a positive selling point so that homeowners no longer needed to feel put down or overlooked by the younger generations. Other selling points included building new friendships within the same age group and activities such as golf, exercise classes, and art workshops. Elders could now build their own world devoted to leisure and recreation. At the opening of Sun City in 1960, 100,000 enthusiastic golden-agers appeared.

This redefinition of retirement life caught on and expanded so that today retirement is directly linked with the leisure lifestyle and almost seen as part of the American Dream. No longer one step from the grave, retirement is now viewed as a chance to enjoy life without the responsibilities and burdens thrust upon younger people. And Social Security helps guarantee those leisure years are spent with at least some level of financial security.

Time for a Change
Things have, once again, changed.

1. The continued extension of life expectancy in the next few decades could nearly double the senior population. (See Figure 8.2.)

2. The financial wherewithal of older Social Security beneficiaries could mean that society's poorest are subsidizing its wealthiest segment.

3. Now just over three workers, not 40, support each retiree, and those numbers are shrinking.

THE LONGEVITY REVOLUTION

According to best-selling author and feminist Betty Friedan, "The idea of retiring at age 65 is obsolete. It is based on an outdated life expectancy." Today we have extended average life expectancy in the United States all the way to 77—and the United States is hardly the most long-lived of nations. The United States is ranked number 35 worldwide in life expectancy, behind Montenegro, Ireland, and Denmark.

The National Institute of Aging, a rather conservative prognosticator, predicts by the year 2050, average U.S. life expectancy will be between

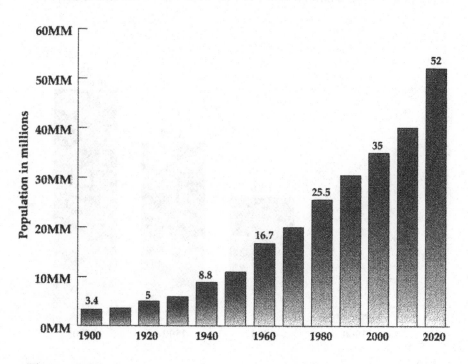

Figure 8.2
Growth of 65+ U.S. Population, 1900–2020
Source: United States. Bureau of the Census, 1996.

90 and 95. And that doesn't even take into account any new biotechnology breakthroughs. National Institute on Aging demographer James Vaupel believes that we are about to enter "a new paradigm of aging" where average life expectancy could soon reach 100 or more. Robert Butler, former director of the National Institute on Aging, suggests that in this new paradigm "work expectancy" needs to increase along with "life expectancy."

But Dr. Butler's rational proposition flies in the face of what is really happening in America. Today's average retiree spends almost 20 years in retirement and that number is projected to go up. That means if we were to opt for early retirement at, say, age 55 and live until age 90, we'd be spending more than half of our adult lives in retirement. (See Figure 8.3.)

In addition to living longer and retiring earlier, today's retirement realities involve the financial status of the over-65 population. As I earlier pointed out, Franklin Roosevelt established the Social Security Act,

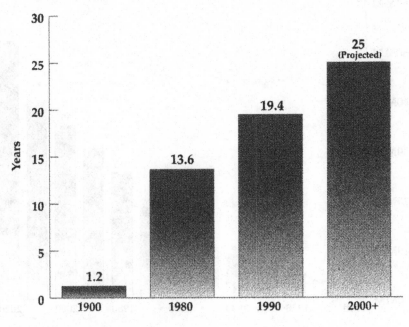

Figure 8.3
Years in Retirement, 1900–2020

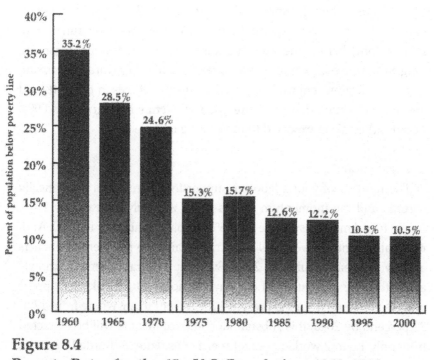

Figure 8.4
Poverty Rates for the 65+ U.S. Population, 1960–2000
United States Bureau of the Census, Current Population Reports, 2000.

in part, to "prevent a poverty-ridden old age." However, during the past half century, this group has gone from being the poorest segment of society to being the richest through a combination of saving, investing, pension programs, and the windfall profits from rising home costs. In the United States, for instance, the over-65 population has the highest level of per capita household wealth of any age group. There are nearly 1 million millionaires receiving Social Security payments. And the sad news is that, at the same time, the under-18 population has become the poorest segment of our society.[5]

In the leisure lifestyle paradigm, we must reevaluate whether it makes sense for the less affluent segments of our population to struggle to support the more affluent segments because of a contract between generations put into place under a different and outdated set of demographic and economic realities.

However, many of today's retirees never expected to live as long as they will and their planning reflects it. Although they were diligent savers and are careful spenders, these retirees may still run out of money long before they die, because their expectations regarding longevity were based on yesterday's realities. In other words, the luxury cars and vacations enjoyed by today's youthful retirees in their 60s and 70s may be costing them a secure financial picture in their 80s and 90s, decades they never expected to fund in the first place.

POPULATION SHIFTS

The number of young laborers supporting retirees has dramatically shrunk, and the momentum of this trend will only increase. By 2040, one in four Americans will be over 65, double the number in 1990. And, if Social Security as we know it today prevails, the number of beneficiaries will at least double by 2040. Even the Federal Reserve acknowledges that the percentage of our payroll income it will take to support retirees will jump from the present 11.5 percent to anywhere from 17 to 22 percent. By 2040, this substantial chunk of income will be extracted from only 1.6 to 2 workers per retiree, a considerable shortfall from the 40:1 worker-to-retiree ratio that ushered in the era of Social Security in Roosevelt's day.

Translating this to financial terms, we are heading toward a financial deadlock. We now spend about one-third of the federal budget on the elderly through Social Security, Medicare, and Medicaid. (See Figure 8.5.) If we maintain the status quo, four out of every five dollars in the U.S. budget will go to supporting the elderly. At the same time, the funds to pay for the war on terror are coming directly from the Social Security trust fund, further eroding the financial wherewithal of that institution.

THE BOOMER VARIABLE

There is, of course, another variable to factor into a new retirement scenario, and it's a big one. Boomers, the largest population segment ever, rarely follow the status quo. The idea that they'll just disappear or recede when they hit age 65 doesn't seem likely, especially as more of them become LifeCyclers. And just because the government tells them they're old at 65, they are not likely to agree.

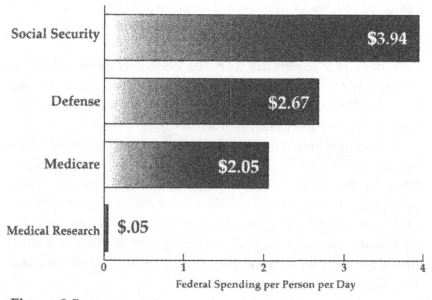

Figure 8.5
U.S. Spending Priorities
Source: NCHS, 1999.

Health conscious, vital, and productive, many see themselves as at least partly defined by their work. They are not about to remove themselves from mainstream society into an enforced vacation simply because they're encouraged to do so.

Not surprisingly, even though traditional retirement is the only model we presently have for what to do after age 65, 80 percent of boomers say they plan to do some form of work well after that age, according to a recent AARP/Roper Starch Worldwide survey. According to Yankelovich Monitor, among those employed, more than half like the idea of starting a new career or job when they reach traditional retirement age. One in 20 boomers plans to work full-time in a new job or career. One in six expects to start a business if he or she does retire.[6]

Eric Greenberg, director of management at the American Management Association, summarizes: "Boomers are going to be in the workforce far longer than their parents were. Boomers marry later, have children later and encounter college costs later than their parents. That, combined with low saving rates and the fact that most people can't sustain their lifestyles on Social Security payments alone, is going to result in people working longer."[7]

In reality, most boomers will not be able to afford retirement even if they wanted to take the traditional route. Savings rates today are at an all-time low. (See Figure 8.6.) A full 40 percent of boomers have less than $10,000 in personal savings. Practically speaking, only about one-third of those inching toward age 65 today have saved enough for the traditional form of retirement. To make matters worse, The Retirement Confidence Survey of 2001 found a drop in the percentage of workers saving for retirement as well as a drop in confidence in their ability to meet retirement income goals. And, when the events of September 11, 2001, coupled with the corporate accounting scandals drove us further toward recession and a bear market, those of us who had invested saw huge losses.

Nearly nine out of ten boomers recognize that "the government has made financial promises to their generation that it will never be able to keep." Further, five out of every six boomers agree that individuals, not the government, should be the ones primarily responsible for providing their own retirement income.[8]

And, what about pensions? As I've pointed out in Chapter 3, with the changing direction of our work lives, fewer than half of all workers have pensions of any kind. Defined-benefit pensions, the status quo in the past, have been replaced by defined-contribution programs, requiring employees to take the lead in contributing money while their employers sometimes match funds. This further puts both the financial burden and responsibility of retirement directly on the shoulders of each of us. It's a good thing that 8 of every 10 boomers intend to keep working to some degree after the age of 65; they'll need to.

RETIRING RETIREMENT

Retirement as we know it today is about to retire. In the cyclic life, most people won't seek it and most won't be able to afford it. In its place, the LifeCycle revolution will free us up to move in and out of periods of

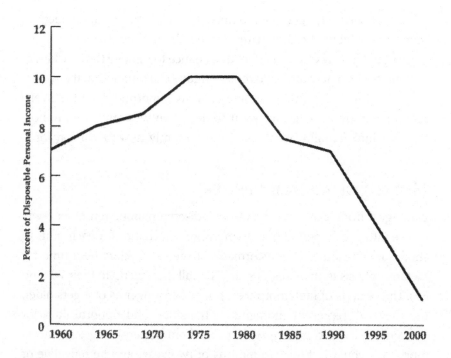

Figure 8.6
Personal Savings Rates, 1960–2000
Source: Bureau of Economic Analysis, Department of Commerce.

work and productivity, as well as leisure or reflection based on our own needs, interests, abilities, and discretion rather than on an arbitrary marker that signals disability and encourages removal from mainstream society. However, each of us will be the primary responsible party for funding that lifestage, at whatever age it arrives and for however long it might last.

The underpinnings of Social Security are based on the notion that old age is a disability, rendering us incapable of earning a living or providing useful contributions to society. Based on yesterday's realities and expectations, this kind of thinking limits our freedom, choices, and perspective of who we might be, how we might contribute to the greater good, how we might live, and how we might feel inspired; and it does so through an arbitrary age marker no longer relevant to anything but history.

Further, we no longer need to make room for the young. In fact, we might face a labor shortage without the help of older workers.

The LifeCycle revolution offers us a chance to remove the shackles of age and create a new model to replace traditional retirement. It empowers each of us to plan these moments of metamorphosis and reinvention for ourselves—what we want to do, when we want to do it, how long we think it might last and, most importantly, how *we* will pay for it.

MODELS OF METAMORPHOSIS

Unhinged from age stereotypes and discrimination, retirement will evolve into a fluid period of metamorphosis, a chance for each of us to shed our old skin and transform. We'll see LifeCyclers take time for metamorphosis in their 20s, 30s, and 40s, all the way up to their 70s and 80s. The periods of metamorphosis might last longer as one gets older, but they will represent moments of transition and opportunities for reinvention *not* a complete withdrawal from society. Stages of metamorphosis could last for two months or two years and be reflective or active, stationary or far-ranging, depending on individual needs and desires. And each of us might go through metamorphoses several times in our lives. They might include a long stretch of leisure time or none at all. They could focus on raising a child, caring for a dying parent or partner, volunteering for an important social cause, studying or teaching, mentoring someone with great potential, living in a foreign land, writing a book, joining the Peace Corps, or planting a garden. Anything we want it to be! Metamorphosis offers a chance for us to catch our breath, take stock, and then reinvent ourselves anew.

John Glenn was ahead of his time on the path to metamorphosis. He reinvented his career many times, each time reaching great heights and contributing something valuable to the world. Growing up in the Midwest in a time where life resembled a Norman Rockwell painting, Glenn attended high school and college in Ohio and married his childhood sweetheart. He entered the Naval Aviation Cadet Academy in 1942. The following year, he started his first career in the military; he was commissioned in the Marine Corps and flew combat missions in World War II and the Korean War. After 16 years as a military pilot, he applied for and was selected as a Project Mercury astronaut. He moved to Houston and worked for NASA for about six years. During that time, he piloted the first manned orbital mission of the United States aboard *Friendship 7* in 1962. At the time he was 40 and there was a lot of concern that he might be too old to venture into space. Glenn retired from his career as an astronaut in 1964 and from the military in 1965.

The next decade Glenn spent as a businessman, but soon found another career that he enjoyed even more: politics. By 1974, Glenn was elected to the U.S. Senate and spent 25 years in that career. But, while still officially serving in the Senate, Glenn took a sabbatical to train for and fly one more time for NASA. At age 78, he flew as a crewmember for 10 days aboard the space shuttle *Discovery.*

Military pilot, astronaut, businessman, senator, and astronaut again. He's also written books, given speeches, and served as part of the board of directors for a variety of corporations. John Glenn has been a pioneer on the path of reinvention.[9]

Scott Oki grew up in a traditional family in Seattle with traditional visions of retirement. His father was a postal worker and his mom a secretary. Since money was always tight, the family would spend hours tying fish flies for extra income. Soon after getting his MBA, Scott went to work at Microsoft as one of only 200 employees. After spending more than nine years at Microsoft, he did what many people only dream of. He retired at age 42, fully expecting to play golf and live a traditional retiree lifestyle.

Instead, Scott spends 80 percent of his time working with charities that he cares about. Two years after leaving Microsoft, Scott and his wife, Laurie, started Nancy & Webster, a baby-blanket company that makes beautiful, all-cotton blankets and donates all its profits to Seattle-area children's charities. Scott also endows the Oki Foundation, which supports child-related causes in the Seattle area. "We wanted to focus on one area and make an impact," he explains. And, recently, his love for golf has motivated him to try his hand at developing a golf course near where he lives. Who knows what else he'll add to the mix in the coming years?

Some of us might take paths similar to Glenn or Oki; others might reinvent themselves a number of times throughout their lives based on needs, passions, and long-term financial wherewithal; still others might

find one path to which they can devote their entire lives. Choice will be
the wellspring of opportunity. And self-responsibility will be the engine
that drives it.

Paths to Reinvention

The many paths leading to reinvention will be as varied and individual
as we are. We can, however, expect those life paths to contain a few
common elements and follow some common themes. Freud wrote that
"love and work" were the two basic needs of man. Maslow expanded
upon this theory and outlined different levels of needs from basic survival up the scale to self-actualization. Level three is described as *living
a life of purpose.* Many of us will find purpose by cycling in and out of
traditional LifeCycles like education, work, and recreation, and also by
discovering the value inherent in giving something back.

LIFELONG LEARNING

As we examined in Chapter 2, *Lifelong Learners,* education will occur
often throughout life. Some of it will be formal, much of it will not be.
For example, when Rebecca Latimer, author of *You're Not Old Until
You're Ninety,* reflected on her life at age 92, she said, "With all honesty,
I'd rather be a very old woman than a very young woman. When I was
younger, I was an unhappy misfit as the wife of an American Foreign
Service officer." Once she and her husband, Fred, settled down in New
Hampshire to retire, her intellectual curiosity woke up. "I don't think I
realized how handicapped I was at 60. I thought only that I wanted to
make the most of the time I had left, but if we think of our starting point
as zero, then I was at minus zero. I was loaded down with inhibitions."

Latimer began her own self-designed education process at that
point. She studied meditation and the human potential philosophers
of her day—Aldous Huxley, Carlos Castaneda, George Gurdjieff, and
Alan Watts. She began to form some important realizations that influenced her life's direction: "the nearer you get to the end of your life, the
less you mind the thought of death." That message liberated her, and
that's when she felt her life truly began. Rejuvenated and inspired, she
adds, "It is positively dangerous to hold opinions we acquired 40 years
ago."

WORK

Cyclic careers will be such an essential ingredient in the cyclic life that I've devoted Chapter 3 to this subject. Most of us will opt to do some form of work throughout our lives, both because we'll still have to earn at least some money, and because we'll also enjoy the challenge. In addition, none of us need to spend 20 to 30 years in enforced leisure. Second and third careers based on our interests rather than society's or family expectations will soon become more the norm. Though their incarnations are myriad, many second or third careers will again contain common threads, embracing such elements as renewed hobbies, increased flexibility, phased retirement, bridge employment, mentoring, and internship.

Trish Millines's second career started while she was still in her first and was something she worked hard to design. She grew up poor in Belmar, New Jersey. Her father wasn't part of her life at all, and her mother cleaned floors for a living. A basketball scholarship offered her the chance to go to college and her love of technology gave her a first career. After graduation, she began work at Microsoft. While she was still working there, she knew she wanted to help kids from low-income backgrounds discover technology. She cashed out from Microsoft and, although she didn't retire a millionaire, she had enough money to live comfortably to pursue her dream. She teamed up with social worker Jill Hull and started *Technology Access Foundation,* a nonprofit dedicated to teaching teens about computer hardware, software, and cyberspace. "This is the best job I've ever had. I've always known that I wanted to do something like this. I love it."[10]

Ideally, our second and third careers will offer the chance to do what we always dreamed of, while we keep our minds active and our pocketbooks full. Turning a hobby into part-time work could become the goal of many. For instance, Kate Burkart had been an advertising executive before her son, Will, was born. Like many new mothers, Kate took a sabbatical from work until Will started school, and then she started her second career as a singer in a rock band that performs at corporate events.

Julie Penfold was a magazine editor until her daughter, Brooke, was born. She wanted to devote most of her time to Brooke, but, once Brooke started school, Julie started freelancing as an editorial assistant.

It quickly dawned on her that she missed being with Brooke, playing and teaching her about life. She immediately realized she much preferred being with children and helping them learn than sitting in front of a computer all day by herself, editing someone else's words. So she went back to school to become a schoolteacher. And now that she's going back to work full-time, her husband, Bart, is taking a sabbatical from his corporate position to try to figure out what he wants to do next.

Similarly, James Cally was an executive with Apple Computers who dreamed of writing books, not managing people. He finally got up his nerve to pursue his dream career as a writer. The examples go on and on. With that in mind, career reinvention counselors will be in high demand as many of us try to adapt our passions and interests into moneymaking exercises.

As we continually gain skills, wisdom, and experience, we may choose to dial down and work less than 24/7. In focus groups with people close to retirement, the one change group members looked forward to the most was the flexibility retirement offers. Work arrangements such as flex time, job sharing, and telecommuting can be a dream come true for an individual who wants to work, but who doesn't want to work that long or hard. Many of these workplace innovations that caught on first with the working young (especially women) are now gaining popularity with older workers. As another example, the virtual workplace not only offers us the freedom to work from anywhere we choose—a mountaintop, oceanside, college town, a leisure community, or even an assisted-living facility—but helps us to spend more time with family and friends or pursuing other interests, a very real benefit whether we're 34 or 64.

Phased retirement—the gradual reduction in work hours and responsibilities—is another approach that many LifeCyclers might choose. Today, only about 16 percent of U.S. firms offer anything like this according to a Watson Wyatt survey. However, as moments of metamorphosis become more common for all working adults, the concept of phased retirement may catch on. In fact, the idea may morph into phasing in and phasing out of retirement. For instance, Nancy Hilliard was an executive headhunter working long hours and commuting to work. She decided to dial it down when her children were born, but she didn't want to give up work completely. Her boss didn't want to lose her talents, so they agreed that she would take on only the most important projects and work from home a few hours a day. Once her children started school, she dialed it back up to a part-time position. She hopes to someday start her own firm.

Bridge employment, a term coined by Robert Atchley, describes the jobs we fill between leaving full-time careers and entering full-time retirement. It's born out of the idea that we will soon retire completely, but need a transition period both psychologically and economically. However, it's a concept that might soon apply to anyone of any age experiencing work transition. We've all heard of "actors in waiting" who are temporarily waiters or telemarketers. However, this is usually associated with young adults on their way into the workforce. Soon it could also apply to adults of all ages in-waiting for their next career. It provides needed income, social involvement, and a better sense of structure and self-worth while we figure out what we really want to do. It is, in fact, transition employment, applicable to anyone of any age.

Mentoring neophyte workers may become one of the most satisfying career moves that any of us might make. If we master a particular position, passing on the critical pieces of knowledge that can help someone else take on a similar role with success only improves the system. Mentoring will take on many forms including recruiting, training, and managing, all of which hearken back to the Jeffersonian ideal of the wise old sage.

Internships, usually reserved for the young testing the waters of a particular industry or career path, is another innovation that might be applied to people of all ages. When considering a new career path why not see what it really is like up close with little to no compensation but the opportunity to experience the job or industry firsthand? For instance, why do White House interns need to be young people exclusively? Why not offer the opportunity to a newly divorced man who wants to start anew or a woman whose kids have just left for college who wants to start a new career? These innovative work opportunities need to be opened up to neophytes of all ages.

Another aspect of the new, cyclic retirement model has to do with play. That's what we first fantasize about when we imagine retirement. But, as we described in depth in Chapter 7, most of us don't want to save leisure activities until the last phase of life. On the contrary, we want to integrate recreation and reflection throughout our life span as we realize it's not just okay but necessary to rejuvenate our spirit to succeed in the new model of long life.

Some LifeCyclers are already experimenting with this by taking midlife sabbaticals to pursue a hobby, explore the world, or follow a dream. However, most of us don't feel we have the time or even the right to do that and, instead, save it until the end of life or blow it off completely. The ironic thing is that making the time for moments of metamorphosis like this is often life changing.

Danny Katz, a hard-driving, 40-year-old portfolio manager with a lifetime passion for basketball, decided to take time off from work for six months to pursue his fantasy. A lifetime superachiever, Danny went to college at Duke University where he played basketball and got excellent grades. At 6 feet, 2 inches, he knew he'd never be a pro basketball player, but he loved the game and stayed with it recreationally as he achieved success in the business world. When he turned 40, he was invited to play basketball in the 1999 Maccabee Games (the Masters—over 40—Division) in Mexico City. Danny trained for these international amateur athletic games for months, working only part-time while basketball became his full-time occupation. He got into the best shape of his life. Going to Mexico City and taking part in this event was one of the defining moments in his life. Even though the proverbial wisdom would have been, "Forget basketball. That's a game for kids," it didn't turn out that way for him at all. Instead, it changed his whole perspective. "I realized that I'm about a lot more than what I do for a paycheck. That ambitious, athletic kid I used to know is still there. I found out that playing competitive basketball makes me feel happier; going to Mexico and playing ball has made me a much better husband, father, friend, employer, and guy."

GIVING BACK

As Danny Katz makes clear, not all rewarding work need be for financial payback. Many of us will set aside time throughout our lives to help create a better world just because it makes us feel good to do so. And as we get older and less time trapped through the multiple commitments of jobs, raising a family, and building a nest, we may choose to give back more of our time rather than less. Once again, the boomer generation will lead the way in developing this trend.

When boomers were young, they were rebellious and idealistic with strong beliefs; they were not afraid to take action on behalf of issues and causes they cared about. Whether it was protesting the Vietnam War or marching for women's rights, boomers were cause-oriented, searching for something to believe in and care for. That hasn't gone away.

Boomers volunteer in higher numbers than any other age cohort, with 55 percent donating at least some of their time to worthy causes.[11] Increasing numbers of boomers have begun to seek experiences outside of work that make them and their children (they motivate their children here as well) feel like they are bigger than just their own lives. This takes many forms and includes activism, volunteering their time and energy, and contributing generously to causes they believe in.

About half of all boomers expect to devote more time to community service or volunteer activities as they reach traditional retirement age.[12] Although my husband and I are nowhere near retirement, a few years ago we decided to take two weeks to volunteer our time for something other than our family and work. We felt the need to give back to a world that has been very generous to us. We flew to Houston to help build houses as part of a Habitat for Humanity project. We had the rare privilege of working side-by-side with Jimmy and Rosalyn Carter building a house from the ground up. It was Houston in the summer—at least 100 sweltering degrees every day with humidity to match. But both of the Carters worked as hard as anyone on the project, never complaining, never even seeming to sweat. In their 70s, they served as an inspiration to every volunteer and the people whose house we were building, Wade and Shalina Gibson and their three small children. The Gibsons, too, were working on the house even though Shalina was very pregnant at the time. Although they were shy around the other volunteers, every day they would open up just a little more.

Toward the end of the project, when the house was completed, former President Carter gathered us all into the cozy living room we had helped to build with our own hands. Together we stood in a close circle, holding hands. We all looked around the room and were amazed at what we had accomplished. Shalina and Wade both had tears streaming down their faces. Jimmy Carter led us in a prayer and handed Wade and Shalina the first gift for their new home, a beautiful white bible. Jimmy Carter then asked Wade if he could remember what Jesus did. Wade gave the answer he probably had to recite every Sunday as a child: "He died for our sins." But that wasn't what Jimmy Carter was looking for. Carter said, "But what did he do before he heard the calling of the Lord?" Wade immediately replied, "He was a carpenter." Carter nodded, "He worked with his hands. He was a builder. By allowing us the chance to build this house for you, you have given each of us the chance to do the work of the Lord. Thank you for that opportunity." At that point, we all had tears streaming down our faces. We knew we had just done something we could be proud of. It was an experience I will always cherish.

In *PrimeTime: How Baby Boomers Will Revolutionize Retirement*, Marc Freeman writes that we need to think more about the potential roles and responsibilities of older adults in our society. He believes it doesn't really matter what form work takes—paid or unpaid, part-time or full-time—but what does matter is the content of that work. He suggests that we "must cultivate those contributions that promise to provide the greatest benefit for individuals and society. Most people," Freeman argues, "can't just walk out the door and make a difference. There needs to be someplace to go, a well-developed avenue to help channel good-will into good deeds." That's why he's been instrumental in developing the Experience Corps, aimed at—but not limited to—older adults.

The Experience Corps is active in schools throughout the United States. In San Francisco, one of the volunteers is a former attorney, Mr. Sapiro. He is 85 years old and helps out at A. P. Giannin Middle School in three social studies classes. When the seventh-grade class was studying World War II, the teacher, Anne Bjornson, asked Shapiro to describe to the class his experiences during that war. So he did, memorably and with enthusiasm. A retired Army colonel, Shapiro had seen action in Africa and Europe. He pulled out maps, brought in photographs, and made the material come alive for everyone in that class. More than that, he helped to build a bridge between the generations by doing what

Thomas Jefferson had hoped to do, "to recount to those around him what he had heard and learned in the heroic age he had lived through."

WHAT WE WILL NEED TO PULL THIS ONE OFF

The previous examples make opportunities for metamorphoses seem like a no-brainer. "Where," we might ask, "do I sign up?" Attractive as it seems, however, this new paradigm depends on accepting, planning, implementing, and revising, on a regular basis, lifelong plans and life-long investment programs. This is a new undertaking that wasn't really required when we lived a linear life dictated by societal norms. But as we move away from that model toward a new cyclic form of life, there are more curves in the road and some unexpected bumps. There may even be some wipeouts requiring us to back up and start a slightly different path to get to the same endpoint. For instance, no one could have predicted that on September 11, 2001, terrorists would attack the World Trade Center and the Pentagon, successfully changing our lives and our economy forever. Dealing with that tragedy has required all Americans—some much, much more than others—to rethink our options and directions.

In similar but far less horrific fashion, new wealth accumulation and depletion cycles will need to change and grow as we live longer, work harder, and save for the unexpected. We'll need to save and invest more, for longer. In fact, with life growing longer all the time, financial planning will become an ever more complicated puzzle requiring more help and direction, starting at even younger ages. This concept ought to be introduced in elementary school with more sophistication being built in as people move through the LifeCycle. Dire warnings to the contrary, we haven't been doing a great job of financial planning to date.

The financial services industry has only begun to scratch the surface in helping us plan for long life and moments of metamorphosis, whether they are expected or unexpected, desired or dreaded. New financial planning, investing, and insurance products and services will need to be developed to better meet the needs of an aging workforce comfortable with changing employers often and cycling in and out of the workforce throughout their lives.

We'll need vacation and sabbatical planners, career reinventors, life-long education managers, and volunteer opportunity coordinators. Travel agents will need to do a lot more than just book flights if they want to thrive. Human resource directors will have to do more than push papers, too. Easy access to volunteer opportunities should be available to everyone at every age. The government and private enterprise ought to create an elder corps to give our oldest and wisest citizens easy access to volunteer opportunities whether they be close at home or far away. These might even include some financial remuneration so that money doesn't become the issue holding them back from sharing themselves.

CONCLUSION

Retirement as we know it will be retired. In its place will come cycles of metamorphosis that will arrive at whatever age we choose, occur as often as we choose, and last for as long as we want. These moments of reinvention will offer us a chance to change directions, renew our spirits, try on a different lifestyle, give of ourselves, or just have fun. The cyclic life will offer each of us the freedom to explore metamorphosis, but the price we will pay is being responsible for planning and paying for it. It will require far more sophisticated planning, decision making, and financial wherewithal. It will offer the financial services industry vast opportunities for new relationships with clients that could last for decades and involve many generations of one family. It will also challenge that industry to create new products and services that might better meet our needs for a long life in the cyclic life arrangement.

THE CYCLIC SELF

In exploring the cyclic life path, we've taken a good look at a variety of ways the circle of life is replacing the linear life path, transforming many dimensions of our lives, including education, work, play, love, family, health and well-being, and the notion of retirement. My hope is that this exploration has sparked a variety of new ideas or directions for every person who has picked up this book. Such ideas may have to do with how we'll pursue a particular career trajectory or plan for our own financial futures. Or maybe it will provide reassurance that going back to school, taking a work sabbatical, or marrying that special someone is the right move. It might bring a business idea to light that we know fits who we are and our talents precisely. Wherever it takes us, I believe the cyclic life can be like a breath of fresh air, offering us tremendous opportunities at every turn.

In large part, what we make of those opportunities is up to us. But, as I touched on in the introduction, seven strategic guideposts can help us prepare for living in the cyclic society. Now I'm not positioning myself as a self-help guru, but I feel these are almost like mantras to keep in mind when venturing down the cyclic path. They are as follows:

1. We are longevity pioneers paving the cyclic life path.
2. The cyclic life is *dynamic*, not *static*.
3. Be a beginner at any age.

4. The rhythm and cadence of life will change.

5. Setbacks and detours are inevitable.

6. Late bloomers may bloom best.

7. The pressure's off.

WE ARE LONGEVITY PIONEERS PAVING THE CYCLIC LIFE PATH

I've said it before but it bears repeating: We are at the dawn of a longevity revolution that is one of the crucial underpinnings of the new cyclic life. Over the last century, we've nearly doubled our life span. There's no doubt that scientific and medical breakthroughs will continue to raise life expectancy and might even allow us to look and feel far younger than our chronological ages. According to Peter Schwartz, cofounder and chair of the Global Business Network, "Science and medicine will not only extend more people's lives to their full Hayflick span of 120 years, but advances in biology will lengthen human life even beyond that. If we look at the current work on stem cells and phenomena like telomerase, an enzyme in the DNA, we find we're learning a great deal about the control mechanism for aging."[1]

As a result, most of us will live even longer than we might expect with more health and vitality. It's a large part of *why* the cyclic life makes so much more sense now. If we're to live added decades, chances are that we may want to try more than one lifestyle and set of circumstances on for size. That's the beauty of a long life; there's time for second chances, new beginnings, and comebacks. We can experiment and move on, accepting what works and letting go of the rest.

There is no doubt, however, that this cyclic path, which has not been heavily traveled, will also challenge us at every turn. Different than for past generations, there is no longer a straight and narrow thoroughfare clearly marked by those who came before us to help navigate these additional decades. Few role models exist. Yes, there are some enigmas like Ben Franklin who toiled in a multitude of careers, but he certainly was not typical of his era. John Glenn, also not typical of his generation, stands out as a role model who has kept learning and growing, shifting careers successfully and maintaining a loving family relationship all the time. There are other John Glenns out there who have been quietly experimenting with the cyclic life to varying degrees of success. Overall, though, we are truly venturing into unexplored territory where what lies around the bend does not necessarily appear on our maps. The truth is that each of us will bear some of the responsibility for blazing this new trail.

This is both exhilarating and frightening. We will be the role models for future generations, showing how living cyclic lives should and should not be done. As we pave the path, we'll need new tools to help make the journey easier.

One of the tools that we'll have to rely on in this new journey of cycles will be wisdom. With longer lives, we hold the potential of gaining more wisdom and maturity than any generation before us, becoming a culture of experienced LifeCyclers who fluidly move in and out of phases of growth, learning, and personal reinvention. Author Theodore Roszak calls it, "the wisdom of a maturing America," and believes it "promises to be our richest resource." In Berlin the Max Planck Institute for Human Development defines wisdom as "expert knowledge about life in general and good judgment and advice about how to conduct oneself in the face of complex, uncertain circumstances."

Wisdom, we can only hope, will be one positive outcome of long life lived on a cyclic path. One of the most relevant pieces of wisdom we can acquire and pass on to future generations is that whatever we might be doing with our lives at any given moment does not define our whole lives but just that exact moment in time. In the next moment, the details could change. On the cyclic path, the picture of who we really are is never complete. We can remain a work in progress throughout our long and varied lives.

Wisdom is only one tool we'll find valuable to help us navigate the challenges and opportunities of a longer, cyclic-life path. The capacity to change and adapt is an acquired skill developed though practice, revision, and, sometimes, even failure. The courage to move forward, even when we're unsure of what lies ahead, is also an acquired skill gained through practice. On a more pragmatic note, some tools are already out there for us to take advantage of—such as lifelong financial planning and health maintenance. As we become more experienced and adept at living a long life, we will unearth a retinue of additional tools we have yet to imagine.

THE CYCLIC LIFE IS DYNAMIC, NOT STATIC

In many ways, this credo of the cyclic life captures both how it will change each of us and how it will, in turn, alter each stage of life we pass through. The linear life path demanded that each stage of life hold us captive for a particular period of time: Young people had to learn what they could to quickly move on to be a productive part of society. Adults married, raised the next generation, and found some useful role that would give them the resources to provide for that family. And the end of life came early with older adults moving off to the sidelines of life to make room for the next generation when that time came. There was an assumption that we could keep growing and changing until about age 50, and then the downward slide began, with little opportunity for growth or change after that. Instead, we were offered a reprieve in retirement: a little time to rest and reflect before death came knocking on our door. In a long-lived society where the cyclic life path prevails, we need to be open to ongoing change, improvement, and growth, at 15, 25, 45, and 85—and all ages in between.

One example of the dynamic growth and change available in the cyclic path is easily seen in the life of former governor of Massachusetts Bill Weld. During one four-year period, he transformed almost every major aspect of his life. He described his personal motivation as "fear of boredom." To keep boredom at bay, he quit politics for a new career in investment banking, which he jokingly refers to as his thirteenth or fourteenth career. This required that he move from Boston to New York while his wife, Susan, stayed behind so their youngest child could finish high school and his wife could keep her career in full swing. Ultimately, this complex arrangement—two strong individuals, each fully engaged in a cyclic life—led to the breakup of their 26-year marriage. In true cyclic fashion, a new romance bloomed for him with a working mother of three, Leslie Marshall. Along the way, he took up an old hobby— writing—which resulted in a novel, *Stillwater*, published in 2001. New career, new love, expanded family extensions, new home, and renewed hobby. Mort Zuckerman, *Daily News* chairman and close friend, describes Bill Weld as "voracious in terms of learning, doing, experimenting." I would say he's a role model for living a more a cyclic life.

Just as our lives become less static and more dynamic, the lifestages we pass through will also become more diverse and less homogenous. For instance, it used to be that if we got a horrible disease such as cancer or heart disease, the end of life was in sight. We tended to believe that cycling out of illness was nearly impossible and full recovery wasn't even an option. Today, however, we can see examples of those who have survived illness, experienced full recovery, and then cycled back into other lifestages.

Frank Tillman, for instance, has cycled in and out of serious illness several times, coping with both heart disease and serious back problems. He's recovered from two heart bypass surgeries and three back surgeries. Through it all, work has been a steady compass in his life. A systems consultant for the Newhouse newspaper group, at age 67 he continues to learn about the newest software for the newspaper industry and to apply that knowledge to help his company determine which software is strategically worth the investment. He says, "I'm not ready to give this up." According to Tim Schmidt, a 30-something client of Frank's who runs production operations for a Newhouse chain in Ohio, "Of course Frank's age is a factor. Anyone with a brain would recognize his knowledge of the industry is a tremendous resource."[2] Each of us knows someone who has survived heart disease, cancer, or surgery of some kind to come back, like Frank, to live full lives.

Illness and recovery are far from the only dynamic lifestage events we will pass through. Careers, education, marriage and remarriage, midlife parenting, grandparenting, even retirement—or the absence of it—can open doors for us to cycle in and out of at our own discretion. Flexibility and agility—both emotional and mental—will be essential skills to cultivate to cope effectively with our dynamic lives. So think *dynamic* rather than *static*.

BE A BEGINNER AT ANY AGE

The cyclic life expects dogs of all ages to learn new tricks. Most of us will have the experience of being a beginner again and again. Increasingly age won't matter. That means we might be very experienced at something when we're 25 and start something new when we're 50.

Vincent Carpano has been a beginner several times, very successfully. At 82, he's knee-deep into learning and living his fourth career as a sculptor. His past careers have included chemical engineering, environmental engineering, and statistical programming. Each career required a slightly different set of knowledge and skills, which was exciting to him. With multiple pensions and a solid investment program, he doesn't need to earn money anymore, so he chose to pursue a passion that was new and different, completely unrelated to what he had been doing before. He discovered this passion when someone brought a sculpture by his office to show him. He took one look at it and decided, "Boy, I'd like to do that."

For the past 10 years, he's regularly attended fine arts courses at Virginia Commonwealth University in Richmond. "I make at least four sculptures a semester," he says. And his learning has led to art shows where he sells his sculptures for anywhere from $500 to $1,100 per piece. Virginia Commonwealth University department head Joe Seipel, a well-known sculptor himself, says, "It's just gorgeous stuff." But the motivator is not the money. Carpano says, "I get a lot of pleasure out of just getting the work done."[3]

My two children, Casey and Zak, are already experts at playing pool at age 15 and 12. They learned the game from their dad, my husband, Ken, who was a pool shark in his youth. They really can play! I, however, can't play at all—or couldn't until I allowed myself to be a beginner at age 50. Until recently, though, every time Ken and the kids would play together, I'd opt out so they could have some time, just the three of them (and to avoid humiliating myself). This year, however, I was with the kids on vacation, while Ken was on a business trip. There wasn't much to do in the late afternoons *except* play pool. So I reluctantly agreed to let them teach me as long as they promised to be kind. They patiently taught me the basics. I was the beginner; they were the experts. I wouldn't go so far as to say I got good, but now at least I can hold my own in friendly family competitions. And, in truth, learning a new skill was fun.

Just like I did with pool, I've noticed that many of us fear looking bad, losing status, or failing when we try something new. I've even seen this in children; if they're not immediately good at hitting a baseball or playing the guitar, they might just give up. But the cyclic life demands that we try new things, dare to be a fumbling beginner until we can learn enough to seem competent, no matter how young or old we might be. Only then do we get to experience what it's like to improve from bad to good, an unbelievably satisfying experience.

I remember when my son, Zak, was learning to play basketball. A natural athlete, Zak had excelled at most sports he tried, but basketball was the first contact sport he played. At first, Zak enjoyed shooting hoops but was frightened by the physical contact of the game, which kept him from improving. He preferred not touching the ball to risking physical contact. (As a mother, I personally thought, smart boy!) But, he kept practicing and playing which took a lot of courage in the face of his fear and uncertainty. Little by little, he realized that the players on the other team didn't want to hurt him; they just wanted to get the ball away from him. Once he realized that, he could apply his skills to keeping the ball from the other team and getting the ball either in the basket or to one of his teammates. Zak's revelation seems obvious but the experience of acting on it and seeing it succeed was exhilarating to him. He's since become a really good player, but more than that, he now loves to play the game with others, just to feel himself improving incrementally all the time.

As my son and I both learned, developing the skills of risk-taking, humility, and just being comfortable with being a beginner, no matter how old or experienced we might be at other things, will be an important tool on the cyclic life path.

THE RHYTHM AND CADENCE OF LIFE WILL CHANGE

A fundamental law of physics states the shortest distance between two points is a straight line. This is a good thing to know when the emphasis is on speed and efficiency in reaching a prescribed destination. Certainly it was indispensable information on the linear-life path when no one could afford to be unaware of where he or she stood on the line, where they must go next, and *exactly* how much time they had to get there.

Not too long ago, unmarried women faced despair, desperation, and the disparaging label of *spinster* or *old maid* as early as their late twenties. College students who spent more than the prescribed four years in school were seen as somehow lacking, either in academic potential, ambition, or self-control. And imminent retirees who hadn't firmly established their nest eggs by their late fifties were regarded with pity and some disdain. They were out-of-step, off-balance, and the rest of the world was passing them by. Not anymore.

On the cyclic path, we are freed from the onus of getting from the linear point A to point B as punctually as possible. Our new, longer lives—and the medical advances that accompany them—provide room for variety and innovation over speed and single-mindedness. We simply don't need to be in such a hurry anymore. And we don't need to move in lockstep with everyone else. Perhaps most importantly, there is no longer a single finish line. There is no penalty in the cyclic life for slowing down, speeding up, or starting over. And there's no valid reason why we can't change our minds and create all new goals in accordance to the new wisdom we gain along the way. We can each have our own goals and objectives (note the plural) and aim to reach them according to our own rhythm and time clock.

Sarah Dunlap is a great example of how the cyclic life allows more freedom of choice and rhythm than the linear path. Sarah was a very driven college student determined to graduate at the top of her class in the field of communications. Single-mindedly, she pursued internships in her field and worked every day and most weekends to establish an impressive resume before she ever even graduated. As everyone expected, Sarah graduated with honors and landed a great job right away. However, to everyone's surprise, Sarah quit her job less than a year later to return to school, this time to be a nurse.

"I just didn't feel like I was doing anything really important," Sarah says about her media job. "But as a nurse, I can really improve the lives of other people every single day." Sarah jokes that she's lucky to have experienced her midlife crisis—at least her first one—in her early twenties. But she's also grateful to realize, she says, that those four years pursuing her communications degree weren't wasted. "Luckily, my parents and I both think that getting an education and learning what you really want aren't really a waste of time. Besides, I have the rest of my life to do what I want . . . I'm not in any big hurry." And, since nursing includes a great deal of interpersonal communications, Sarah realizes her dual training will help her to excel in her chosen profession.

Of course, the classic example of moving at our own pace through a cyclic life is found in the many women—and many of my own friends—who defied the linear path's demand that they get married and have children right after school (in the old days, the pursuit of a college degree was even referred to as getting one's "MRS. degree"). I don't have enough fingers to count the number of bright, driven women in my neighborhood who possess law degrees and executive titles and are currently driving carpool. I don't know a single one of them who would give up the years she invested and may reinvest in her career, or who would give up the gift of being a full-time, mature mom.

Like many women, Academy Award–nominated actress Debra Winger took a hiatus from acting in movies to raise her family, which included a son from her former marriage to Timothy Hutton, and a son from her current husband Arliss Howard's first marriage. She enjoyed it so much, she and Arliss Howard decided to have another baby. She, however, hardly stopped working. In between being a full-time mother and wife, she performed in a few theatre productions and taught a course at Harvard University. Like many educated, experienced career women, she kept her hand in interesting projects related to her knowledge-base but experimented with her work while she focused the majority of her time on enjoying her growing family.[4] Although it might have seemed like she disappeared completely from acting, she just changed her priorities: The rhythm and cadence of acting shifted down while the level of family activity moved up, at least temporarily.

Annette Bening lost her desire to work when she started having babies with her husband, Warren Beatty. In 2000, she told *Good Housekeeping* magazine, "I thought, 'Is this going to go away and not come back?' Now I realize there's an ebb and flow."[5]

When Karen Hughes, President George W. Bush's former communications director, quit the White House to move back to Texas with her family, everyone was quick to assume that she was just another woman who couldn't handle the pressures of work and family. Sylvia Hewitt, author of *Creating a Life*, said, "If Karen Hughes can't handle keeping the balancing act together, who can?" But I see it a little differently. In fact, Karen Hughes *is* handling the balancing act with intelligence and good judgment. Like many of us, Ms. Hughes didn't give up her career, she just reprioritized. She is working for President Bush . . . from Texas instead of Washington, D.C. Telecommuting is a commonly used practice to add flexibility and control to our lives. She chose to temporarily put family first.[6]

More and more women are realizing that their identity as a career person won't erode just because they decide to take some time to raise a family. Part of the beauty of the longer, more cyclic life is that we can decide to push on all fronts at one time, or pull back on our career while we raise a family. We don't have to do it all simultaneously, but we can, if that's what we want. The choice is ours.

SETBACKS AND DETOURS ARE INEVITABLE

Because of its adaptability and range of options, the cyclic life is more complex and less predictable than the linear-life path. There will be moments when we'll feel like we've lost our way or, perhaps, made some questionable choices. That's okay. The cyclic life offers ample time to assess the damage, pick ourselves up, dust ourselves off, and move ahead, on whatever road we choose.

My husband, Ken, has had the rare privilege of being singled out by *Time* magazine as a role model for this core truth. And he's proud of it. Me, too. *Time* magazine interviewed him as an expert on aging and the mature market when he was 52. *Time* asked what it was like to pass 50 and become part of the very age segment he had so long researched. He told them the truth, "It was a terrible year for me."

At 50, Ken's life was in turmoil. He was traveling all the time for business, so he spent little time with his wife (me), family, or friends and became distant from all of us. His mother, with whom he is very close, had a serious bout with cancer that required his constant interaction with both his emotionally overwrought parents and her harried doctors. His home base had become a blur of hotel rooms where he never ate a home-cooked meal or saw the outside world. His businesses, a constant headache, were not performing well and offered no signs of improvement. The wealth he had worked so hard to accumulate on paper seemed to be evaporating before his eyes with the market's massive downturn. With extremely high cholesterol—more than twice the level deemed healthy—and weight gain from his lifestyle, his health teetered on the brink of rapid deterioration. Plus, he struggled most nights to sleep, his mind racing with worry. It was such an extreme set of negative circumstances that he knew he had to take radical action, and he did.

He said, "I may not turn out to be a big financial success, but I'm going back to what I love most." He had hit a wall and knew that radical change was the only answer. He took off a few months from work to take stock. He detoured from the path he was on to rediscover his own home and worked hard to rebuild his relationships with our children, his closest friends, and me. He began to exercise, lose weight, and lower his cholesterol with prescription drugs. All this helped him to sleep better. And, luckily for us all, his mom recovered from her bout with cancer. He even reinvented his career by transitioning out of his business ventures and going back to what he loved most, exploring the future of aging and giving world-class presentations to business and government leaders. The irony of it is that he's not only happier but he's also more successful both psychically and financially than he was before. However, he also knows that this reinvention might be just one of many in his cyclic life.

Kamran Elahian also believes that setbacks are a necessary detour on the road to success. He knows firsthand. He hit a major one on April Fools' Day 1992, the day he was fired from the company that he had started. He describes it like this: "I felt like I'd lost my child. I went numb."

"Months after he was fired at 38, Elahian realized that his most spectacular failure was his most precious gift. It toughened him for even greater risk-taking in his life as well as in his career. Failure steered him to eventually launch six Internet and telecommunications startups from 1993 to 1999. Failure propelled him to start a venture capital fund, Global Catalyst. And failure spurred him to embark on his most audacious mission: to wire every school in developing countries and countries in conflict for the Internet, including Bulgaria, Cambodia, and Israel."[7]

Setbacks and detours aren't just inevitable; they are great learning experiences that often give us back more than they take. While we process the pain and frustration of a failure or setback, however, we need to stay alert to the doors opening to new opportunities, learning, and skill-building.

LATE BLOOMERS MAY BLOOM BEST

When the average human life span was 47, less than a half century ago, there was little opportunity for many of us to apply the kind of wisdom, clarity, and talent that absolutely required decades of experience and observation to obtain. Until recently, history offered us its examples of genius as anomalies—both unusually talented youths like Mozart or uncommonly long-lived artists like da Vinci.

Ray Kroc, founder of McDonald's Corporation, was a failed salesman before he dreamed up the franchise at age 52. Dr. Ruth Westheimer didn't even show any interest in sex education until she was 39 years old and didn't appear in the media until she was well into her 40s. Norman Cousins was a success as the editorial director of *Saturday Review* for 30 years. However, he felt he didn't really find himself until he'd lived through a life-threatening illness that changed him completely and steered him to a new career path as an author of inspirational books. These late bloomers were considered enigmas who had beaten the odds and made something of themselves very late in the game. The cyclic life, however, delivers this potential opportunity to each of us.

I recently picked up the newsletter sent out by Rancho La Puerta, a health spa in Tecate, Mexico, that has been owned by the Szekely family since its inception more than 60 years ago. My husband and I have known and respected Deborah Szekely, the matriarch of the family, and her children for over 20 years. After her husband died, she took over his dream of building one of the first real health spas in North America. With little money but a lot of commitment, she transformed the ranch from a modest health farm to one of the most wonderful health spas in the world. In a newsletter, Deborah wrote, "On May 3rd, I will be 80!

Incredible! Impossible! But reality nonetheless. What makes it weird is that I feel no different now than when I turned 50. I am filled with as many dreams for the future, and I still do not have the time, or patience or willingness to become old, thus the number feels alien and incomprehensible."

Like Deborah Szekely, many of us will choose to keep challenging ourselves throughout our lives with new projects, new goals, new friends and loved ones, new careers, and, as Deborah goes on to say in her open letter, "a new *raison d'etre*—with all the attendant exciting, challenging reasons to stay awake at night and ponder how best to bring them all to fruition." Some of us may never feel *old*; others might feel old for a while and then find something that brings us back to the wide-eyed excitement that we identify as youth and vitality. The choice will be ours.

Imagine, though, how many more men and women will have the opportunity to bloom now that our life spans have nearly doubled! Do you, for example, view the world the same way now as you did at 19? Could you have possibly understood the alchemy of your successes without the counterpoint of your failures? Don't you know more about what truly matters now than you ever have? And don't you expect to know just as much more in the future? And how in the world could you have focused on the meaning of life when you were so busy changing diapers or paying the rent?

The good news in the cyclic life is that you don't have to be famous like these examples to bloom late, or to bloom repeatedly. Because, ultimately, the cyclic life is a picture of optimism where the best—whatever *we* decide that is—is yet to be.

THE PRESSURE'S OFF

One of the advantages of stepping away from a prescribed linear path is that the urgency to be at any given point along it, at any given time, begins to fade away. This last guidepost tells us that we can relax a little on the cyclic path; in fact, it may actually help us to achieve our goals.

My friend, Jessica Callen, was desperate to have another child. A psychologist by training, Jessica had a clear picture in her head about how she wanted her life to unfold, and she had methodically set about manifesting this picture. Family was the centerpiece. She wanted to be happily married with two or three children running around, laughing and jumping. Her own father had died when she was still a child, which had forced her to grow up fast and made her aware of how important family was.

Jessica married a great guy, moved to a beautiful home, and set about having children. She was thrilled when she got pregnant almost as soon as she and her husband tried. She knew she could have the family she always dreamed of! Her daughter was born, and she soon set about the task of conceiving her second child. She figured that if they were two or three years apart, that would be perfect. But, this time, Jessica didn't have such an easy time conceiving. She tried for three years with no luck. Then she desperately tried every fertility drug and procedure available, including some experimental ones with no success for another two years. Having another baby became her obsession, but nature was not cooperating.

Finally, in frustration, she gave up. She was in poor health from all the fertility treatments. And she had been so focused on getting pregnant, that her husband and daughter felt ignored. It began to dawn on her that her goal of building a real family was built around a picture she had in her head that was different than what her actual family might be. She began to relax and reconnect with her husband and daughter. Soon she was feeling better than she had in years.

One day, though, she didn't feel so well. She was a bit nauseous, and she couldn't eat a thing. So she went to the doctor worrying that maybe all those fertility treatments might have taken their toll and caused some horrible illness. That wasn't the case. To her surprise and joy, Jessica found out that she was pregnant.

Jessica now realizes that she had to take the pressure off to reach her goal. As a footnote, she now has three beautiful children: two girls and a boy. After her second daughter was born, she decided that she didn't want to ever go through anything like what she had gone through again. She and her husband decided that two children were a blessing. But nature took its course, once again, and she had a boy two years after her second daughter was born.

Jessica is a wonderful—but far from unique—example of how living a longer life takes the pressure off us to do it all right away. Among my circle of close friends alone, I count a 40-something professional woman getting the teaching degree she's always wanted, a former hard-charging executive who's supervising his daughter's playdates, and four or five people who are learning long-dreamed-of skills like playing a musical instrument, speaking a new language, taking really beautiful photographs, or working full-time for charity. The point is that in the old linear paradigm, a person had to decide what he or she wanted, and go after it to the exclusion of almost everything else in the relatively short time allotted them. In our new, longer, freer LifeCycles, however, delaying a dream doesn't mean giving it up. Nor does pursuing one dream exclude the possibility of fulfilling several others in one lifetime.

Ultimately, then, what the new cyclic life offers us is time. Time to relax. Time to explore. Time to reconsider. Time to reinvent. Time to fire up our engines and time to dial them down again. The outcome, and the way we feel about it, is for the first time, increasingly up to us. And that, my friends, is truly revolutionary.

THE CYCLIC SOCIETY

There's no doubt that the cyclic life path holds the potential to transform each of our lives in a multitude of ways. Just as importantly, we LifeCyclers will collectively have a tremendous impact on society as a whole. Through the transformation of millions of individual lives, a new cyclic society is being born. The elements of society and commerce that thrive in this new environment will be those willing and able to meet the evolving wants and needs of consumers continually reinventing themselves.

Each chapter of this book delineates a variety of ways in which the new cyclic life paradigm will impact businesses and organizations in the for-profit and non-profit sectors. I've described some of the industries, products, and innovations that are poised to benefit from cyclic lifestages such as lifelong learning, cyclic careers, and rehirement/retirement. I've also mentioned some of the products and marketing strategies that might no longer be relevant.

Since the inception of modern advertising and product positioning, business has had the luxury of clearly defining its target audience according to its position on the linear-life path, and blasting out messages that easily hooked linear-lifestage-captive consumers. But, in a cyclic society, where brand loyalty is short-lived and LifeCycles are no longer defined exclusively by age, companies will only be as good as their current ability to keep pace with a constantly morphing consumer.

It's a lot more work to try to invent new ways of reaching customers who are cycling through life at their own pace, involved in the LifeCycle events they choose, and for a duration they determine.

Clearly age-based mass marketing is passé. Flexibility, adaptability, creativity, and the willingness to discard outdated but comfortable ideas will all figure into the marketing success stories of our cyclic future. Adapt or be left behind is fast becoming a maxim of the cyclic society.

That maxim will also be evident in the workplace, where employers will need to work harder to recruit and retain LifeCycling workers. Many of us are used to a hierarchical power structure where most of the authority and decision-making capabilities are held by the few at the top of the pyramid. Flexibility, adaptability, and creating individual solutions for employees weren't necessarily encouraged. But a cyclic life pattern demands that employers pay close attention to employees' needs and utilize just these concepts to attract and retain valuable employees.

Similar to the preceding chapter, these seven key strategic guideposts can help companies and organizations thrive in our increasingly cyclic society. I would emphasize that they apply not only to corporate product developers and marketers but also to those interested in launching entrepreneurial ventures or simply looking for new career directions. Non-profit organizations, associations, educational institutions, and scientific fields such as medicine will also find relevance in understanding the cyclic society. And government might upgrade its relevance if politicians understood the emerging needs, challenges, and opportunities of our cyclic society. These guideposts are:

1. Embrace the new ageless consumer.
2. Target lifestyle and LifeCycle, not age.
3. Reinvention is a constant in the cyclic life.
4. Empower consumers.
5. Needed: lifestage navigation.
6. Target freedom and security.
7. Optimize a cyclic workforce.

EMBRACE THE NEW AGELESS CONSUMER

Freedom from age stereotypes feels like a breath of fresh air to consumers, no matter how old they are. It should also feel like one to businesses that can now look beyond their narrow, age-defined target to attract and delight new consumers of all ages. To define the bull's-eye of the market as *youth* and to do so in strictly chronological terms, limited to 18 to 24 or 18 to 34, is an idea whose time has come—and now clearly—long gone. How liberating—and profitable—to be able to sell products and services to people for 50 years rather than just 15.

Throughout this book, we've repeatedly seen that age is losing its significance in defining who we are and what we want. We all know 18-year-olds who are mature beyond their years while we probably know a few 60-year-olds who are youthful in every way. The number of years someone's been alive has become one of the least defining characteristics of individual consumers. It is no longer the main axis for targeting the consumer, either. And, with the demographic and economic balance-of-power moving away from youth and toward the middle and later years of life, this more *ageless consumer* is very good and timely news for business.

Yet, many advertisers and product managers still chase the young out of a long-instilled habit that told us that youth was where the action was, the only market really worth pursuing. The media itself is both the perpetrator and the victim of this kind of thinking. The value of a television show, for instance, still tends to be judged not by its ratings or even the spending power of its viewers, but by the age of the eyeballs it attracts. Although 35+ adults have far more economic clout than teenage boys, television executives, producers, and the advertisers they covet still think teenage boys are the more valuable audience because they *used to be* the market that was largest and spent the most. In spring 2002, ABC was considering replacing Ted Koppel's long-time news show, *Nightline*, with *The David Letterman Show* because Letterman could attract more young male viewers. Letterman, ultimately, rejected ABC's overtures and openly referred to TV suits as "colossal boobs" for this very behavior. I'd characterize missteps like these as pure age-based, linear life thinking, foolishly offtrack for the challenges and opportunities of the twenty-first century.

With every day that passes, more and more savvy business leaders are beginning to welcome the ageless consumer with open arms. For instance, the nightclub industry, estimated to be around $74 billion by *The Wall Street Journal*, has traditionally been linked to the young and hip. However, after the September 11, 2001, terrorist attack, nightclubs saw business plummet by anywhere from 25 to 40 percent. They had to come up with new strategies and new target markets to rebuild their business. Rather than just going after the usual young hipsters, many clubs tried using entertainment to attract both "easily bored young-sters and older folks who don't like to dance. 'It's a totally different market,' says Noah Tepperberg, co-owner of Suite 16 in New York where business almost doubles the night it holds Burlesque a Go-Go," which is designed to appeal to those looking to be entertained, old and young alike. Similarly, Rumi, a club in Miami's trendy South Beach area, has featured everything from a classical violinist to a trapeze artist. Q Nightlife in Chicago has had salsa instructors and Club Clearview in Dallas hires performance artists to liven up the scene with patrons of all ages.[1]

Some producers and writers in the movie industry work hard to cre-ate films with universal, transgenerational appeal. The classic example would be the *Star Wars* series. When *Star Wars: Attack of the Clones* was released in spring 2002, theatres were filled with people of all ages. Most of the young audience members weren't even alive when the original *Star Wars* was released while others have been fans since they themselves were teens or young children. No matter how much or how little we may like the movie, its universal appeal attracts a transgenera-tional audience. And it's not just true for the big franchise movies like *Star Wars*. The same weekend *Star Wars: Attack of the Clones* opened, so did a British comedy, *About a Boy*, starring Hugh Grant. It was strictly an old-fashioned relationship movie that attracted teens and adults of all ages, male and female. It had universal appeal through a well-told story filled with humor and poignancy.

As these examples demonstrate, some businesses are already gear-ing up for the ageless consumer. And as the success stories of ageless marketing multiply, it will soon seem almost humorous that we once defined our target markets according to chronological age.

TARGET LIFESTYLE AND LIFECYCLE, NOT AGE

If age no longer defines who we are, what does? Identity now has much more to do with an individual's current interests, affinities, affiliations, and LifeCycle. People 22, 42, and 62 might covet sports cars or skiing equipment. Fiber pills are a staple of many under-30s as well as the stereotypical over-50s. And along with the high school seniors, potential students read college catalogs in any decade of their lives.

For example, although my husband and son are exactly 40 years apart in age, have very different net worths, different education levels, marital status, and just about every other metric used to define who they are in this world, they're both huge basketball fans. If an advertiser tried to sell them anything to do with basketball, from a seat at an NBA game to a dribbling workshop, chances are that both of them would buy it.

In similar fashion, I exercise at a fitness club, which attracts all levels of fitness aficionados, broadly spanning the chronologic life span. What I particularly like about this, is that no one pays much attention to the age range we represent. We all just enjoy exercising. In one of the kickboxing classes I attend regularly, I've become particularly friendly with a 70-year-old woman, a 29-year-old man, and a 16-year-old girl/woman. (I only know their ages because I've talked about writing this book; as a result, people volunteer their ages to me.) Not only are we different ages, we're different in most ways—incomes, marital status, family structure, careers—but we all love fitness and everything to do with it. Often we'll enjoy a latte together before we leave the gym to tackle our diverse daily schedules. And when a fitness-clothing manufacturer shows up at our club to sell their clothes at trunk shows, we're all there with credit cards waving. Likewise, when a local hospital offered health-screening tests for cholesterol, diabetes, or bone density at the gym, we all showed up. Our mutual interest in exercise, fitness, and good health binds us together, not our birthdates.

The same could be said for diabetics, menopausal women, and cancer survivors. Ditto those in the lifestage of parenting, grandparenting, and work. It's also true of hikers, scuba divers, stamp collectors, knitters, cooks, wine connoisseurs, and political activists.

I know an 80-something woman who's wealthy and conservative. She endorses the old school way of doing things in all cases and still wears white gloves to church each Sunday. One of her favorite friends is a young woman with dread locks and multiple piercings. This odd couple is united in their affinity for animal rights; they both respond to messages that support the ethical treatment of animals. They lobby their friends and politicians; they support the same associations and buy from the same manufacturers. They boycott the same restaurants and eat in the same ones as well; both dress only in clothing that doesn't hurt animals. One has donated all of her minks and lives in a mansion; the other wears shirts made of hemp and rents a room in a group home. But their affinity ties them together and precisely targeted ageless messages get through to them both.

LifeCycle, too, can act as a magnet to attract consumers. For instance, grandparents come in all sizes and shapes. Some are in their 80s while others are in their 40s. What they all have in common is a strong desire to connect with their grandchildren. And research has long shown that this desire for emotional bonding often expresses itself in purchasing power. The average grandparent spends about $500 annually on each grandchild, an estimated total of $35 billion annually. What a bonanza for companies as diverse as toy retailers; clothing manufacturers; financial service companies; travel and leisure resorts; and private schools, colleges, and universities! More than half of all grandparents contribute to the funding of private school and college educations for their grandchildren. To target grandparents of all ages, making it easier for them to figure out which gifts their grandchildren might really appreciate as they move through their youth and early adulthood, is definitely one way to increase sales in a cyclic society.

As interests, affinities, affiliations, and LifeCycle draw like-minded people together, we are morphing into a transgenerational, *ageless society*. In considering the products, services, and messages we direct to cyclic consumers, then, we should look not to age but to lifestyle interests, affinities, affiliations, and LifeCycle.

Educators would do well to keep this in mind when designing curriculum and marketing their schools' programs. Human resource directors need to factor this into their plans when hiring and designing

compensation and benefit programs. And, of course, consumer marketers—whether they're selling non-profit giving programs, vacations
in Hawaii, training programs, or cosmetics—need to break free of their
ageist stereotypes and integrate this multigenerationality into their
messages.

REINVENTION IS A CONSTANT IN THE CYCLIC LIFE

One of the most liberating themes running through this book is the
notion of personal reinvention. It might take the form of losing 20
pounds to create a new body image, going back to school for that college degree we always dreamed of, having a second family, finding the
perfect mate long after we thought it possible, or turning a hobby into a
career. The opportunity for personal reinvention will probably knock at
our doors many times throughout our lives, changing who we are, our
interests, and of course, our product and service preferences.

One glaring example can be found in the very public life of Liza Min-
nelli. We've all witnessed the ups and downs she has experienced. In
2002, after two hip replacements, a bout with encephalitis, and multiple
drug and alcohol rehabilitations, she is once again attempting to reinvent herself at age 56. She lost weight, got married, decided to start a
family, and revived her singing career with a concert tour, "Liza's Back."
At the London show, the audience was thrilled to see her dancing "like
an 18-year-old." John Kander and Fred Ebb wrote the title song for this
tour which included the heartfelt lyrics: "No longer a kid, but I'm beat-
ing the clock and happy and steady and ready to rock."[2]

Not all of us will attempt to transform so much at one time, but often
one small change can lead to another. For instance, losing weight can
bring about new exercise and eating habits, which then might result in
the purchase of new clothes. New marriages often mean fusing two
households, which can result in buying new household goods and furnishings, and maybe even a new house. Starting school in adulthood
often means utilizing conveniences like a cleaning service and home
delivery of precooked foods. The domino effect of change becomes
obvious.

Responding appropriately to the ever-morphing cyclic consumer's needs and demands requires vigilance in knowing and reassessing the customers we serve. It means ongoing interactive communications to better understand our consumers, and it also requires a nimble willingness to repeatedly adapt our business to match that consumer's evolving needs. Those dollars spent several years ago to understand consumers' wants, needs, habits, and hot buttons? They don't necessarily apply to the new cyclic consumer of the twenty-first century. As men and women of all ages repeatedly make course corrections and reinvent themselves, it's becoming necessary to reexamine and reformulate again and again. What about the minivans and SUVs that spoke so perfectly to the proverbial soccer moms and frustrated off-roaders of the late 90s? Young families with kids in 2004 might just consider these gas-guzzlers unethical. The fat-free snacks the product development team came up with in response to overwhelming consumer demand? They're sitting on shelves. Consumers are eating low carb now and it's time to send the product developers back to the drawing board. Quickly. And again and again. In a cyclic society, one market study per product Life-Cycle simply isn't enough. Not anymore.

We'll need to protect ourselves and our families from those unexpected bumps in the road. Everything from health, long-term care, and disability insurance to powers of attorney and living wills will need to be thought through, put into place, and then revisited as we transition into new LifeCycles. It's an opportunity for business to rise up and create products for long-lived LifeCyclers.

As our consumers change, our businesses will need to factor in their reinvention and respond to it to maximize effectiveness as marketers. For instance, Discover Financial Services, a division of Morgan Stanley & Company, has come to realize that reinvention and many of the twists and turns in life can impact the personal cash flow of even their best credit card customers. In response, they have been sending greeting cards to some of these customers with a message of hope and an offer to help them. The greeting cards have messages like this: "The new day is another beginning . . . a chance to start over . . . a time of hope and promise."[3] These cards are personally signed by employees of Discover Card and include their direct phone numbers to encourage customers to contact them for help in managing payment of their accounts. True, it's a form of collections, but without the aggressive, unfriendly tone of traditional collections agencies. Discover has come to realize that these customers will usually bounce back from life transitions or financial hard times and be good, reliable customers again. If they're treated with respect, courtesy, and a helping hand during these turning points, they might remember it and remain loyal customers when their finances improve.

Whatever business we are in, we would do well to remind ourselves from time to time that our consumers are growing and changing rather than perpetuating the status quo. To stay competitive, we will need to be vigilant in repeatedly reassessing those needs and respond to them quickly so we can better serve our cyclic customer.

EMPOWER CONSUMERS

One of the essential outcomes of life on a cyclic path is that consumers of all ages and economic levels will be better educated, more self-reliant, and less inclined to depend on external authority to make decisions. We're no longer passive participants in the game of life; we're more empowered than any consumers that have ever come before and, as a natural outcome, we seek to continuously increase and fortify our empowerment.

Gone are the days when a physician could prescribe a course of action without patients getting second opinions and doing research on their own; when the fashion mavens could describe what was in or out and expect everyone to run to the stores to buy just that; when our job opportunities were limited to those available only with our present employer.

The traditional product marketing model of the past implicitly handed control to manufacturers. They determined which products they would offer consumers through retailers of their choosing. In turn, retailers dutifully stocked and advertised the products that manufacturers chose to provide for consumers. Then, consumers willingly bought what the manufacturers had created and the retailers had advertised.

During the past decade, this model has been turned upside down by increasingly empowered consumers. Consumers can no longer be herded like sheep to buy what manufacturers predetermine they need. Instead consumers send clear signals about their preferences to the manufacturers and retailers. If consumers don't like products, they don't buy them. Period. Manufacturers that develop the preferred products, succeed. Retailers that stock and advertise those products, prosper.

For instance, in spring 2002, national apparel sales slumped 7 percent among the affluent 35- to 54-year-old woman. Many women in that age group are in great physical shape and report that they love fashion, but they were not buying the prairie skirts, hippie shirts and belts, and see-through tops that were deemed in. Were they looking to buy frumpy clothes? Not on your life! In fact, many women like Stevie Wilson, for instance, a 41-year-old writer and mother, loves to wear leather pants and corset tops. But she passed completely on the spring fashions because the look "makes it hard to be taken seriously."[4] The Gap acknowledged the mistake, saying, "Our customer is miffed. We kind of got too trendy," and they swiftly moved back to clothes with more universal appeal. Their television commercials had the tag line, "For Every Generation." They are responding to their real boss—the empowered consumer.

Gone, too, are the days when manufacturers could prosper simply though churning out the same product or service for decades, even centuries. Even powerful brands like Coke and Pepsi are experimenting with new products like Vanilla Coke and Pepsi Blue. In an attempt to align with morphing consumer needs, they are also expanding their offerings through the acquisition of newer products like Sobe and Propel. Savvy business leaders know that cookie-cutter formulae will not address the needs of empowered cyclic consumers. And the satisfaction inherent in making a purchase with a logo from IBM, Levi's, or Hyatt is increasingly being replaced by consumers' delight in products and services that have been tailored just for them.

That's right. We've all seen products that are custom designed. Maybe we assumed it was a fad that would come and go, but the technology is catching on. General Mills, for example, has gotten the tailor-made message. At their website, www.MyCereal.com, consumers can literally make their own cereal. "For years we've gotten calls from consumers asking for very specific mixes of cereal ingredients, but most of those ideas are very 'niche' and wouldn't warrant mass merchandising. But customizing cereals gives us a chance to provide consumers with what they really want while we learn more about consumers' tastes," says General Mills spokesperson, Greg Zimprich.[5] The direct interaction with consumers also helps General Mills keep their hands on the pulse of consumers' changing needs. And it's an effective way to test-market new products with a friendly audience, a cornerstone for success in the cyclic marketplace. Customized products cut across many industry sectors to offer empowered consumers exactly what they want.

Products of all kinds can offer empowerment. For instance, health screenings can detect disease early enough so it can be successfully treated before it wields its destructive force. Personal emergency response systems can allow the elderly to live independently and still feel safe. Self-help books, which have dominated the best-seller list for decades, can teach us everything from how to short stocks to how to find a new career. In the coming decades, consumers will become more and more empowered and, in so doing, will seek products and services that can further increase their level of control and power.

NEEDED: LIFECYCLE NAVIGATION

In the linear life model, where many decisions and actions were prescribed by society and aligned with age, life was simpler to navigate. With fewer options to consider, we didn't need a lot of course correction or guidance after we got through the teenage years and reached adulthood. Everyone knew where they needed to go next, and there were generations of role models exemplifying how best to get there.

Today, things are different. To successfully travel the cyclic life path filled with its innumerable choices, complexities, and turning points, we will need to continuously steer our lives through myriad twists, turns, and options again and again—not just when we graduate high school, start our career, or have a baby. Sometimes we'll face the challenge of too many choices rather than no choices at all. These choices might involve complex considerations for which we'll have insufficient knowledge or experience. In addition, we may not know anyone else who has experienced the exact same set of challenges. As a result, continuous education and expert advice from a new class of professional guides, coaches, counselors, and navigators will become a strategic resource of great value in our increasingly cyclic society. It's part of our need for more and more empowerment.

Asking for help in navigating our adult lives is not something that we currently do very well. In fact, many of us have the notion that we're not quite up to snuff if we need advice from any sort of professional. Remember that the rich and famous have always depended on professional guidance to get a leg up with their fleets of lawyers, accountants, therapists, and agents. Now we all might have to consider looking for some expert guidance to successfully navigate life's increasingly complicated journey.

Our lifelong navigation process could include an emphasis on finances and investing, health and wellness, family and interpersonal relationship management, and personal development. And the hardest task might be to find advisers with integrity we can really trust. Even that might require expert advice. If we're not yet familiar with the term *life coach*, we'll definitely hear it more and more as we self-navigate the cyclic path. For example, as the burden of financial preparedness increasingly falls on us, we'll seek out financial planners with a set of LifeCycle navigation skills that reach beyond anything we've seen before. These professionals will be a blend of investment strategist, career counselor, education counselor, marriage counselor, and life planner. And financial life planning should probably start while we're young as part of the curriculum in our public schools. If we consider algebra (which I have yet to find a practical use for) a necessity for graduating from high school, why don't we also teach budgeting, finance management, and the basics of lifelong investing?

Just the other day on National Public Radio the crisis in education in California was discussed. One of the ongoing problems raised was that many of the elected school board members who are fiscally responsible don't have the financial expertise to make and manage budgets. Through their lack of knowledge and the financial bumbling that has resulted, they were contributing to the very crisis they were supposed to be solving. One school board member proclaimed, "No one ever taught me about budgeting or financial plans. The learning curve is enormous.

How can anyone expect us to do this job effectively?" She's right about her lack of skills, and it's obvious that we all need to have basic money management skills to run our lives effectively. It needs to be part of life-long education that rightfully begins in our youth and continues throughout our long and cyclic lives.

How about help with navigating the constantly morphing health care and medical insurance system? The last decade was all about managed care, now health care is transforming its shape once again to offer us more choice. The new buzz-phrase is *defined-contribution health plans*. Although these new plans encourage us to choose our own doctor, hospital, and other health care options, how do we actually figure out what our ever-changing needs are? And how do we choose the plan that will best meet our unique needs? These are complexities that cry out for the expertise of a well-informed, unbiased consultant who understands the ins and outs of the constantly changing health care maze and can match a solution to our particular circumstances.

To help shed light on this frustrating challenge, data–based rating systems are beginning to appear that make shopping for doctors and hospitals easier and less complicated. Ultimately, these artificial intelligence–based expert reviews could take much of the guesswork out of the selection process. For instance, Health Grades, a Lakewood, Colorado, company, issues report cards on hospitals and nursing homes nationwide, available on the Internet. The ratings are designed to measure quality, cost, and effectiveness.[6] This is clearly a much-needed first step, but still needed are enhanced educational guidance, referral services, and professional advice in this area to help consumers navigate their way. My guess is that many people would be willing to pay for a framework where options and references about individual doctors, hospitals, nursing homes, and health insurance plans can be better understood.

Navigating the job market, too, has become more complex and confusing with our cyclic lifestyles. With single career paths a remnant of the past and loyalties felt by both employees and employers evaporating, career management is now an individual responsibility. According to Shannon Kelley, marketing director of the Association of Executive Search Consultants in New York, "Executives are being a lot more proactive about their careers than ever before. I think it's a mind-set that's developing, independent of any economic cycle. People know companies won't necessarily be loyal and they also want a varied career, not necessarily within the same company." This trend goes beyond executives to impact all of us in the workforce. Proactivity and career navigation will be the new watchword for most of us, whatever our job or rank. And seeking professional help and brainstorming when considering a move in this complex maze of career challenges and opportunities will become more and more common.

As our lives become less predictable and more flexible and as reinvention and empowerment become staples of life, there will be increasing demand for trusted advisors of all colors and stripes across a variety of fronts. This will create tremendous opportunities for those companies, individuals, or software programs that can offer the much-needed help and advice we will all crave on the liberating—but sometimes confusing—cyclic life path.

TARGET FREEDOM *AND* SECURITY

These two concepts may seem contradictory and at odds with each other, but the cyclic life makes both of them highly relevant to cyclic consumers. Although the linear-life path was highly restrictive, it did offer us predictability, comfort, and security. In stark contrast, the cyclic life path offers us tremendous freedom to choose, but at a price. The price is that many of the moorings that provided predictability, comfort, and security have become unhinged. For many, there is no longer the stability and structure of one job, one skill set, or even, necessarily, one family for life. We will now have to take much of the responsibility of managing a variety of aspects of our lives on our own, something that few of us have had to do in the past. Yes, we are better equipped to handle this shift—more educated, empowered, and free to reinvent our lives in a multitude of ways—but, as humans, we definitely crave a degree of security to complement our freedom. Many of us will enlist LifeCycle navigation tools, which will provide some comfort and security; even then, the task will be daunting.

For some, this untethered ride will be emotionally exhilarating; for others it will feel a little bit like being on the high ropes without a net. Remember that some of us will seek out a cyclic life path while others will be thrust onto it through a job loss, a divorce, or an illness. Many will actively seek the freedom and flexibility that the cyclic life offers while balancing the gaps that this lack of security creates with carefully crafted solutions that offer some degree of security and comfort. Others will grab for the solutions that offer the most security and comfort and later realize, with a sigh of relief, just how good the freedom and flexibility of the cyclic life feels.

Some product choices can offer us *freedom with security*, a strange new brew that's exactly right for the cyclic consumer. For example, over the last several decades, the financial services industry has recognized the empowered consumers and acknowledged them by providing more and more diverse options to the individual investor. At the same time, most employers shifted to defined contribution pension programs like 401(k)s instead of the traditional defined benefits programs. This may again change, but until it does, we now have the added freedom—and responsibility—to choose where to invest that money. We're now being offered lots of freedom, but little in the way of security. As a result, large numbers of us feel overwhelmed by the dizzying spectrum of options and decisions it requires from us. We're so afraid of making a mistake that we freeze, choosing to do nothing at all rather than act foolishly. Ironically, we're choosing the security of doing nothing to the freedom of taking a risk and possibly making a mistake.

The result of this mind-set of fear and avoidance is that it undermines the likelihood that we'll enjoy freedom and security over the long term. According to a recent study, *Re-visioning Retirement,* conducted by The Dychtwald Group and Harris Interactive and commissioned by AIG/Sun America, most of us don't plan adequately for the financial ramifications of a long life and eventual retirement, whenever that might come and whatever shape it might take. The study concludes that "Satisfaction in the later years is directly linked to the number of years one saves for retirement. This is true across all age and income levels."[7] Which means that many of us are making a huge mistake in neglecting to put a financial plan in place to invest in our own financial future. We're limiting both our own chance for financial freedom and security in later life.

This points to a tremendous opportunity for the financial services industry to provide us with a solution that can satisfy both of our opposing needs: freedom and security. Like it or not, individual investors now have the freedom to manage their own lifelong financial saving and investing. At the same time, they want to do so with carefully crafted solutions that are easy to understand, trust, and implement with some degree of safety and comfort. If we felt secure knowing we have the best investment option for us with the smallest amount of risk attached, we might more readily save and invest, especially if we trust that advisor, not always a given. And, if we make saving and investing a lifelong habit, we'll give ourselves a better shot at enjoying freedom and security as we get older.

Another example of how an entire industry can both offer freedom and fill this comfort and security gap can be found within the banking industry. Over the last decade, banks have consolidated into mega-banks that offer a whole retinue of products from checking to life insurance but have sacrificed personalized service in the process. Megabanks determined that they just couldn't profitably provide such a variety of products while offering a high level of customer service. So they dropped the service. Ironically, that personal connection was one of the most sought-after features that customers look for in dealing with their money. They feel secure, comfortable, and even empowered if they have personal relationships with those to whom they entrust their money. And this need for trusted advisors is more important today than ever before.

Small retail banks saw the opportunity and seized it. Many decided that if they specialized in offering customers such freedoms as no minimum balances, extended hours, free checking, customized loan terms, and combined this with such securities as ready access to credit lines, quick decisions on loan applications, and most important, personal attention from bank executives—just the services the megabanks were dropping—they could build their local customer base effectively.[8] They worked hard to fill the customer service gap left by the big banks. As a result, many customers switched brands.

Another result: Small banks' profits have grown by 11.8 percent for the last five years, according to analyst Anthony R. Davis at Ryan Beck and Company, a boutique investment bank. Michael Berk is just the kind of customer the small banks wooed successfully. For years he had been a loyal customer of a large bank. As the CEO of H&SYacht Sales in San Diego, California, which sells more than $60 million in luxury boats annually, Michael had grown weary of the low level of service from his large bank. For example, he had waited for three months for approval for a simple line of credit. While waiting for that credit line approval, his bank changed his contact person several times, making him feel frustrated, insecure, and uncomfortable. So, when given the option, Michael switched his business to a smaller bank, which gave him his line of credit in four days. The comfort and security this new level of service offered him, combined with the freedom to get quick business decisions on credit lines and loans, made him feel comfort, trust, and loyalty to that small bank, at least for now.[9] Providing customers with personalized, red carpet service is definitely one tactic that combines a sense of freedom with comfort and security that can prompt a brand loyalty shift.

As empowered consumers become more the norm, they will thrive on the freedom offered through the cyclic-life path. At the same time, they will instinctively seek large doses of security to make their journey more comfortable. Successful businesses will recognize this contemporary paradox of needs and respond to it.

OPTIMIZE A CYCLIC WORKFORCE

"If employers thought the '90s were the decade of the worker, the next decade will be even more that way," says Harvard University economist, Dale W. Jorgenson.[10] With single career paths mainly a remnant of the past, guaranteed pensions evaporating, and the responsibility of career planning falling squarely on the individual employee, the loyalties felt between employers and employees have been slowly withering. Add to this, the fact that the demographic shifts I've described in this book—more older adults and fewer younger ones—will begin to create a labor shortage in most of the industrialized world if we continue to think of the workforce in those limited terms.

Fertility has fallen below replacement rate in more than 60 nations, representing about half the world's population. "The average worker in the United States is close to 45 and by the year 2005, 15 percent of the workforce will be over age 55."[11] In Italy the number of people of traditional workforce age is shrinking by 7 million from 1990 to 2025; in Japan, it's shrinking by 10 million. In the United States, the labor force growth began slowing in the 1990s, too, and will drop to a mere 0.8 percent over the next decade, according to Watson Wyatt Worldwide, a benefits consultancy. Recently, Colorado's Aspen Institute, a well-known group of political and business leaders, undertook a study on the upcoming labor shortage. James E. Oesterreicher, one of several executives involved in the study, reported we "face a worker and a skills gap—both are right around the corner."[12]

What might it take to optimize our cyclic workforce in the twenty-first century? In Chapter 3, *Cyclic Careers*, I discuss this challenge in depth. The bottom line is that we will need to find ways to creatively attract and retain a multiethnic, multigenerational workforce to effectively implement our business or organizational plans. At the same time, employers will need to expand or contract their workforce at a moment's notice. Balancing these two needs will be the challenge.

The best and the brightest will need to be wooed with everything from educational opportunities and training to flexible hours and telecommuting, from employee benefits like child care and elder care to opportunities for career growth and change. Salaries, bonuses, and stock options will count, too. And remember, our employees will be living cyclic lives and will want all the bells and whistles that come along for the ride. They will expect their work lives to offer both personal growth and satisfaction along with that paycheck.

The era of the male dominated, 18- to 64-year-old worker is a remnant of the past. Diversity of age, gender, and race will be the norm. Early retirement programs will soon be replaced by incentives to keep workers employed for longer. Flexible hours and the virtual workplace will encourage women to stay in the workforce while other personal demands tug at them. And employee benefits that include child care and elder care will help those of us busy caring for young children and elderly parents to juggle effectively.

Child care and elder care will be benefits that many cyclic workers will seek, particularly women who are generally the ones taking on these emotional, stress-laden responsibilities. According to the Employee Benefits Research Institute, 85 percent of companies today provide some level of child care for employees while only a third of those companies provide any type of elder care. That will change. Just as child care gained support from employers in the '80s and '90s, elder care will gain support from employees in the coming decades. "More than half of all Americans think they will care for an elderly relative in the next 10 years."[13] Some employers have already responded in kind. "Ford Motor Co. now offers free house calls by geriatric-care managers to its 150,000 workers in North America to help employees develop care plans for vulnerable elderly relatives; AT&T has *elder care one-stop shops* to coordinate care and services for their workers' older family members; and Fannie Mae employs a full-time elder care manager to assist their employees at their Washington, D.C., headquarters."[14] In the coming decades, creative solutions for both child care and elder care will emanate from many employers who want to win over employees.

Continual education and training will also be highly sought after by employees of all levels. As I've emphasized throughout this book, education is no longer a prerogative in a cyclic society. It's a lifelong necessity with the power to add strength to individuals and to the companies that offer it to their employees. Most of us are well aware of this at the executive level, but all levels of workers will be needed and will want to move up the ladder of success. For example, since the 1990s, Bank of America has partnered with Goodwill Industries International to train welfare recipients to become cashiers and tax processors. "We're mindful of the labor-shortage projections and see these populations as continuing to provide a wonderful source of labor with higher retention rates," says Karen B. Shawcross, a senior vice president at Bank of America.[15] Similarly, New York Presbyterian Hospital offers $10,000 in tuition assistance to any of their present employees, even unskilled laborers such as housekeepers and laundry workers, who are willing to go back to school to learn skilled jobs that are hard to fill such as ultrasound and X-ray technicians and histotechnologists.

Flexibility in the workplace will become an even bigger draw. Some employees will want to work from home and telecommute while others will want to work part-time or flexible hours. Older workers in particular may want to continue to work but take on fewer responsibilities and put in fewer hours and days. James E. Oesterreicher sums it up like this: "For most of our lifetime, people have worked hours their employers wanted them to. Now employers will have to become more flexible."[16] For instance, Deloitte Consulting has created Senior Leaders Program to retain some of their senior partners who are tired of the long hours and constant travel, no longer need the money, but enjoy the challenge of the work itself. Sandy Aird, the program designer, is himself only working part-time at 64. He says, "We want to help them find a second career within our firm." Cigna offers its retirees the opportunity to return to work part-time through a formal program, Encore. Mark Jacobs, a staffing executive at Cigna, says, "There is a real value in not having that talent walk out the door." Herman Knoll, a former vice president of international claims, is just such a talent. After retiring from Cigna, he still works there two mornings a week, analyzing international claims and has the freedom to spend his afternoons volunteering at a soup kitchen. This way, he no longer has to travel or even work full time. "It's on my terms," he says.

In the coming decades, recruiting and retaining employees, at all levels, will be one of the critical challenges employers will face. According to Bob Proctor, a senior organization specialist at McKinsey & Company, "Right now, at most companies, the majority of time and effort is focused on consumers. In the future, competition for talent might mean you have to first win in the labor market, before you're ever going to have the chance to win customers."[17] As pioneers on this new cyclic path, we need to show future generations how to build successful relationships between employers and employees that are a win-win for both parties.

CONCLUSION

As Claremont Graduate University's Peter Drucker says, "The best way to predict the future is to create it." This cyclic life and the revolution in living, working, and buying creates a brand-new territory, and we are the pioneers, creating our collective future. Whether it's our first year in business or our centennial, how well we know and respond to our consumers and employees will be the measure of our success.

In the business world, the prize will belong to those among us who best understand and then best serve the members of our cyclic society, many of whom are self-navigating through life at their own pace, taking part only in those activities they choose. They're out there and they're buying, but they're in a process of constant change. In a cyclic society, the onus is on business not just to keep up, but to stay a step ahead.

ENDNOTES

INTRODUCTION

1. Holly J. Morris, "Extreme Hobbies," *U.S. News & World Report,* April 22, 2002. (Howard Means coauthored with Susan Sheehan, *The Banana Sculptor, the Purple Lady, and the All-Night Swimmer: Hobbies, Collecting, and Other Passionate Pursuits.*)

CHAPTER ONE: THE PATH TO LIFECYCLE LIBERATION

1. John W. Rowe and Robert L. Kahn, *Successful Aging* (New York: Pantheon, 1998).

2. *New York Times,* 1992.

3. Population Division of the Department of Economic and Social Affairs, *1998 Revision of the World Population Estimates and Projections* (New York: United Nations, May 4, 2000) and www.un.org/esa/population/worldaging.

4. "Superaged," *San Francisco,* November 1998.

5. "The Economics of Aging: The Luxury of Longer Life," *The Economist,* January 27, 1996.

6. Ken Dychtwald, *Age Power: How the 21st Century Will Be Ruled By the New Old* (Los Angeles: Tarcher/Putnam, 1999).

7. United States Census Bureau International Data Base.

8. United States Census, 2000.

9. Ibid.

10. Ibid.

11. Landon Jones, *Great Expectations* (New York: Coward, McCann & Geoghegan, 1980).

12. Dychtwald, *Age Power.*

13. Yankelovich Monitor Minute, "Driving the Trend," January 7, 2002.

CHAPTER TWO: LIFELONG LEARNERS

1. Pamela Paul, "Time Out," *American Demographics,* June 2002.

2. Peter Drucker, *Post-Capitalist Society* (New York: HarperBusiness, 1993).

3. Associated Press, "Greenspan Promotes 'Lifelong Learning,'" June 20, 2001 (Web).

4. Age Wave/Roper Study, 1997.

5. *Journal of the American Medical Association,* February 13, 2002.

6. David L. Marcus, "A Scholastic Gold Mine," *U.S. News & World Report,* January 24, 2000.

7. Sam Lubell, "Gotham: The New Human Capital," *New York,* January 2002, p. 16.

8. Pamela Paul, "Time Out."

9. Ken Dychtwald, *Age Wave* (Los Angeles: Tarcher, 1986).

10. Cindy Blanding, "Have Pension, Will Travel," *Parks and Recreation,* September 1993.

11. James M. Pethokoukis, "E-learn and Earn," *U.S. News & World Report,* June 24, 2002.

12. David L. Marcus, "A Scholastic Gold Mine."

13. Joseph E. Hight, "Boomers Want to Know the Answers," *The Boomer Report,* October 1998.

14. "Those Who Can, Teach," *Economist,* October 28, 1995.

15. Michael Meyer, "Just Don't Shoot the Client," *Newsweek,* November 30, 1998.

16. Joseph Weber, "School Is Never Out," *Business Week,* October 4, 1999.

17. Toddi Gutner, "Financial Education for Undergrads," *Business Week,* May 21, 2001.

18. Ibid.

19. Heather John, "Learning Takes a Holiday," *Age Wave Report,* July 1999.

20. Greg Schmid, "The New Sophisticates," *American Demographics,* December 1999.

21. Rebecca Saunders, *Business the Amazon.com Way, Get Big Fast* (New York: Harper-Business, 2000).

CHAPTER THREE: THE DA VINCIS: CYCLIC CAREERS

1. www.mos.org/sln/Leonardo/LeoHomePage.html
2. Anne Kate Smith, "Charting Your Own Course," *U.S. News & World Report,* November 6, 2000.
3. Howard Schultz, *Pour Your Heart into It* (New York: Hyperion, 1997).
4. Pamela Paul, "Time Out," *American Demographics,* June 2002.
5. Smith, "Charting."
6. Kim Clark, "Why It Pays To Quit," *U.S. News & World Report,* November 1, 2000.
7. "The Untapped Resource: The Final Report of the Americans over 55 at Work Program" (New York: Commonwealth Fund, 1993), p. 28.
8. www.heldrich.rutgers.edu/
9. Nina Munk, "Finished at Forty," *Fortune,* February 1, 1999.
10. "Never Too Old to Be a Rookie," *U.S. News & World Report,* April 30, 2001.
11. Rochelle Sharpe with Ann T. Palmer, Joann Mueller, Elizabeth Hayes, and Deborah Rudin, "Teen Moguls," *Business Week,* May 29, 2000.
12. Nancy Ann Jeffrey, "The Mid-Life Intern," *Wall Street Journal,* July 12, 2002.
13. Barbara Sher, *It's Only Too Late If You Don't Start Now* (New York: Delacorte Press, 1998).
14. Michelle Conlin, "And Now, The Just-In-Time Employee," *Business Week,* August 28, 2000.
15. Ibid.
16. "A Worker's No-Fault Divorce," *The Economist,* February 2, 2002.
17. Kate Rope, "Tomorrowland: Manage," *San Francisco,* January 2000.
18. Ron Winslow, "Health Benefit Trend: Give Workers Money, Let Them Buy a Plan," *Wall Street Journal,* February 8, 2000.
19. Munk, "Finished at Forty."
20. Ken Dychtwald, *Age Wave: The Challenges and Opportunities of an Aging America* (Los Angeles: Tarcher, 1986).
21. "News You Can Use," *U.S. News & World Report,* November 6, 2000.
22. Pamela Paul, "Time Out."
23. Rebecca Gardyn, "All in a Day's Work," *American Demographics,* July 2001.

24. Pamela Paul, "Time Out!"

25. Stephanie Armour, "Timeout," *USA Today*, November 21, 2000.

26. Kim Clark, "You're Laid Off! Kind of. Firms Look Beyond Pink Slips," *U.S. News & World Report*, July 2, 2001.

CHAPTER FOUR: LOVE CYCLES

1. www.marriage.about.com/library/weekly/aa070198.htm

2. Harriet Shaklee, "In the Good Old Days: Fact or Fiction on the Nostalgia Trip," The University of Idaho Cooperative Extension.

3. Amy Dickinson, "Positive Illusions, Personal Time: Your Family," *Time*, September 1999.

4. Tara Parker-Pope, "Health Journal: How Eye-Rolling Destroys a Marriage; Researchers Try to Predict Divorce Risk," *Wall Street Journal*, July 2002.

5. "The Bridget Jones Economy," *The Economist*, December 22, 2001, pp. 68–70.

6. Ira Matathia and Marian Salzman, *Next: Trends for the Near Future* (Woodstock, NY: Overlook Press, Peter Mayer Publishers, Inc., 1999).

7. Joanne Y. Cleaver, "Good Old Dad," *American Demographics*, June 1999, pp. 59–63.

8. Pamela Paul, *The Starter Marriage and the Future of Matrimony* (New York: Villard Books, 2001).

9. The National Marriage Project, "The State of Our Unions, 2001," Rutgers, the State University of New Jersey, June 2001.

10. Tara Parker-Pope, "Eye Rolling."

11. The National Marriage Project, "The State of Our Unions, 2001."

12. George Wayne, "Q & A: The Devil and Kim Cattrall," *Vanity Fair*, January 2002.

13. F.M. Esfandiary, "Intimacy in a Fluid World," *In Context*, Summer 1985.

14. Scott M. Stanley and Howard J. Markman, "Facts About Marital Distress and Divorce," University of Denver and PREP, Inc., www.smartmarriages.com/7.html.

15. Joan Raymond, "For Love of Money," *American Demographics*, July 2000.

16. June Fletcher, "The Big-House Backlash," *Wall Street Journal*, March 17, 2000.

17. John Carroll, "My (Other) House," *American Demographics*, June 2002.

18. Sandra Cavallo and Lyndan Warner, *Widowhood in Medieval and Early Modern Europe: Women and Men in History* (New York: Addison Wesley Longman, 1999).

19. Kimberly Blanton, "Golden Illusions: Baby Boomers Are Already Looking Forward to the Prospects of a Carefree Retirement, but for Many Women of the Generation, Realizing the Dream Will Be Elusive," *Boston Globe*, October 28, 2001.

20. Alex Tresniowski and Gerald Burstyn, "Sweet Charity," *People*, October 19, 1998.

21. Lani Willis, "Hear Them Roar: Single Women in the Housing Market," www.HomeStyles.com/library/BuildingLifestyTrend/001120/001120.html [cited May 2000]; updated information available from www.homeplans.com

22. "My Dinner with Andre," *Wall Street Journal*, July 19, 2002.

CHAPTER FIVE: THE VIRTUAL FAMILY

1. Josh Schonwald, "Marriage Wanes as American Families Enter New Century, University of Chicago Research Shows," The University of Chicago News Office, November 24, 1999.

2. Bonnie Blackburn, "Moms Starting Families in 40's Test Odds," *USA Today*, September 24, 1997.

3. "The Aging of the American Mother," *Harper's Bazaar*, August 1997.

4. abcnews.go.com/sections/primetime/index.html, "The Gift of Life," August 22, 2002.

5. The Segal Company, "The Aging of Aquarius: The Baby Boom Generation Matures," February 2001.

6. Landon Jones, *Great Expectations* (New York: Coward, McCann & Geoghegan, 1980).

7. Betsy Morris, "Tales of the Trailblazers," *Fortune*, October 12, 1998.

8. D'Vera Cohn, "Percentage of New Mothers in Workplace Fell Last Year," *Washington Post*, October 18, 2001.

9. Ibid.

10. Alan Shipnuck, "Behind Every Great Woman . . . a Taste of What Life's Like for the Men of the LPGA," *Travel & Leisure Golf*, March/April 1999.

11. Joann S. Lublin, "Managing Your Career: Working Dads Find Family Involvements Can Help Out Careers," *Wall Street Journal*, May 30, 2000.

12. Ethan Watters, "The Way We Live Now: In My Tribe," *New York Times Magazine*, October 14, 2001.

13. Tait Trussel, "Seniors Have to 'Be Prepared,'" *The Orlando Sentinel*, January 6, 2002.

14. Julie Baumgardner, "Stepgrandparents Can Create Rewarding Bonds," *Chattanooga Times*, January 20, 2002.

15. Jim Steward, "Step Aside, Grannies and Grandpas, with Divorces, 2nd and 3rd Marriages, Kids Are Getting Swamped by Multiple Grandparents," *Montreal Gazette*, December 31, 2001.

16. Ibid.

17. Pamela Paul, "Echoboomerang," *American Demographics*, June 2001.

18. Ibid.

19. Ibid.

20. Ibid.

21. Sue Shellenbarger, "Up Next: Juggling Care for Grandpa, Mom, and Aunt Pat," *Wall Street Journal*, October 13, 1999.

22. Ken Dychtwald, *Age Power: How the 21st Century Will Be Ruled by the New Old* (Los Angeles: Tarcher/Putnam, 1999).

23. www.arp.org/press/inthemiddle/July, 2001.

24. Metropolitan Life Insurance Company Survey, 1997.

25. Greg Loper, "Universal Design: Homes That Meet Life's Changing Needs," www.store.homestyles.com/library/BuildingLifestyTrends/010101/010101.html [cited May 2000]; updated information available from home plans.com

26. Sue Shellenbarger, "Technology Holds Promise for Easing Families' Worries Over the Elderly," *Wall Street Journal*, July 25, 2002.

27. Yumiko Ono, "An Army of 'Home Helpers' Is Ready to Descend on Us," *Wall Street Journal*, October 7, 1999.

28. Lisa McLaughlin, "Extended-Family Vacation," *Time*, June 12, 2000.

CHAPTER SIX: RE-CREATION

1. "Finding the Best Camps for Grown-Ups: Fantasy Camps Cater to Adults with Music, Sports, Nature," *Investors Business Daily*, March 9, 1999.

2. Wendy Bounds, "Work, Work, Work. Give Me a Break!" *Wall Street Journal*, November 1, 2000.

3. www.celebrationfl.com/press_room/faq07.html

4. Walter Gibbs, "When Home Is Not a Castle but a Cruise Ship," *The Christian Science Monitor*, October 8, 1997.

5. Dean Takahashi, "Tech Toys: Video Games for Grown-Ups," *Wall Street Journal*, April 28, 2000.

6. Bart Eisenberg and Gijutsu-Hyoron, "Pacific Connection," *Software Design*, September 1999.

7. Bonnie Pittman, American Academy of Arts and Sciences, *Daedalus*, "Muses, Museums, and Memories; Review," June 22, 1999.

8. "15 Ideas That could Shake the World: Singing and Dancing," *Utne Reader*, March-April, 1999.

9. Jeff Wise, "Personal Fortune: Life Beyond Work: The Type A Vacation: Take a Few Days and Destroy Yourself," *Fortune*, August, 16, 1999.

10. Susan Carey, "For Added Fee, Superagents Book High-End Trips," *Wall Street Journal*, November 19, 1999.

11. Ibid.

12. Janet-Rae Dupree, "Dig That Crazy Diggler," *U.S. News & World Report*, June 24, 2002.

13. "Extreme Retailing," *BusinessWeek*, December 20, 1999.

14. Simon Berry, "The Future of Destination Leisure," *Leisure Industry Week*, September 27, 2000.

15. Eileen Daspin, "Discomfort Food," *Wall Street Journal*, April 28, 2000.

16. Carol Emert, "Play with Your Food," *San Francisco Chronicle*, Business Section, October 16, 1998.

17. Tenaya Darlington, "Slow Is Beautiful (and Delicious)," *Utne Reader*, November-December 2000.

18. Trish Deitch Rohrer, "Sweat Salvation," *New York Magazine*, April 6, 1998.

CHAPTER SEVEN: RECOVERERS AND REJUVENATORS

1. Bruce B. Auster, "The Fountain of Youth," *U.S. News and World Report*, April 24, 2000.

2. http://www.cancer.org/eprise/main/docroot/CRI/content/
CRI_2_4_1x_Who_gets_cancer?sitearea=CRI

3. http://www.nhlbi.nih.gov/health/public/heart/index.htm

4. Stephen Smith, *Miami Herald*, November 25, 2001.

5. www.lancearmstrong.com

6. www.realage.com/racruise

7. www.census.gov/population/socdemo/statbriefs/agebrief.html

8. James Fries, M.D., *The Case for Healthy Aging and Compression of*

Morbidity: Healthy Aging (Aspen, CO: Aspen Publications, 1999), p. 47.

9. *Journal of the American Medical Association,* November 1998.

10. The Harvard Study defines alternative medicine treatment as acupuncture, herbs, homeopathy, naturopathy, energy healing, folk remedies, megavitamins, massage, self-help remedies, chiropractic care, and yoga. Conducted by professors from Harvard Medical School, the study said that "visits to alternative practitioners are up 47 percent since 1990." The research study estimated that Americans visited alternative health professionals 629 times a year and primary-care physicians 386 million times a year. Already one in three Americans buys alternative health care, and boomers are the most likely to seek alternative medical treatment— and they pay for it out of their own pocket. For 1997 alone, that translates into $27 billion in spending as compared to $27 billion paid out of their own pocket for all traditional physician services.

11. Jerry Adler and Joan Raymond, "Fighting Back, with Sweat," *Newsweek,* Fall/Winter 2001.

12. Ibid.

13. Ellyn E. Spragins, "So What's the Score?" *Newseek,* October 19, 1998.

14. From an interview aired on Oregon Public Broadcasting, "High-End Health Care," by Tom Banse, September 5, 2001.

15. Dennis Normile, "Heart and Home," *Popular Science Flash Forward,* Summer 2001.

16. *Living Longer,* Summer 1999 [electronic newsletter]; available from www.agingresearch.org.

17. David Stipp, "Engineering the Future of Food," *Fortune,* September 28, 1998.

18 Catherine Arnst, "The New Era of Lifestyle Drugs,". *Business Week,* May 11, 1998.

19. Rachel K. Sobel, "Futures: Viagra in a Virus," *U.S. News & World Report,* November 19, 2001, p. 59.

20. Dr. Ronald Klatz, *Grow Young with HGH,* Harper Perennial, 1998.

21. Ivan Carvalho, "Every Breath You Take," *Wired Magazine,* March 2000.

22. Ibid.

23. www.roperasw.com/newsroom/retail/r0104002.html, April, 2001.

24. Barbara Thomas, *Los Angeles Times,* January 21, 2000.

25. Peg Tyre, "Turning Back the Clock," *Newsweek,* Fall/Winter 2001.

CHAPTER EIGHT: METAMORPHOSIS: RETIRING RETIREMENT

1. David McCullough, *John Adams* (New York: Simon & Schuster, 2001).

2. Carole Haber and Brian Grattan, *Old Age and the Search for Security: An American Social History* (Bloomington: Indiana University Press, 1993).

3. Marc Freedman, *Prime Time: How Baby Boomers Will Revolutionize Retirement and Transform America* (New York: PublicAffairs, 1999).

4. Ibid.

5. Peter Peterson, "Social Insecurity," *Atlantic Monthly,* May 1996.

6. Harris Interactive, "Baby Boomers Head for Retirement."

7. Karen Hube, "Help Wanted," *Wall Street Journal,* November 29, 1999.

8. Peterson, "Social Insecurity."

9. www.jsc.nasa/gov/Bios/html/glenn-j.html

10. William Plummer and Tina Kelley, "The Givers," *People,* October 27, 1997.

11. The Independent Sector, "America's Senior Volunteers," 1997, and "American Volunteers," 1998 (Washington, D.C.: Independent Sector, 1997 and 1998).

12. AIG/Sun America, The Dychtwald Group, and Harris Interactive, "Re-visioning Retirement Study," April 2002. (This quote is from "Baby Boomers Envision Their Retirement," according to the study.)

CHAPTER NINE: THE CYCLIC SELF

1. Peter Schwartz, *Wired Magazine,* May 2002.

2. Pamela Sherrid, "Retired? Fine. Now Get Back to Work," *U.S. News & World Report,* June 5, 2000.

3. Ibid.

4. Carla Meyer, "What You See Is What You Get," *San Francisco Chronicle,* March 31, 2002.

5. "Lights, Camera . . . Cut!" *People,* April 1, 2002.

6. Karen S. Peterson and Karen Thomas, "Is Hughes' Exit Sign of a Trend?" *USA Today,* April 25, 2002.

7. Bill Been, "Starting over . . . and over . . .," *Fast Company,* January 2002.

CHAPTER TEN: THE CYCLIC SOCIETY

1. Sarah Collins, "Velvet Ropes, Bouncers—Bingo?" *Wall Street Journal*, May 10, 2002.

2. Jeannie Williams, "Liza May Just Kiss New York Goodbye," *USA Today*, May 14, 2002.

3. Ruth Simon, "'Dear Debtor, Please Forgive Our Asking,'" *Wall Street Journal*, May 17, 2002.

4. Lauren Lipton, "Too Trendy for You?" *Wall Street Journal*, May 17, 2002.

5. Rebecca Gardyn, "What's Cooking," *American Demographics*, March 2002.

6. Bernard Wysocki Jr., "New Ratings Let Patients Shop for Hospitals," *Wall Street Journal*, May 1, 2002.

7. AIG/Sun America, The Dychtwald Group, Harris Interactive, "Re-visioning Retirement Study," April 2002.

8. Mara der Hovanesian and Heather Timmons, "For Small Banks, It's a Wonderful Life," *Business Week*, May 6, 2002.

9. Ibid.

10. Aaron Bernstein, "Too Many Workers? Not for Long," *Business Week*, May 20, 2002.

11. "How to Prepare for the Coming Older Workforce," *Safety Directors Report*, April 2001.

12. Bernstein, "Too Many Workers?"

13. Lee Fletcher, "Eldercare: A Concern of Aging Workforce," *Business Insurance*, March 5, 2001.

14. "Eldercare as a Benefit Gains Attention of More Employers," *Boston Business Journal*, March 1, 2002.

15. Ibid.

16. Ibid.

17. Jay Stuller, "Ready for the Other Millennium Bomb?" *Chief Executive*, July 2000.

ABOUT THE AUTHOR

One of the nation's leading authorities on generational marketing, Maddy Dychtwald has been actively involved in analyzing and forecasting lifestyle and consumer trends for nearly twenty years.

In 1986, she co-founded Age Wave with her husband, Ken. Age Wave is the nation's premier think tank and strategic consulting group focused on boomers and the mature market. During her decade of work there, she helped grow the company from the ground up to a multi-million-dollar enterprise with a reputation as the best in its field.

Maddy took a sabbatical from Age Wave in 1997 to focus her time on speaking engagements, research and writing this book, and raising her two children. She has delivered speeches to more than 200,000 people worldwide, including a diverse group of clients such as Allegiance Healthcare, Allstate Insurance, Chevron/Texaco, Direct Marketing Association, IAI Mutual Funds, International Council of Shopping Centers, International Foundation of Employer Benefit Plans, National Association of Educators, New Balance Athletic Shoes, Washington Wine Commission, and Touchstone Mutual Funds.

In keeping with the cyclic life pattern herself, Maddy recently cycled back into working at Age Wave as senior vice president. She and her family live, work, and play in the San Francisco Bay Area.